D1568568

PROFILES IN AMERICAN HISTORY

Significant Events and the People Who Shaped Them

(Continued on inside back cover)

PROFILES IN
AMERICAN HISTORY

Westward Movement to the Civil War

1803
▼
United States purchases Louisiana Territory, expanding west.

1820
▼
Missouri Compromise admits Missouri into the union as a slave state; bans slavery in Louisiana Purchase north of latitude 36°30'.

1845
▼
The United States annexes Texas.

1836
▼
Ralph Waldo Emerson writes *Nature,* a short book that outlines the basic beliefs of the transcendental movement.

1835
▼
José Navarro signs Texas declaration of independence from Mexico. Texas Revolution begins.

1821
▼
Mexico gains independence from Spain, honors agreement made by Spain for Americans to colonize Texas.

1846
▼
President James Polk declares war against Mexico.

1848
▼
United States gains from Mexico one million square miles of the Southwest and California in Treaty of Guadalupe Hidalgo.

1848-1848
▼
Gold is discovered in California; gold rush attracts 80,000 immigrants over land and sea.

1854
▼
Kansas-Nebraska Act overturns Missouri Compromise.

1865
▼
Lincoln is assassinated.

1865
▼
Congress approves Thirteenth Amendment, ending slavery in the nation.

1865
▼
Robert E. Lee surrenders to Ulysses S. Grant at Appomattox Courthouse. War ends.

1863
▼
President Abraham Lincoln delivers Emancipation Proclamation.

1861
▼
South secedes from Union; Civil War begins.

PROFILES IN AMERICAN HISTORY

Significant Events and the People
Who Shaped Them

4

Westward Movement to the Civil War

JOYCE MOSS
and
GEORGE WILSON

U·X·L

AN IMPRINT OF GALE RESEARCH INC.

PROFILES IN AMERICAN HISTORY:
Significant Events and the People Who Shaped Them

VOLUME 4: WESTWARD MOVEMENT TO THE CIVIL WAR

Joyce Moss and George Wilson

Staff

Carol DeKane Nagel, *U•X•L Developmental Editor*
Thomas L. Romig, *U•X•L Publisher*

Christine Nasso, *Acquisitions Editor*

Shanna P. Heilveil, *Production Assistant*
Evi Seoud, *Assistant Production Manager*
Mary Beth Trimper, *Production Director*

Mary Krzewinski, *Cover and Page Designer*
Cynthia Baldwin, *Art Director*
Arthur Chartow, *Technical Design Services Manager*

The Graphix Group, *Typesetting*

Moss, Joyce, 1951-
    Profiles in American history : significant events and the people who shaped them / Joyce Moss and George Wilson.
        p. cm.
    Includes bibliographical references (p. 265-266) and index.
    Contents: 4. Westward expansion to the Civil War
    ISBN 0-8103-9207-0 (set) : $225.00. — ISBN 0-8103-9211-9 (v. 4) : $29.95
    1. United States—History.   2. United States—Biography.
I. Wilson, George, 1920–.   II. Title.
E178.M897 1994
973—dc20   94-6677
                                                                                                                    CIP

∞™ This book is printed on acid-free paper that meets the minimum requirements of American National Standard for Information Sciences—Permanence Paper for Printed Library Materials, ANSI Z39.48-1984.

Printed in the United States of America

Published simultaneously in the United Kingdom by Gale Research International Limited
(An affiliated company of Gale Research Inc.)

I(T)P™

The trademark ITP is used under license.

Contents

Westward Movement   1

Mexican War   38

Transcendental and Romantic Movements   90

Pre-Civil War Controversies   130

Civil War   168

Reader's Guide

The many noteworthy individuals who shaped U.S. history from the exploration of the continent to the present day cannot all be profiled in one eight-volume work. But those whose stories are told in *Profiles in American History* meet one or more of the following criteria. The individuals:

- Directly affected the outcome of a major event in U.S. history
- Represent viewpoints or groups involved in that event
- Exemplify a role played by common citizens in that event
- Highlight an aspect of that event not covered in other entries

Format

Volumes of *Profiles in American History* are arranged by chapter. Each chapter focuses on one particular event and opens with an overview and detailed time line of the event that places it in historical context. Following are biographical profiles of two to seven diverse individuals who played active roles in the event.

Each biographical profile is divided into four sections:

- **Personal Background** provides details that predate and anticipate the individual's involvement in the event
- **Participation** describes the role played by the individual in the event and its impact on his or her life
- **Aftermath** discusses effects of the individual's actions and subsequent relevant events in his or her life
- **For More Information** provides sources for further reading on the individual

Additionally, sidebars containing interesting details about the events and individuals profiled, ranging from numbers of war casualties to famous quotes to family trees, are sprinkled throughout the text.

Additional Features

Maps are provided to assist readers in traveling back through time to an America arranged differently from today. Portraits and illustrations of individuals and events as well as excerpts from primary source materials are also included to help bring history to life. Sources of all quoted material are cited parenthetically within the text, and complete bibliographic information is listed at the end of the entry. A full bibliography of scholarly sources consulted in preparing the volume appears in the book's back matter.

Cross references are made in the entries, directing readers to other entries in the volume that elaborate on individuals connected in some way to the person under scrutiny. In addition, a comprehensive subject index provides easy access to people and events mentioned throughout the volume.

Comments and Suggestions

We welcome your comments on this work as well as your suggestions for individuals to be featured in future editions of *Profiles in American History.* Please write: Editors, *Profiles in American History,* U·X·L, 835 Penobscot Bldg., Detroit, Michigan 48226-4094; call toll-free: 1-800-877-4253; or fax: 313-961-6348.

Preface

"There is properly no History; only Biography," wrote great American poet and scholar Ralph Waldo Emerson. *Profiles in American History* explores U.S. history through biography. Beginning with the first contact between Native Americans and Vikings and continuing to the present day, this series offers a unique alternative to traditional texts by emphasizing the roles played by individuals, including many women and minorities, in historical events.

Profiles in American History presents the human story of American events, not the exclusively European or African or Indian or Asian story. The guiding principle in compiling this series has been to achieve balance not only in gender and ethnic background but in viewpoint. Thus the circumstances surrounding an historical event are told from individuals holding opposing views, and even opposing positions. Slaves and slave owners, business tycoons and workers, advocates of peace and proponents of war all are heard. American authors whose works reflect the times—from Walt Whitman to John Steinbeck—are also featured.

The biographical profiles are arranged in groups, clustered around one major event in American history. Yet each individual profile is complete in itself. It is the interplay of these profiles—the juxtaposition of alternative views and experiences within a grouping—that broadens the readers' perspective on the event as a whole and on the participants' roles in particular. It is what makes it possible for *Profiles in American History* to impart a larger, human understanding of events in American history.

Acknowledgments

For their guidance on the choice of events and personalities, the editors are grateful to:

Jonathan Betz-Zall, Children's Librarian, Sno-Isle Regional Library System, Washington

Janet Sarratt, Library Media Specialist, John E. Ewing Junior High School, Gaffney, South Carolina

Michael Salman, Assistant Professor of American History, University of California at Los Angeles

Appreciation is extended to Professor Salman for his careful review of chapter overviews and his guidance on key sources of information about the personalities and events.

For insights into specific personalities, the editors are grateful to Robert Sumpter, History Department Chairman at Mira Costa High School, Manhattan Beach, California.

Deep appreciation is extended to the writers who compiled data and contributed the biographies for this volume of *Profiles in American History:*

Diane Ahrens
Erika Heet
Dana Huebler
Lawrence K. Orr
Robert Sumpter
Colin Wells

The editors also thank artist Robert Bates for his research and rendering of the maps and Paulette Petrimoulx for her careful copy editing.

Introduction

During the first half of the nineteenth century, different social systems grew firmly entrenched in the North and the South. The regions struggled to coexist for a time, balancing the number of free states and slave states in the nation. But as Americans ventured westward, fears mounted over which system would prevail in new territories entering the Union. This westward migration aggravated the discord between the regions and helped propel the nation down the road to civil war.

An 1837 proposal to annex Texas, where rich cotton land attracted slave owners, raised a clamor in Congress. In the eyes of some representatives it was a suspicious proposal—a plot to extend slavery westward—that would give the South more states and senators than the North, leaving the South to dominate the central government. Similar fears were raised when the United States gained more than one million square miles after the Mexican War. With this new territory came proposals, debated in Congress, over how to handle slavery in the area. There were other issues too. The territory included a sizeable population of Mexicans who suddenly became American citizens. They struggled to adjust, in some areas losing lengthy battles—legal and military—over land that had been granted to them by Mexico and almost everywhere losing social standing.

Meanwhile, the North saw the rise of a movement whose members objected to slavery, to the limits placed on women, and to the common American quest for riches. Called transcendentalism, its followers, through writings and lectures, advocated plain living and high thinking. Their views affected public opinion and widened the gulf between North and South. The transcendental writer Henry David Thoreau, for example, objected to the Fugitive Slave Act, a part of the Compromise of 1850 that encouraged the capture of runaway slaves. Meanwhile, other writers of the period embraced the romantic style, creating fictional tales that at times looked critically at events in America's past.

As the issue of slavery grew more heated, Americans explored different solutions. Individuals proposed legislation, brought into the Supreme Court questions about freedom and property rights over slaves, and conducted violent raids in attempts to abolish slavery abruptly. In the end, North and South resorted to war to settle their differences.

Southern states seceded, believing they had voluntarily entered into the Union and could lawfully leave it. They did so, convinced that their liberty and property (slaves) were threatened after the Republican party, which was made up of Northerners, won the 1860 presidential election. At first the North fought to preserve the Union and to establish the idea that in a democracy a minority must submit to government by the majority. Events that transpired in the first two years of warfare led to the adoption of an additional war goal: the abolition of slavery.

Picture Credits

The photographs and illustrations appearing in *Profiles in American History: Significant Events and the People Who Shaped Them,* Volume 4: *Westward Movement to the Civil War* were received from the following sources:

On the cover: **Courtesy of the Library of Congress:** John Charles Frémont, Zachary Taylor.

Courtesy of the Library of Congress: pages 4, 9, 29, 36, 41, 55, 61, 63, 64, 75, 79, 81, 95, 107, 119, 137, 175, 191, 199, 212, 213, 223, 241, 245, 247, 249, 252; **courtesy of the Kit Carson Museum:** page 7; **courtesy of the Texas Collection, Baylor University, Waco, Texas:** pages 45, 53; **courtesy of the Concord Free Public Library:** page 102; **Harper's Weekly:** page 134; **courtesy of University of California at Los Angeles Library, Special Collections:** pages 149, 201; **courtesy of Boston Athenaeum:** page 159; **AP/Wide World Photos:** page 183.

Westward Movement

1803
▼
U.S. purchases Louisiana Territory, expanding west.

1803-1806
▼
Lewis and Clark make first cross-continental journey.

1819
▼
Spain signs Transcontinental Treaty, giving up claims to the Pacific Northwest.

1836
▼
Missionaries **Marcus Whitman** and **Narcissa Prentiss Whitman** journey to Oregon.

1829
▼
Christopher "Kit" Carson becomes an apprentice trapper in the Rocky Mountains.

1825
▼
Erie Canal connects New York City to the Great Lakes and the Old Northwest.

1821
▼
Moses Austin wins permit from Spanish to bring American families into Texas.

1839
▼
John Augustus Sutter builds fort in California.

1846
▼
British-U.S. treaty is signed, settling the dispute over Oregon Territory; the 49th parallel becomes the boundary.

1846-1847
▼
1,600 Mormons migrate from Illinois to Utah.

1848
▼
U.S. gains from Mexico one million square miles of the Southwest and California in Treaty of Guadalupe Hidalgo.

1864
▼
Civil War ends; many Southerners migrate westward.

1862
▼
Congress passes Homestead Act, offering free land to settlers; dealers, not farmers, grab the best parcels.

1861
▼
Civil War slows westward movement.

1848-1849
▼
Gold is discovered on Sutter's land in California; gold rush attracts 80,000 immigrants over land and sea.

WESTWARD MOVEMENT

From the time of the first European colonists, there was a movement westward across North America that involved native and immigrant peoples. American Indians were slowly pushed west until the 1830s, when thousands were relocated hundreds of miles to Oklahoma. In contrast, immigrant Americans moved west voluntarily. Their movement was a response to the rapid growth of the immigrant population in the East, which limited opportunities there.

The building of transportation systems—canals in the 1820s and railroads in the 1830s—encouraged the movement west, linking the frontier to distant markets and goods. In time, settlement of the West by whites fell into a pattern. Mountain men, or trappers, migrated first, along with a handful of missionaries bent on converting native peoples. Temporary farmers came next; often they would build a rough cabin, clear a small parcel of land, then sell these "improvements" to a permanent farmer, who fenced in fields, replaced the rough cabin with a frame house, and

Why Immigrant Americans Moved West

- Start their own farms on low-cost land
- Conduct trade on the frontier
- Mine for gold or silver
- Buy and sell land for profit
- Bring Protestant beliefs and education to the frontier
- Practice the Mormon religion freely
- Improve their health

1

carved out roads over which merchants, lawyers, and others would move into the area. Falling outside this pattern were the Mormons, who escaped westward to observe their religion in peace.

Among the first group of mountain men to the Far West was **Christopher "Kit" Carson,** who blazed routes and guided pioneers. The missionary **Marcus Whitman** played this same role in 1843, guiding 120 ox-driven wagons and several thousand cattle on the 2,000-mile journey over the Oregon Trail. The country had suffered a business slowdown, or depression, brought on by a sudden collapse in prices during the Panic of 1837. Lured by glowing reports of lush frontier land, easterners caught the Oregon Fever and streamed west to improve their fortunes. Most of them were white Americans in their late twenties to early forties who brought their families.

In 1846 Britain decided to accept the 49th parallel as a boundary between British and American territory if Vancouver Island would remain in British hands. Congress agreed, and Oregon, already settled by 5,000 Americans, officially became U.S. territory. Meanwhile, pioneers streamed west over the Oregon Trail, stopping in Willamette Valley, where **Narcissa Prentiss Whitman** unhappily endured the hardships of pioneer life. Nearby lived Cayuse Indians, half of whom died from measles brought on by a new flood of 5,000 pioneers in 1847.

The pioneers traveled west by sea around Cape Horn in South America or made the less costly overland journey on the California and Oregon trails. Wagon trains would form into a great circle at night for protection from Indian raids. Yet the Indians were in perhaps more dire need of protection.

The westward movement was disastrous for native Americans. Thousands died of diseases caught from pioneers, and others suffered as the incoming whites fed their oxen on grasses needed by Indian ponies and, for sport, hunted buffalo, on which the Indians depended for food and clothing. Moreover, the movement sparked warfare between tribes. As

▲ **Trails west**

hunting grounds shrank, tribes battled one another for the dwindling resources. The Sioux raided the Kiowa, Crow, and Pawnee tribes and thus gained new territory.

In 1851 the U.S. government held a council at Fort Laramie to win guarantees of safety for pioneers on the Oregon Trail and to repay the Plains tribes for their losses. Not all tribes attended, and some who came were angered by the outcome. The Fort Laramie Treaty, the first U.S. treaty with Plains tribes, promised them yearly payments. In exchange, they had to give up their right of free movement and live within

▲ **Buffalo hunting as the Great Plains were opened**

agreed-upon tribal boundaries. Black Hawk, a Sioux Chief, angrily refused. He would not have his people restricted to an area north of the Platte River. His resistance foreshadowed warfare in the near future.

Meanwhile, it became easier and easier for whites to buy western land. Prices collapsed again in the Panic of 1857, which led to a movement to give away acreage for free in the West. In 1862 the Homestead Act gave 160 acres to any citizen over twenty-one who lived on the property, improved it, and paid a small registration fee. In Oregon, a married man could get 640 acres if he lived and worked on the land for four years. Most farms were occupied by parents and one to four children. Loneliness was common, for communities grew slowly.

In contrast, the mining frontier was a lively place. Gold strikes sparked rushes to California in 1849, to British Columbia in 1858, and to Colorado in 1859. The pattern typical of mining-camp settlements was boom and bust. Camps seemed to spring up overnight and fade in short order, occupied briefly by hundreds of miners and by merchants, saloonkeepers, and ladies of the evening. Few prospectors struck it rich since most of the gold was buried deep beneath the surface and could only be extracted with heavy machinery. Still, several miners hit "pay dirt": James Marshall on **John Sutter**'s property in California, for example, and Peter O'Riley and Patrick McLaughlin in Nevada. The California strike spelled disaster for Sutter, who had moved west to improve his fortune and, until then, had succeeded.

Chinese miners in particular proved skillful at finding gold that others overlooked. But even they had no way to get at the rich deposits locked deep in the veins of the rock. Still, miners rushed into the areas in droves, most of them male, young, and unmarried. Some 80,000 came to California in 1849. Unable to succeed in their get-rich-quick schemes, they often abandoned prospecting and went to work as wage earners for the corporations that mined for the deep, hidden gold. Others settled down to farm, or they set up shops to service the ever-growing population. Prejudice against foreign miners and an 1850 tax on them (foreigners had to pay twenty dollars monthly for a mining permit) drove many Mexicans and Chinese into other occupations in San Francisco and Sacramento.

Meanwhile, California Indians suffered the loss of their lands. As they were killed off and their territory taken, bands such as the Nipewai began to die out. One band, the Modoc, resisted being pushed out of California into Oregon, but to no avail. A slowdown in the westward movement would begin with the Civil War, which delayed conflict between the government and western tribes for a time. Afterward, however, the westward movement would resume, leading to a few final struggles between white and native Americans for lands of the Far West and the Plains.

Christopher "Kit" Carson

1809-1868

Personal Background

Christopher "Kit" Carson was born on December 24, 1809, in Madison County, Kentucky, the third son of Lindsay and Rebecca Carson. When Kit was one, the family moved to Howard County, Missouri, where he spent the first fifteen years of his life. Growing up in this rustic environment at the edge of the frontier, Kit learned at an early age to shoot and hunt. Kit's father and older brothers taught him how to protect himself, and he grew to love the challenges of frontier life.

In 1818, when Kit was just nine years old, his father died. Kit's mother remarried in 1822, and Joseph Martin became a second father to Kit. Since Kit had not been given a formal education and could not read or write, Martin sent him off to learn a trade. At age fifteen, Kit was apprenticed to a saddler's shop in Old Franklin, the westernmost outpost in Missouri, to work for David Workman.

Apprenticeship. Kit worked hard at the shop for two years, learning the saddler's trade and listening to the colorful customers. Prospectors, trappers, and scouts came in for supplies and they were full of stories about their adventures in the untamed West. Wide-eyed, Kit heard tales of trailblazing, hunting, and camping on the frontier and of fighting and trading with various native American tribes. The dramatic stories of life west of the Missouri River

▲ **Christopher "Kit" Carson**

Event: Settlement of the West; economic growth.

Role: Through his role as a scout, guide, mountain man, and rancher, Kit Carson promoted economic growth in the United States. Carson guided trappers, miners, and livestock ranchers throughout the Southwest and California. His expeditions forged trade and travel routes from the Midwest to the West Coast, permitting further development and settlement in the region.

captivated the teenager. He longed to join with these mountain men in their settlement of the West.

The West. At the time, the United States extended just to the Midwest, with much of the territory of present-day California and the Southwest belonging to Mexico. Some trails had been forged leading to the West Coast. Spanish missionaries and American explorers such as Jedediah Smith and Lewis and Clark were among those who had mapped the area. But journeys to the West Coast remained perilous for American settlers because of both the roughness of the trails and the presence of local Indian tribes and Spanish settlers. As more and more Americans began heading west, these earlier settlers, who already claimed the territory, were naturally threatened and sometimes terrorized the newcomers, stealing their livestock and looting their ranches and forts. Yet the West became increasingly appealing, luring new settlers with its resources of gold, cattle, fertile farmland, and valuable pelts. Americans continued to risk the dangerous journey to stake their claims in California and the Southwest.

Kit finally decided to quit the saddler's trade. "[It] did not suit me and, having heard so many tales of life in the mountains of the West, I concluded to leave" (Carson, p. 4). Anxious to travel and see the world, Kit resolved at age seventeen to join the first party headed for the Rocky Mountains that would take him.

Participation: Westward Movement and Economic Growth

Taos. In August 1826, Carson talked his way into joining a scouting expedition destined for Santa Fe, New Mexico. The group made it to Santa Fe by November, and from there Carson traveled to Taos, where he sought further employment. Carson took an immediate liking to this undeveloped, awe-inspiring barren land. The horizon was as big and wide as his imagination and the colorful mix of New Mexico's inhabitants—American, Spanish, and Mexican settlers, and Pueblo, Ute, and Apache Indians, among others—appealed to his sense of adventure. Carson made his home in Taos, then a city of just 3,606, and quickly learned Spanish and a few native American dialects.

▲ **Cattle being driven to market**

Though Carson was small, he had ample drive and determination and was known as a tough fighter. He immediately landed a job with Colorado's first cattleman, David Kinkead, who had begun a ranch in Taos. Carson worked as a cook and hunter for Kinkead but craved a more exciting and dangerous occupation. After a few months, Carson convinced an American army colonel, Philip Trammel, to hire him as an interpreter on a journey to Chihuahua, Mexico. He made the journey and got a job in a Mexican copper mine for a few months. But, again, Carson became restless. Longing for further adventure, he packed up and returned to Taos.

Apprentice mountain man. In 1829 Carson landed his first job as an apprentice mountain man, accompanying a trapping party through the Rocky Mountains. He began the trip under the guidance of Ewing Young, a pioneer trader and explorer who was to have a profound influence on the young man's life. Carson quickly proved to be a great asset to the expedition because he spoke several languages and could cook and hunt. He learned to trap beaver as well as anyone on the journey and established himself as a loyal, capable crew member.

Description of a Mountain Man

Carson truly began his frontier life when he became an apprentice mountain man in 1829, under Ewing Young. Learning the importance of being well equipped, the young mountain man was outfitted with the following provisions: He rode a dependable horse and, of course, carried a loaded rifle slung over the front of his saddle. Fastened to his saddle were a buffalo-skin bag of gunpowder and lead, a blanket, extra moccasins, tobacco, needles and medicine. He also carried flint, steel, a butcher knife, a tomahawk, and a whetstone (for sharpening). Mountain men such as Carson usually wore flannel shirts, leather or wool pants, a coat made of blanket cloth or buffalo skin, and a hat of wool, fur or leather. While some mountain men dressed in showy raccoon hats and fringed leather jackets, Carson wore simpler, more practical pieces.

Missions. The trappers eventually made their way through the Rockies to California, crossing the Mojave Desert and coming upon the sprawling Spanish missions at San Gabriel and San Fernando, just outside of the small pueblo of Los Angeles. Carson was impressed by the hundreds of acres of fertile farmland held by the missions and by the size of their operations. San Gabriel, for example, owned 30,000 head of cattle, as well as horses, sheep, and hogs, and sold an annual amount of farm products in excess of $50,000. Carson called this mission "a paradise on earth" and could see the great potential of California agriculture (Guild, p. 39).

The trappers traded with the missionaries, giving them knives and furs for beef. After a few days at the missions, they headed toward northern California in search of livestock and beaver pelts. On this leg of the journey, Carson had his first encounters with Indian tribes and began to establish himself as a fearless fighter and tracker.

Navajo encounter. While camping outside of a mission near San Rafael in northern California, Carson's camp was raided by a group of Navajo. They ran off with sixty head of cattle and horses, which the party was planning to drive back to Santa Fe. Rather than take the loss, Carson resolved to get the animals back. Young organized a group of twelve, headed by Carson, to track the raiders as far as necessary. Carson led the men more than 100 miles through the Sierra Nevada Mountains, a range with which he was wholly unfamiliar, and, amazingly, found the Navajo raiders days later. He recalled:

> We surprised the Indians while they were feasting off some of our animals they had killed. We charged their camp ... and recovered all of our animals, with the exception of six that were eaten. (Carson, pp. 16-17)

Carson guides trappers. After this first expedition through California with Young, Carson's reputation grew. He worked steadily as a guide throughout the area for the next several years. Because trapping had become very profitable, his major clients in the 1830s were fur trappers headed for northern California and the Pacific Northwest. The trails were full of dangerous surprises. Carson's tracking abilities were continually tested. In 1833, while Carson accompanied a trapping expedition in California, a group of fifty Crow Indians stole twelve horses from his camp. Carson's horse had not been taken, yet he tracked down and recovered the stolen animals, but the men responsible for the theft escaped.

With their horses recovered, some of the men were content to return to camp. But Carson was determined to punish the thieves, regardless of the danger involved. From his growing knowledge of native American tribes, he understood that the Crow did not respect anyone who backed down in the face of an attack. Unless he stood his ground against the Crow, Carson figured, he would always be at their mercy. So, though greatly outnumbered by their opponent, Carson's group found and entered the Crow fort and boldly charged those responsible for the theft. They killed almost everyone in the fort until daylight broke and the remaining Crow saw how few men were in the enemy party. The Crow then counterattacked but Carson's men managed to get away through the woods. Some Cheyenne Indians who had accompanied Carson on this raid greatly admired him for his courageous stand against the Crow and rewarded him with the name "Little Chief."

During this stage of his life, Carson became increasingly familiar with the customs and values of native Americans. He made friends and enemies of various tribes and learned many of their languages. Carson always tried to coexist with the native Americans. He would never attack without being provoked, but when property or persons under his charge were threatened, he was the first to retaliate. In 1835 Carson married an Arapaho woman named Waanibe and had two daughters with her. He appears to have spent only seven years with Waanibe, until he returned to St. Louis in 1842 to find another employer and enroll the two girls in a convent school. It is unknown whether Carson's wife died at this time or some years later.

Carson meets Frémont. With beaver numbers greatly diminished in California by 1841, trappers began to move farther north. Consequently, the demand for guides within the Southwest waned. Carson was forced to return to St. Louis to find prospective settlers, ranchers, and gold miners who were beginning to migrate from the Midwest in great numbers. In April 1842, Carson arrived in Missouri, sixteen years after leaving "civilization" for the "wilds of the West." He visited friends and family in St. Louis but within two days became tired of the settlements and took the first steamer out. Truly a frontiersman by this point, Carson had little patience for cities and their throngs of people.

His escape from the city led to a fateful meeting. Colonel John Charles Frémont, sent by the U.S. government to explore and set up military outposts in the West, was aboard the same steamer as Carson. The two struck up a conversation and Carson informed the colonel that he knew well the western landscape. Frémont, who had not heard of Carson's exploits, inquired as to Carson's qualifications and, being told of his solid reputation, hired Carson to be his guide through the Rocky Mountains.

For the next year, Carson served as Frémont's guide, successfully protecting the colonel's party from the Sioux who were warring against American trappers in the South Pass area of the Rockies. In addition, Carson used his knowledge of Spanish and native American languages to great advantage on the expedition, preventing fights and promoting trade. Frémont completed his first expedition by the close of the year, and he and Carson parted company. But Carson had so impressed Frémont that the colonel arranged for him to rejoin the next expedition to California. In the meantime, Carson returned to Taos to marry his second wife, Senorita Josepha

Jaramilla, a beautiful fifteen-year-old girl from a prominent New Mexico family. Though Carson was very much in love with Josepha, he was truly wed to the wilderness. For the next four years Carson and Josepha saw each other only between his expeditions, yet they managed to have several children together. "Like a magnet," she always drew him back to Taos (Carson, p. 68).

Carson no coward. In April 1843, Carson again took the Old Spanish Trail from New Mexico to California to rejoin Colonel Frémont, who had summoned him by letter. While traveling with a Mexican man en route to meet Frémont, Carson was approached by a large band of Ute Indians. His companion advised him to make his escape, saying that the warriors would surely kill him if they captured him. Carson almost heeded the suggestion:

> [I] considered the advice very good and was about to mount my horse, when I thought how cowardly it would be for me to desert this man who had so willingly offered to sacrifice his life to save mine. Upon this I changed my mind, and told him that I would die with him. (Carson, p. 72)

Carson and his compadre stood their ground together as the party approached and encircled them. They held their rifles cocked and ready, determined to shoot the first Ute who raised his gun. The standoff lasted for about thirty minutes until, according to Carson, "seeing but little hope of being able to kill us without losing two of themselves, they left" (Carson, p. 73). Carson's willingness to stand up to an enemy even when greatly outnumbered contributed greatly to his reputation as a true hero of the West and encouraged other Americans that, with Carson's presence, it was safe to settle in the region.

Mexican War. From 1843 to 1844, Carson again traveled with Frémont throughout California, carving trails, setting up military posts, and protecting American farmers and ranchers from attack. Frémont returned east in July 1844, and Carson returned to Taos, where he attempted to settle down with Josepha and start a stock ranch of sheep and cattle. It was a short-lived attempt, however. By August 1845, Frémont again summoned Carson to his aid and, according to the colonel, Carson "sold everything at a sacrifice and not only came himself but brought his friend to join the party" (Carson, p. 88).

War had been declared between the United States and Mexico, and Carson joined in the fight for American control of California.

During the war, Carson repeatedly volunteered for the most dangerous missions, carrying messages between command posts throughout the state. With his knowledge of the territory and its inhabitants, Carson was perfectly suited for the task and completed the deliveries successfully. He also participated in many of the skirmishes, including the battles of San Gabriel and Los Angeles.

Appointed and denied lieutenant rank. By March 1847, Carson was made an official bearer of dispatches for the War Department and carried military information from California to Washington, D.C. Once in Washington, he was appointed by President James Polk as Lieutenant of Rifles and was sent back to California to resume his war efforts. The following year Carson returned to Washington carrying more dispatches for the president but along the way was informed by a friend that his appointment as lieutenant had not been confirmed by the Senate. Many of Carson's friends advised him not to carry the messages any farther in light of the denial of his military appointment but, true to form, Carson replied that he would fulfill his duty:

> If the service I was performing was beneficial to the public, it did not matter to me whether I was enjoying the rank of lieutenant or only the credit of being an experienced mountaineer. (Carson, p. 125)

Fame. Frémont published many of Carson's exploits before and during the Mexican War, and these writings greatly contributed to the tracker's fame. Actually, Carson despised this type of glorification and carried himself so humbly that most people could hardly believe he was the war hero and fearless tracker they had read so much about.

Carson's Dislike of the City

Carson would be greatly disturbed by the number of settlers who thronged to the west in his wake. When Carson first visited San Francisco in 1847, it was a sleepy little Spanish pueblo amidst some of the most beautiful and rugged scenery Carson had ever seen. Its population was about 200. When he returned just six years later, he could not believe the change that had taken place due to the gold rush and American migration. Its population was now 40,000. Carson barely recognized the pueblo and certainly disliked the change that had occurred. Adding to his displeasure, people instantly recognized Carson everywhere he went since by now he had become so well known. He disliked this type of attention so much that he cut his visit short and likely never returned.

Farmer and rancher. After the war, in 1851, Carson was finally able to settle down with Josepha and his growing family, which included adopted Navajo children in addition to their own. With some partners, he began a ranch on the Santa Fe Trail, forty miles south of Rayado, bringing Adaline, a daughter from his first marriage, to live here too. He and his partners successfully raised cattle and produce, which they sold to the local Fort Union outpost. This enterprise proved highly profitable and increased the amount of trade conducted in the region.

Aftermath

Civil War. During the Civil War, Carson served as an Indian agent and a soldier. His heroic efforts finally earned him the official title of brigadier general. After the war, he was made superintendent of Indian Affairs of the Colorado Territory. But, severely weakened from his decades in the saddle, Carson was in poor health by this stage of his life. He barely made it back to Josepha from a trip to Washington in the spring of 1868. Saying that his wife must see him before he died, Carson made the rigorous more than 2,000-mile journey to his family, but it turned out that it was Josepha who was closer to death. On April 11, 1868, the couple was reunited in time for Josepha to give birth to their youngest daughter, Josephita. Two weeks later, Josepha passed away.

After his wife's death, Carson's health and will to live rapidly faded. He spent his last days with a close friend, Dr. H.R. Tilton. Breathing was becoming increasingly difficult, and Carson felt the life draining from his body. On May 23, he called to Tilton from his bed, saying, "Doctor, Compadre, Adios" and died (Guild, p. 282). Carson received a military funeral, and he and Josepha were buried side by side in their hometown of Taos.

For More Information

Brewerton, George Douglas. *Overland with Kit Carson.* New York: Coward-McCann, 1930.

Guild, Thelma S. *Kit Carson: A Pattern for Heroes.* Nebraska: University of Nebraska Press, 1984.

Marcus Whitman

1802-1847

Narcissa Prentiss Whitman

1808-1847

Personal Background

Overview—A hasty proposal. Twenty-seven years old and unmarried, Narcissa Prentiss was considered an old maid by the standards of 1835. Tall and pretty, with curly honey-blonde hair and a beautiful singing voice, she had not lacked proposals of marriage. She, like her mother, however, took religion very seriously. Narcissa decided that she wanted to go to the American West as a missionary, a religious worker who would bring the Christian message to the Indians there. But the missionary service turned her application down because she was not married. The frontier, they told her, was no place for a single woman.

Marcus Whitman was a handsome and energetic doctor six years older than Narcissa. He had recently been appointed as a missionary to the Indians. When he wrote to Narcissa suggesting they meet before he left, she agreed. Marcus had thought of trying to find a wife to share the burdens of life on the frontier. Narcissa needed a husband if she was to fulfill her own dream. Attracted to each other, the two became engaged during Whitman's visit, thinking that God clearly meant for them to be together and to go west to do missionary work.

Early years in western New York. Marcus and Narcissa had grown up near each other in western New York State, Narcissa

▲ Narcissa Prentiss Whitman

Event: Opening of the Oregon Trail.

Role: In settling among the Pacific Northwest's Cayuse Indians, the husband-and-wife missionary team helped prepare the way for the great migration west along the Oregon Trail through Indian territory. Outraged by the loss of their lands, the attempts to make them into "civilized" Christians, and the ravages of disease, Cayuse Indians killed the Whitmans and eleven others in 1847.

in Prattsburg, where her father was a judge, and Marcus in Rushville. The towns lay about twenty-five miles apart, midway between Lake Ontario and the Pennsylvania-New York border. Both children descended from English Protestant families that had arrived in Massachusetts sometime before 1640. Their parents had settled in western New York in the 1790s, when it was still considered part of the frontier. Towns appeared in the area, but it remained rugged in many respects. Even in Marcus and Narcissa's time, roads were rough enough that men usually traveled between the towns on horseback rather than in carriages.

Plainfield Puritans. Marcus's father died when the boy was seven, and he was sent to live with his uncle in Cummington, Massachusetts. He did not see his mother again until he was thirteen, and then only briefly. He spent the next five years at a religious school in Plainfield, near Cummington, visiting his uncle's family during holidays. They were very religious, more so than his own father had been. By the time Marcus returned home to Rushville when he was eighteen, the Puritan beliefs of the Cummington Congregational Church had influenced him deeply. Congregationalists observed the Sabbath very strictly; for example, they stopped all activity from sundown on Saturday to sundown on Sunday. Church members were not even allowed to stroll along the riverbank or go for a boat ride. Years later, in the wilderness of the West, the Whitmans would make a point of keeping their Sabbath observances— even when it was difficult or dangerous.

Prayer and song. Narcissa's mother was an enthusiastic Presbyterian, with beliefs similar to those of the Congregationalists. Many of Narcissa's childhood memories were of Presbyterian services. Though the church was an important center of Prattsburg's social life, the building itself was plain. The simple, unpainted wood structure had no heating, so the members kept on their heavy coats in the wintertime. During evening prayer services, homemade tallow candles provided the only light.

Much of the service was taken up with singing hymns, and the Prentisses took special enjoyment in the music. As a relative later recalled:

▲ Marcus Whitman

Judge Prentiss and his family were all singers. My earliest recol-
lections of him are as choir leader, setting the tone with an
old-fashioned pitch pipe, and now and then giving it a toot ... to
make sure they were keeping up to the pitch.

[Narcissa] seems to have been particularly gifted in speech, and
especially in prayer and song. I well remember her clear sweet
voice, as a leading soprano, in the old church at home. (Drury, pp.
103, 105)

Narcissa's voice became an important part of her missionary work;
Indians from miles around would bring their children to hear her
sing.

Working, studying, teaching. Narcissa later said that she
decided to become a missionary when she was fifteen. She joined
the Female Mite Society, one of several religious women's groups in
Prattsburg, whose members visited poor homes in the community
to offer religious comfort. She also began teaching Sunday school,
where she led young children in singing or in religious discussions
about Bible stories. At the same time, she pursued her own studies,
first at Auburn Academy in nearby Auburn and then at Franklin
Academy in Prattsburg. Later, in her mid-twenties, she taught
school for a few years. In July 1834, when she was twenty-six, her
family moved forty miles away to Amity, a small village deep in the
woods. Again, she threw herself into church and Sunday school
affairs. But she still dreamed of becoming a missionary.

"Are females wanted?" That November, a visiting Congregational minister, Samuel Parker, spoke in Amity's log schoolhouse
about his wish to gather missionaries and money for a mission, or
religious outpost, among the Indians in a place called Oregon.
Authorized to find volunteers for the mission, he had been touring
the Northeast, speaking in various towns and villages in western
New York. Narcissa was immediately interested in the idea.

Unknown to her, Parker had recently spoken to a group in
nearby Wheeler, New York—a group that included a young doctor,
three years out of medical school, named Marcus Whitman. Marcus had volunteered right away. He had already tried once to win a
place as a missionary but had been turned down because of a past
illness. While Parker had welcomed Marcus's response, he was less

hopeful about Narcissa's chances. However, in December he wrote to the missionary board on her behalf, asking, "Are females wanted? A Miss Narcissa Prentiss of Amity is very anxious..." (Drury, p. 111). As Parker expected, Narcissa's application was rejected. Marcus's was accepted.

Engagement. Wheeler was only a few miles from Prattsburg, and Marcus had attended a prayer meeting once in the Prentiss home. That was probably when he and Narcissa met for the first time. Hearing that she had been rejected as a missionary, Marcus wrote to her and then visited Amity. They were attracted to each other because of their shared ideals. They also were caught up in enthusiasm for Parker's missionary cause. Their engagement, quickly decided upon in January 1835, happened not because they were in love, but because each had a dream of the future that seemed to require them to be together.

Narcissa applied again, mentioning her engagement to Marcus in her letter to the board. By the time she heard that she had been accepted, Marcus had already met Parker in St. Louis, the first major stop on his journey west. Their purpose was to scout out conditions for the party of missionaries, which was to be sent out in two years.

Participation: Opening of the Oregon Trail

Time of suspense. Marcus was gone for nearly a year. Narcissa heard nothing from him until his return in December 1835. It was a difficult time for her. She could not help but wonder and worry how Marcus was doing among the Indians and wild mountain men of the West. Would conditions be suitable for a mission among the Indians in Oregon? Her future seemed to hang by a slender thread. When Marcus finally returned, he had only a day or two to visit and tell her about his journey.

Whitman's first trip west. During the long journey, Whitman and Parker traveled with a party of trappers from the American Fur Company, which had outposts in the Pacific Northwest. There the mountain men, as they were called, trapped beaver, sending the furs east to make the high-crowned men's hats so fashionable in the early 1800s. The hard-boiled trappers were increasingly unfriendly to their religious guests until a cholera epidemic killed three of the trappers. Whitman used his medical skills to prevent the feared disease from striking the others down. In the process, he won their respect. The group journeyed through the wilderness beyond the Rocky Mountains to the Green River in present-day Wyoming. There, in August, they joined the Rendezvous, the yearly meeting of trappers and Indians at which furs were traded.

Indians and mountain men. At the Rendezvous, Whitman met Nez Perce and Cayuse Indians from Oregon. He learned from them that these Oregon tribes were eager to welcome missionaries among them. He also met some colorful mountain men, including the legendary Jim Bridger. Whitman won Bridger's undying friendship by removing an Indian arrowhead that had been lodged in the trapper's back for three years. Another trapper, Kit Carson, shot a mountain man in the arm in front of Whitman during a horseback gunfight. After a few days at the Rendezvous, it was decided that, rather than going on to Oregon with Parker, Whitman should return to the East at once. If he could pass on the good news that the Indians wanted a mission, the party of missionaries might be able to go out a year earlier than planned. Whitman brought two young Nez Perce boys back with him, to teach them English and introduce them to Christianity.

Organizing the mission. Whitman returned in December, and in early January the board approved his request to depart ahead of schedule. Marcus and Narcissa had only two months to plan the mission. They would have to leave by the end of February because Whitman had promised to meet Parker at the 1836 Rendezvous and to return the two boys to their families. He and Narcissa now had to find at least two other missionaries, including a minister, willing to go with them. This proved difficult. Finally, Narcissa suggested a friend of hers named Henry Spalding, a minister who had been selected to start a mission among the Osage Indians of Nebraska. Spalding, in fact, had wanted to marry Narcissa, but she turned him down. He had since married, and he and his wife, Eliza, agreed to go to Oregon instead of Nebraska.

Before a large crowd of family, friends, and well-wishers, Marcus and Narcissa married on February 18, 1836. After frantically gathering and packing clothes and supplies, the newlyweds said goodbye to their loved ones and began the long, dangerous trip west in early March.

Across the Great Divide. The party traveled by riverboat as far as Liberty, Missouri, just beyond St. Louis. Even after they began traveling by wagon, Narcissa found the going easier than she had expected. They were well protected and guided by a large group of American Fur Company trappers. Food was plentiful, and the group slept comfortably in tents. Narcissa wrote to her mother that housekeeping on the prairie was not so difficult after all. On July 4, Narcissa Whitman and Eliza Spalding became the first white women to cross the Continental Divide, the line separating the eastern and western watersheds of the Rockies. The four missionaries seemed to be getting along well. At times, however, Narcissa noticed a strain between the two couples. In fact, Henry Spalding still resented her rejection of him, and his jealousy would lead to problems between him and the Whitmans. Somewhere west of the Rockies, Narcissa discovered she was pregnant.

Fort Vancouver. After leaving the two Indian boys with their families at the Rendezvous, the missionaries continued west. They abandoned their wagons at Fort Boise, present-day Boise, Idaho. Having been the first to bring wagons so far west, they were given credit for opening a new section of what would become the Oregon Trail. The party continued their journey on horseback, arriving at Fort Vancouver, near where the Columbia River empties into the Pacific Ocean, on September 12, 1836. They had covered more than 3,000 miles in 207 days.

As western headquarters for the American Fur Company, Fort Vancouver offered the travelers comforts they had not seen since leaving Missouri. They were warmly welcomed by John McLoughlin, the fort's colorful "Chief Factor" (commander). Tall and broad-shouldered, McLoughlin, with his mane of long white hair, was called White-headed Eagle by the Indians. The missionaries enjoyed a refreshing variety of fruits, vegetables and other foods at McLoughlin's elegantly set table. Afterward the two women stayed on in comfort, while Whitman and Spalding went to search for suitable places for each to build a mission.

Waiilatpu. Whitman chose a fertile spot farther east, on the Walla Walla River twenty-five miles upstream from the Columbia, below the wooded slopes of the Blue Mountains. Here, among the cottonwood and birch trees, the Cayuse Indians built their summer lodges. The camping ground itself was a field of tall rye, and the Indians called it Waiilatpu (wye-ee-laht-poo), or "Place of the Rye Grass." For the Spaldings' mission, the men found a site in Nez Perce territory, about 100 miles farther inland, on Lapwai, or "Butterfly Valley," Creek. After four enjoyable weeks at Fort Vancouver, the women traveled east to the sites while the men worked to build houses before the winter.

Early years at the mission. For two years, the Whitmans' missionary work went slowly but without major problems. They built a small but cozy house out of adobe (mud bricks mixed with grass and baked in the sun), set up a mill for grinding wheat into flour, and brought in cattle, hogs, sheep and chickens. Their newborn daughter, Alice Clarissa, brightened both their lives, especially raising the spirits of the often homesick Narcissa. Visitors—mountain men, fur company officials, and a few early settlers—stopped by on their way east or west. Whitman and Spalding began farming, building irrigation systems, and teaching the Cayuse and Nez Perce about agriculture. All four missionaries struggled to learn the Nez Perce language, which the Cayuse also spoke. Eliza had the greatest success. Narcissa in particular found the Nez Perce language frustrating; she usually spoke to the Indians in English, which the missionaries were trying to teach them.

Personality clashes. By 1840 troubles had begun mounting. Disputes between the Whitmans and the Spaldings kept breaking out, and additional missionaries sent by the board only added to the general atmosphere of disagreement. Even small decisions, such as whether to pray aloud or silently, caused bitter arguments. Though all shared in such problems, Narcissa seemed to be most affected. She began to escape alone to her room, often crying, when the others expected her to make household decisions. The problem, in fact, was that the mission had no leader. The missionaries were expected to reach agreement in a spirit of Christian harmony, which they found difficult to achieve when tough decisions had to be made quickly.

Cultural conflicts. Perhaps more significant than personality clashes among the missionaries were the increasing conflicts between white and Indian cultures. Neither group had understood the other's expectations. The Cayuse had thought they could share in the whites' technology, which seemed mysterious and powerful, without giving up their own ways. Living a nomadic life, in which there was no place for settled farming, they did not understand Whitman when he spoke to them of owning the land. To the Indians, land belonged to everyone and to no one. Furthermore, in the eyes of the Cayuse, plowing injured the earth, which they thought of as a mother.

To the missionaries, civilization and Christianity went hand in hand and left no room for nonwhite culture. The Cayuse religion included worship of many spirits—tree spirits, river spirits and the like—so they found it easy at first to add a new god to the list. When they began to understand that the missionaries expected the new god to become their only god, the Indians became uncomfortable. Discomfort soon turned to proud resistance. And resistance only became stiffer in the face of the Whitmans' growing impatience with Indian ways.

Tragedy. For both of the Whitmans, but especially for Narcissa, a turning point came in June 1839, when Alice Clarissa, just over two years old, drowned in the nearby Walla Walla River. Alice had been her mother's strongest source of joy and comfort in her troubling situation. Narcissa fell into a deep depression, which made it even harder for her to deal with the Indians. She began to view them as "filthy" savages (Schwantes, p. 75), ungrateful for what the Whitmans were trying to do for them. They in turn saw her as conceited. Meanwhile, the missionaries' own disputes continued. Worse yet, they had converted few Indians to Christianity. In the fall of 1842, the missionary board decided to close the missions and transfer the Whitmans elsewhere.

Winter ride. When they heard of the board's decision, the Oregon missionaries elected Whitman and a man named Lovejoy to ride east and try to change the board's mind. The two set off on October 3, hoping to reach St. Louis by December. Hearing that Indians between Oregon and St. Louis were hostile, they made a detour south through Taos in present-day New Mexico. Winter caught up with them, and they were lucky to survive the season. Yet they kept on their way, reaching Boston by April. There Marcus succeeded in persuading the board to keep the missions open.

"Oregon fever." By the early 1840s, accounts of Oregon's fertile, apparently unclaimed land had created great excitement in the land-hungry east. The Whitmans themselves proved that women could survive the trip. A few settlers had ventured to the Northwest in previous years, but the first great migration occurred in 1843, the year that Marcus returned to Oregon. The mission of Waiilatpu lay close to the route that would be called the Oregon Trail and Marcus volunteered to serve the group of migrants—nearly 1,000 men, women, and children—as doctor and guide.

Epidemic. The Cayuse, seeing Marcus return with hundreds of families, assumed that he had brought them on purpose to take control of the region and change the Indians' ways. Most of the pioneers continued west to the fertile Willamette Valley, but new immigrants would continue to use the mission as a rest stop. Each year brought more, until in 1847 nearly 5,000 settlers flooded across the Blue Mountains on their way west. That year, they brought with them diseases against which the Indians had no immunity, or natural defenses. The measles killed half the Cayuse in two months alone.

The Whitman Legacy

In the early 1800s, it was not clear whether Britain, as colonial ruler of Canada, or the United States would control the Oregon Territory (present-day Oregon, Washington, and Idaho). The thousands who followed the Whitmans' example gave the United States a powerful claim on the region.

Whitman tried in vain to nurse the Indians back to health. Children were especially hard hit. The white children who fell ill seemed to recover, but the Indian children did not. To the Indians, it appeared that the Whitmans might actually be poisoning their children. Showing open hostility, they began throwing stones through mission windows at night and carrying out other acts of vandalism.

Violent end. The worsening situation reached a tragic climax on a cold, foggy November morning in 1847. Just after the last of the previous day's pioneer wagons pulled away to continue their journey west, a group of Cayuse entered the mission compound. While one man distracted Whitman by starting an argument about land, another crept up behind him and laid several blows on his skull with a tomahawk. The missionary collapsed and died within minutes. Other Indians then attacked the main house, shooting Narcissa in the chest. She too died immediately. Eleven other whites were killed, and more than forty (mostly immigrants who had stayed there to rest) were captured.

Aftermath

Failure and success. As missionaries, the Whitmans were not, in fact, successful. In over a decade, they converted only about twenty Indians to Christianity. They also failed to understand the Indians they were dealing with, though warned by McLoughlin and others that the Nez Perce, for example, might be more open to adopting white ways than the proud, independent Cayuse. In fact, by the early 1840s, Narcissa herself had begun to doubt whether she was really meant to be a missionary at all. In a letter to her parents, she confessed, "I feel every day ... that I am entirely unfitted for the work, and have many gloomy, desponding hours" (Jeffrey, p. 158). However, the Whitmans did serve as an example and a guide to the thousands of white settlers who came west after them. Their experience showed that the trip could be made, and that a determined farmer could prosper in the West.

Waiilatpu is now known as the Whitman Mission National Historic Site. A college in Oregon and a county in Washington also bear the name of the pioneering missionaries. Descendants of the Cayuse live on a small reservation near Pendleton, Oregon.

For More Information

Drury, Clifford M. *Marcus and Narcissa Whitman and the Opening of Old Oregon.* 2 vols. Glendale, California: Arthur H. Clark Company, 1973.

Jeffrey, Julie Roy. *Converting the West: A Biography of Narcissa Whitman.* Norman: University of Oklahoma Press, 1991.

Schwantes, Carlos A. *The Pacific Northwest: An Interpretive History.* Lincoln: University of Nebraska Press, 1989.

John Augustus Sutter

1803-1880

Personal Background

John Sutter was born Johann August Suter in the small village of Kandern, Grand Duchy of Baden, Germany, on February 15, 1803. He was the eldest of three boys born to Johann Jakob and Christine Wilhelmine Suter. Though John's twin brothers, Heinrich and Friedrich, were five years his junior, the three were inseparable during their childhood in Germany.

Military academy. John's father operated a paper mill in Baden. It did poorly, partly because of a slow business climate in Germany, so in 1819 Johann Jakob relocated his family to Neufchatel, Switzerland. John, aged sixteen at the time, was sent to a military academy for the next four years. As a young cadet, he learned all he could about weaponry and war games. Early on, the glare of military brass and the roar of the cannon attracted him far more than arithmetic or reading and writing. He loved the outdoors and the uncertain life of a soldier and hoped to continue a career in the military. But John's father had other plans for his eldest son. Upon graduation, the young man reluctantly joined his father's printing business as a book clerk.

Book binding. While Heinrich and Friedrich learned the printing trade, John was taught book binding. Working indoors for his father, he began to detest the drudgery of his daily routine,

▲ John Augustus Sutter

Event: Growth of the American economy; Gold Rush of 1848-49.

Role: An enterprising pioneer of the Sacramento Valley in northern California, John Sutter carved a personal empire out of the wilderness. He built a trading post on 50,000 acres at the foot of the Sierra Nevada Mountains, complete with a ranch, vineyards, and a sprawling farm. In 1848 the property became the site of the first gold discovery in the region. Ironically, the gold rush that followed led to Sutter's downfall.

longing instead for "the open drill-ground and the black guns and the sun-bright sky" (Dana, p. 4). But travel and adventure would have to wait a decade.

Marriage. Sutter worked for his father for the next several years and, during that time, fell in love. In 1824 he married Anna Dubelt. The couple lived on the meager salary of a book clerk and raised four children: Johann Augustus, Jr., Anna Elisa, Emil Victor, and William Alphonse. Sutter joined the Swiss Army reserves in 1826, earning some extra income and at least partially fulfilling his military ambitions.

Growing increasingly restless working for his father, Sutter left the printing house after about six years and joined first one, and then another, printing firm. But hard times were again plaguing the trade, eventually forcing Sutter to join the Swiss Guard for stable income. He discovered that a guard's pay was worse than a book clerk's. Debt overtook the struggling family and Sutter was forced to make a crucial decision. Faced with imprisonment for bankruptcy, he began to think about the opportunities in the United States, particularly in the "Wild West." To Sutter, the West offered boundless land and endless opportunity. He had always dreamed of owning his own land and America seemed the only place where that remained possible.

After careful thought, the family decided to stake their future in America. Younger brother Friedrich agreed to watch over Anna and the children until Sutter could afford to send for them. At age thirty-one, he sailed for New York in search of a new beginning.

Participation: Economic Growth

Arrival in America. When John Sutter arrived in July 1834, New York was a budding, bustling city. The United States included twenty-six states, the Midwest beyond the Missouri River was free territory, and Texas had just become an independent republic. Mexico controlled most of the Southwest, and Britain, Russia, and the United States were vying for control of the Oregon Territory. There was an undercurrent of excitement in the air, which could be sensed even by an immigrant who spoke no English.

Name changes. Sutter, who was fluent in German, Spanish, and French, quickly learned English and, as was common among immigrants, Americanized his name from Johann Suter to John Sutter. He also began calling himself Captain Sutter, insisting that he had been an officer under Charles X of France. Sutter was determined to found a community in the West, of which he would be in control. So he ventured west, toward St. Louis, to begin building his dream.

St. Louis—Santa Fe. An outgoing, confident man, Sutter easily won friends in America. He traveled to St. Louis with some French and German men and stayed there through the winter of 1834. However, St. Louis was not the "Garden of Eden" he had expected it to be (Chidsey, p. 10). The weather was cold, the soil dusty, the city already populated. He wanted space, sun, and a fertile homestead—a frontier of his own to tame.

For some months, Sutter tried his hand at farming outside St. Louis but found this life too slow for his liking. By 1835 he had heard of the prosperous Santa Fe trade, where goods from St. Louis were sold at great profit at outposts in the Southwest. With a German partner, Sutter decided to become a trader. They packed up some goods, including cattle, blankets, and tools, and joined a caravan headed for Santa Fe. Finding this venture profitable and the climate of the Southwest to his liking, Sutter continued his life as a trader through 1838. During this time, he periodically sent money back to Anna and the children.

While in Taos, a trading town northeast of Santa Fe, Sutter met a French-Canadian fur trapper named Popian who had just come from an expedition in California. Popian was full of stories about "the land that was ever golden with sun-warmth" where "every fruit and tree and living thing grew with miraculous rapidity" (Dana, p. 15). Then under Mexican control, California was rumored to be a sort of Promised Land, still undeveloped, with an abundance of natural resources and unclaimed territory. Sutter was mesmerized by Popian's tales and decided California was the land of his dreams. Without hesitation, he joined the first expedition west, hoping to gain passage to California.

California. Because of the danger of attack by native Americans along the Old Spanish and Santa Fe trails, Sutter traveled by

way of the Oregon Trail. He accompanied the American Fur Company into the Oregon Territory and then joined a Hudson's Bay Company trapping expedition to Fort Vancouver. Though an indirect route, Sutter learned he could travel by ship from Vancouver to California. However, there were no ships sailing directly to Yerba Buena (present-day San Francisco) when Sutter arrived in Vancouver, just one to Honolulu, Oahu, in the Hawaii Islands, which were then called the Sandwich Islands.

Sutter sailed aboard the *Columbia* to Honolulu and, while awaiting a ship to California, met the king of the islands, Kamehameha III. Sutter told Kamehameha, as well as a group of merchants he was traveling with, of his plans for building a community and trading post in California. The king took an immediate liking to Sutter. A good storyteller and natural leader, Sutter's confidence easily inspired others around him. Intrigued by his ideas, Kamehameha offered to send with Sutter ten men (Kanakas) to help in his venture. Most of the merchants, in turn, eagerly vowed their support. Kanaka soldiers and Russian, German, French, and Swiss merchants all pledged to join Sutter in his venture. Sutter began to feel that his dream was within reach. Now he just had to make it to California.

After a few weeks, the men finally obtained passage on the ship *Clementine*. Traveling via Sitka, Alaska, Sutter and crew arrived in Yerba Buena in July 1839.

Dream realized. When Sutter landed in present-day San Francisco, the Bay City had a population of under 200. It was called Yerba Buena and was governed by Juan Bautista Alvarado. Yerba Buena was described as having "only one real house ... [and] a scattering of huts" and was still overrun by herds of deer and other wildlife (Chidsey, p. 11). While the coastline was sparsely populated, territory east of Yerba Buena remained totally undeveloped, and it was this property that Sutter sought to claim for his own.

Once in port, Sutter was ordered to the capital of Monterey to meet with Governor Alvarado. With a few of his partners and letters of introduction from various U.S. and Swiss officials, Sutter went to see Alvarado about obtaining a land grant in northern California. As Alvarado listened to Sutter's plan to build a vast fort and trading post at the foot of the Sierra Nevada Mountains, he too became inspired. Alvarado offered Sutter the land if he would become a Mexican citizen. The Mexican governor supposed that with Sutter developing the area for Mexico, the country could benefit from a thriving community in the midst of the wilderness without any risk or expense of its own. The agreement stated that Sutter must develop the land within one year and that at the end of that time period, he would officially become a Mexican citizen and legal owner of the property. Mexican citizenship appealed to Sutter because he thought it would make him more readily acceptable to Californians and would give him legal rights to the land. Sutter agreed to Alvarado's terms and was granted 50,000 acres near the Sacramento River.

Sutter's land was considered "the wildest part of the wilderness" (Chidsey, p. 12). Located at the junction of the American and Sacramento rivers, it lay sixty miles from the Pacific Ocean and the nearest city. The site was a virtual no-man's land, but that is exactly why Sutter chose it. At such a distance he could truly be on his own. Truly this was an area where he could build a new future for himself and his family.

New Helvetia. On July 10, 1839, Sutter left Monterey for his new home. But first he traveled throughout northern California, visiting all the local Mexican, Russian, and U.S. outposts in order to set up trade deals and request advice concerning settlement of the Sacramento Valley.

Having secured steady trading partners, on August 9, 1839, Sutter chartered a boat to carry his men and supplies up the Sacramento River. When the ship reached the juncture of the American and Sacramento rivers and Sutter saw the fertile valley that spread out before him, he cried, "Here is a likely spot! Pull in! Pull in!" (Dana, p. 80). Sutter had finally made it. The Sacramento Valley was a wild but lush land, carpeted with green grass and lined with giant Sequoia trees that led up to the mammoth Sierra Nevada mountain range. Where others looked and saw the home of grizzly bears and herds of deer and elk, Sutter saw farmland, ranchland, and the foundation of a new community. Yet he realized that taming the area would not be easy.

Finding a hill for the site of the fort, Sutter named the area after his homeland, calling it New Helvetia, which means "new Switzerland." He posted the Kanakas as guards around the camp and began building the fort. Attracted by the construction and influx of people in the region, native Americans from the Consumne, Yalesumne, Ochocumne, and other area tribes came to visit. Addressing them in Spanish, Sutter said: "I come in peace. I am your friend and I have come to live with you forever" (Dana, p. 79). Sutter distributed presents to the native Americans and offered them employment building his fort, which many accepted.

Sutter's Fort. At first, modest dwellings were built to house the men while Sutter's Fort, a massive 500- by 150-foot military-style structure, was under construction. Sutter was overjoyed to see his vision daily becoming more of a reality and wrote to Anna, saying, "Man can fashion this land into a paradise" (Dana, p. 89). He promised to send for her and the children as soon as the fort was completed.

Outfitted with three brass cannons, courtesy of Hawaiian King Kamehameha, Sutter's Fort was completed in the first year and he received title to it as well as Mexican citizenship. The fort's eighteen-foot-high, three-foot-thick walls enclosed a vast trading post, including shops, small "factories," and personal dwellings. Outside the fort, farmland was cultivated, vineyards planted, and livestock set to roam the fields. Sutter's Fort soon became a stopover for all who traveled through the area, including trappers, frontiersmen, traders, and rancheros. As New Helvetia grew and the trading post prospered, settlers began to arrive and the wilderness of the Sacramento Valley was transformed.

Sutter's empire. Sutter ran his budding New Helvetia empire with military precision. The men in his employ "were obliged to appear well washed, tidied and neatly clad every Sunday morning

---

Sonoma Wineries Owe Homage to Sutter

When Sutter began building his sprawling ranch in the Sacramento Valley in 1840, he laid the foundations for the multibillion-dollar-a-year California wine industry. Though lacking proper planting and distilling equipment, Sutter cultivated wild grapes throughout his property of New Helvetia and started producing brandy. Native Americans were hired to tend the vineyards and pick the grapes. Sutter planned to one day expand the distillery, but plans were cut short. However, the vineyards remain.

for drill" (Dana, pp. 138-39). With judicial and military power vested in him by the Mexican government, Sutter had the authority to arrest thieves as well as assemble his own army of 200 men. Sutter recalled: "The adult soldiers of my infantry and cavalry personnel had regular uniforms ... purchased from the Russians" and "military discipline was always strict at the fort" (Dana, p. 139).

Once Sutter's fort was completed, he began to acquire and cultivate more land. In 1841 he purchased Fort Ross from Russians who were being driven out of California by the Mexicans and bought an area called Bodega from Mexico. With these purchases, Sutter tripled his landholdings. Soon Anna and the children joined him in California and his dream seemed nearly complete.

Mexican War. Sutter was officially a Mexican citizen. Yet by 1845 he had joined the United States in its fight for control of California. Sutter both led his army of men into battle against Mexico and housed American soldiers in his fort. For his efforts, he was made an American citizen in 1847 when California became U.S. territory.

Gold rush. In the fall of that year, just as Sutter was reaching the peak of success, an out-of-work carpenter by the name of James Wilson Marshall drifted through Sutter's Fort. With the war over and increased settlement sure to follow, Sutter was interested in building a sawmill in order to provide more housing on his land. Sutter and Marshall forged an agreement in which Sutter would furnish the tools, manpower, and food if Marshall would choose the sawmill site and manage the operation.

Sutter Meets Carson a Second Time

Though Sutter had encountered Kit Carson while on the Oregon Trail en route to Fort Vancouver, the men were formally introduced in 1841, when Carson and John Frémont stopped at Sutter's Fort. Carson and Frémont had been mapping the Sierra Nevada, struggling through rough winter snow and ice. Their horses were skeletal and the men were exhausted. Sutter heartily welcomed the scouts into his fort and fed and boarded them for two weeks. Though they had virtually no money, Sutter said, "I have never yet fattened my purse on the distress of others," and he provisioned Frémont's expedition out of his own pocket. (Dana, p. 157)

The sawmill was built in Coloma, an area fifty miles upriver from the fort. But Marshall found something more valuable than timber at the site. In January 1848, he discovered gold washing through the sawmill, and Sutter's life was suddenly thrust into chaos.

Prodded by congressional announcements and newspaper

▲ California gold diggers

reports, gold-diggers from throughout the world flocked to Sutter's property and "squatted" on his land for the next three years. Ignoring his property claims and destroying his farm and ranch land, the squatters even took Sutter to court to challenge his property claims. Since the land was granted to Sutter under Mexican authority, and California by 1847 belonged to the United States, the rights to Sutter's empire were in question. Forced into expensive and lengthy court battles, Sutter began to sell what he could of his property and mortgaged the rest. Sutter's Fort was soon mortgaged beyond its value, and by 1852 Sutter was bankrupt—again.

Aftermath

Sutter took his case all the way to the Supreme Court, believing "surely something can be done" (Dana, p. 380). But nothing was done to spare Sutter. The Supreme Court ruled that "it is against public policy for one man to hold the fee of so much land" (Dana, p. 380). Dejected but not wholly defeated, Sutter replied to the decision: "Are all my labors to come to nothing? I cannot believe the United States capable of such action. Surely something must be misunderstood" (Dana, p. 381).

Feeling guilty about the decision, the state of California paid Sutter a pension of $250 a month, but that small sum could hardly repay the man who settled the entire Sacramento Valley and greatly aided the United States in gaining possession of it. Sutter, with the support of his family and many friends, petitioned Congress through 1873 to make up for his tremendous loss. However, petitions to aid the "Old Gentleman" always seemed to get lost in committee and never resulted in favor of Sutter. On June 18, 1880, Sutter checked into a Washington hotel for one last attempt to petition Congress. But at seventy-nine, he was worn out from his many trials and died in his sleep before Congress could hear his last plea. Anna died one year later.

For More Information

Carson, James H. *Bright Gem of the Western Seas.* Lafayette, California: Great West Books, 1991.

Dana, Julian. *Sutter of California.* New York: Halcyon House, 1934.

Dunbar, Edward E. *The Romance of the Age.* New York: D. Appleton & Co., 1867.

Mexican War

1820
▼
Population in U.S. territory reaches about 9,600,000; 200,000 Mexicans and Indians live in Spanish-controlled West.

1821
▼
Mexico gains independence from Spain, honors agreement made by Spain for Americans to colonize Texas.

1829
▼
Mexico abolishes slavery.

1845
▼
John L. O'Sullivan coins the term *Manifest Destiny;* the U.S. annexes Texas.

1836
▼
Led by **Sam Houston,** Texas rebels win independence at Battle of San Jacinto.

1835
▼
José Antonio Navarro signs Texas declaration of independence from Mexico and writes constitution. Texas Revolution begins.

1834
▼
Antonio López de Santa Anna becomes dictator of Mexico.

1846
▼
President James Polk declares war against Mexico. **Zachary Taylor** leads army to the Rio Grande River. **Jessie Ann Benton Frémont** translates Spanish documents for the U.S.

1847
▼
Taylor leads troops to victory at Battle of Buena Vista. Andres Pico surrenders to **John Charles Frémont** in California. Winfield Scott captures Mexico City.

1848
▼
Treaty of Guadalupe Hidalgo ends war; U.S. gains California, Arizona, New Mexico, and the disputed Texas.

1856
▼
John Frémont runs for president; Jessie Frémont continues to write books and articles about life in the West.

1853
▼
The United States makes Gadsden Purchase, buying final strip of southern Arizona and New Mexico.

1851
▼
Gwinn Land Law passed to handle claims made by Mexican Americans on lands in California.

1850
▼
Compromise of 1850 organizes former Mexican lands of Utah and New Mexico as territories and lets them decide slavery for themselves. California admitted to the Union as a free state.

MEXICAN WAR

In the 1820s the northwest portion of Mexico stretched from Texas to New Mexico, Arizona, and California. The entire region was distant from the capital, Mexico City, and only lightly populated by Mexicans and native Americans, who outnumbered Mexicans in the area by two to one. Anglo-Americans slowly began to penetrate the region. They trekked to Santa Fe, New Mexico, with trade goods, and a few settled there. More Anglos moved into Texas, attracted by its prime cotton land. In 1821 Stephen F. Austin carried out a plan begun by his father, Moses Austin, leading 300 Anglo families into sparsely settled Texas. The new American settlers joined Texas's Mexicans, who lived mostly around San Antonio.

Mexico abolished slavery in 1829. At the time 15,000 Anglos, 3,000 Mexicans, and 1,000 slaves lived in Texas. Anglo cotton growers managed to get around the law by freeing their slaves, then forcing them to sign life contracts as servants. By outlawing slavery, however, Mexico showed that it intended to limit the growing power of the American settlers in Texas. The settlers, in turn, objected to conditions of life under Mexican rule. They had to use Spanish as their official language. They were not entitled to trials by jury, and in 1830 Mexico closed Texas's borders to more American settlers. The atmosphere grew tense. In 1834 Antonio López de Santa Anna seized control of Mexico's central government and abolished the constitution, taking power away from local leaders. It was an explosive move. The Texas Anglos, led by Austin, and the Texas Mexicans, led by **José Antonio Navarro,** joined forces and rebelled. **Sam Houston** took command of their rebel army. Marching north to crush the Texans, Santa Anna defeated them at the Alamo but lost the final battle at San Jacinto. By this time, the Texans had declared their independence, but Mexico did not recognize it. Threatened with death by lynching, Santa Anna signed a treaty that confirmed independence for Texas and moved its boundary from the Nueces to the Rio Grande River. Mexico's congress, however, refused to accept this agreement; it would not recognize the Rio Grande boundary or Texas independence.

The dispute continued for a decade, ending in the Mexican War. Meanwhile, Texas adopted a constitution and asked to be annexed to (or become a possession of) the United States. There was heated debate in America over the wisdom of annexing another slave state. Northerners, such as John Quincy Adams, argued that it was a conspiracy by the South to extend slavery into the West and upset the balance of power in the nation, which had thirteen free and thirteen slave states. Against Adams were leaders such as John L. O'Sullivan, who argued that America's manifest destiny, or future role, was to spread its democracy across the continent. They believed that people living in the West, Mexicans and native Americans, were inferior to Anglo-Americans and that it was their duty and unquestionable right to bring into the area their superior form of government.

After nine years of controversy, Congress finally annexed Texas, which led Mexico to cut ties with the United States. Meanwhile, President James Polk, who was determined to gain western territory, sent John L. Slidell to Mexico. Slidell was to purchase New Mexico and California and to convince Mexico's government to accept the Rio Grande as Texas's border. Rebuffed, he could not even make his offers.

An angry Polk ordered General **Zachary Taylor** to Texas's disputed area between the Nueces and Rio Grande

ANTI-TEXAS MEETING
AT FANEUIL HALL!

Friends of Freedom!

A proposition has been made, and will soon come up for consideration in the United States Senate, to annex Texas to the Union. This territory has been wrested from Mexico by violence and fraud. Such is the character of the leaders in this enterprise that the country has been aptly termed "that valley of rascals." It is large enough to make *nine* or *ten* States as large as Massachusetts. It was, under Mexico, a free territory. The freebooters have made it a slave territory. The design is to annex it, with its load of infamy and oppression, to the Union. The immediate result may be a war with Mexico—the ultimate result *will be* some 18 or 20 more slaveholders in the Senate of the United States, a still larger number in the House of Representatives, and the balance of power in the hands of the South! And if, when in a minority in Congress, slaveholders browbeat the North, demand the passage of gag laws, trample on the Right of Petition, and threaten, in defiance of the General Government, to hang every man, caught at the South, who dares to speak against their "domestic institutions," what limits shall be set to their intolerant demands and high handed usurpations, when they are in the majority?

All opposed to this scheme, of whatever sect or party, are invited to attend the meeting at the Old Cradle of Liberty, to-morrow, (Thursday Jan. 25,) at 10 o'clock, A. M., at which time addresses are expected from several able speakers.

Bostonians! Friends of Freedom!! Let your voices be heard in loud remonstrance against this scheme, fraught with such ruin to yourselves and such infamy to your country.

January 24, 1838.

▲ **Many U.S. citizens objected to the annexing of Texas**

river, which at the time was inhabited by Mexican citizens. War erupted on three fronts: in Texas, New Mexico, and California. Taylor scored the first clear victories in Texas. General Stephen Kearney followed in New Mexico, taking Santa Fe without a fight; several months later, Mexicans in Taos rebelled but were finally put down. Meanwhile, **John Charles Frémont,** encouraged Anglo-Americans to stage an uprising in California called the Bear Flag Revolt. His wife **Jessie Ann Benton Frémont** was hired by the U.S. government to translate Spanish documents during the war. (Most of Jessie Frémont's other writings concerned her husband's adventures in the West.)

Winfield Scott led an army of 10,000 Americans deep into Mexico, ending the war with the capture of Mexico City. The Treaty of Guadalupe Hidalgo, signed February 2, 1848, stated the final terms. Mexico gave up all claims to Texas and would collect $15 million from the United States for New Mexico and California. Altogether, the nation gained more than one million square miles of territory, which was inhabited by 75,000 Spanish-speakers and 150,000 native Americans. Five years later, the United States would pay another $10 million for the Gadsden Purchase, a strip of southern Arizona and New Mexico. Added to these expenses was the high cost of the war itself: $97 million and 13,000 American lives.

There had been great controversy in the United States over the justice of this war. One of General Taylor's aides, a colonel named Ethan Allen Hitchcock, wrote in his diary when first stationed in the disputed area of Texas:

Some Causes of the Mexican War

- Mexico considers Texas her territory; United States annexes Texas.
- President James Polk wants to acquire New Mexico and California.
- Americans feel bound to spread democracy through the continent.
- United States seeks control of trade from the Pacific Coast to China.
- Mexico will not recognize Rio Grande River as the Texas border.

I have said from the first that the United States are the aggressors.... We have not one particle of right to be here.... It looks as if the government sent a small force on purpose to bring on a war, so as to have a pretext [excuse] for taking California and as much of this country as it chooses ... My heart is not in this business.... (Howard Zinn, *A People's History of the United States,* [New York: Harper & Row, 1980], p. 149)

In Congress, Abraham Lincoln introduced the so-called spot resolutions, which were challenges to Polk asking whether the spot at which fighting broke out really was on American soil. Writers joined the controversy, with Henry David Thoreau protesting the war and Walt Whitman supporting it. There were even some who wanted to permanently occupy and rule Mexico.

Despite the bickering, the United States voted for funds to support the troops once the fighting began. More than half of Taylor's army were immigrants, mostly Irish and German, who probably joined up for the salary and to prove their loyalty to their new nation more than to spread democracy through the continent. Hundreds died of diarrhea and other diseases, and 9,207 soldiers deserted during the war.

The consequences of victory ranged from more unrest over slavery to severe losses for some of the Mexican inhabitants. Once the United States gained the former Mexican territory, it had to decide how to deal with slavery in the area. The dilemma would be the subject of much controversy, escalating tensions between the North and South. There were disputes over land rights in the newly acquired territory too. By the treaty of Guadalupe Hidalgo, the Mexican inhabitants became U.S. citizens entitled to full property rights, yet many would lose their lands. They were thrust into the unfamiliar maze of U.S. court procedures to prove they were the rightful owners. In 1851 California passed the Gwinn Land Law, under which Mexicans could confirm their title to land in the California courts. Such a trial on average took seventeen years and cost the landholders huge fees. In the end, the Mexican Americans were forced to pay the bills with their lands, so that by the early 1860s they had lost most of their large holdings in the state.

José Antonio Navarro

1795-1871

Personal Background

In 1756 a young Spanish soldier from the Mediterranean island of Corsica landed in Mexico, which at that time was still a colony of Spain. His name was Angel Navarro, and he was a private in the royal Spanish army. Soon after arriving, he was assigned to the deserted but strategic outpost of Saltillo, in northern Mexico. Over the next twenty years, he rose to the rank of colonel and in 1777 married a woman named Maria Josepha Ruiz y Peña, from the town of San Antonio, farther north, in the Mexican province known as Tejas, or Texas. Probably because of this connection, Navarro was soon posted to San Antonio and given the mission of controlling and, if possible, enslaving the rebellious Indians of the area. It did not take him long, however, to decide that the Indians did not deserve to have anyone controlling or enslaving them. He resigned from the army, built a home, opened a store in town, and began raising a family with his wife.

Native Texan. The Navarros had twelve children in all, of whom José Antonio was eighth. By the time he was born, in 1795, San Antonio had been in existence for almost 100 years. Originally founded as a mission, the city later became a military headquarters for Spain. San Antonio's population grew in 1731 with the arrival of 400 immigrant families from the Spanish-owned Canary Islands. In

▲ José Antonio Navarro

Event: Settlement, independence, and statehood of Texas.

Role: Soldier, political leader, and businessman, Navarro was among the most prominent of the Tejanos, or Texan Mexicans, who sided with the American immigrants in fighting for independence from Mexico (1836). Afterward, he devoted much of his energy toward easing relations between the Tejano and Anglo-American (white) communities in the new state.

1795 it boasted between 2,000 and 3,000 inhabitants, who thought highly enough of Angel Navarro to elect him their first alcalde, or mayor. Little is known about José's childhood, but he must have learned some important lessons from his father, whose respect for human dignity was clear in his refusal to treat the Indians badly. About 1805 José was sent south to Saltillo for a year of schooling. He returned to work in a general store in San Antonio. Two years later, Angel Navarro died. Like many of his neighbors, he had felt more loyal to Texas, with its rolling hills and fertile prairies, than to Spain. He passed on this love of Texas to his children. One of his final requests was to ask them to devote themselves to Texas and to the freedom of its people. Many years later, as an old man facing the pain of racial discrimination against Hispanics, José Antonio would ask the same thing of his own children.

Witness to revolution. José soon saw for himself how most San Antonians felt about Spanish rule. From 1811 to 1821, as he grew from adolescence to adulthood, Mexico fought a war to win independence from Spain. Later, José would recall San Antonio's first moves to join the rebellion. Rebel commanders won the support of the town's sizable army garrison. Then, in José's words, they

> made prisoners of Governors Salcedo, Herrera and other Spanish officials who still slept in the peaceful slumber of the morning twilight, confident that no one would dare to attempt any offense against their omnipotent [all-powerful] persons. This memorable day of January 22, 1811, was the first time the Mexicans of San Antonio de Bexar had made public their desire to break forever the chains of their ancient colonial slavery. (Dawson, p. 18)

Massacres at San Antonio. In 1813 a combined force of Mexicans and American volunteers won a major battle against the Spanish at Rosillo, near San Antonio. The Spanish forces were nearly wiped out, and a number of Spanish officers were captured. In the excitement of their triumph, however, a group of the victorious rebels got carried away, with tragic results. As Navarro later told it:

> A company of sixty Mexican men under the command of Antonio Delgado led out of San Antonio fourteen Spanish prisoners, including four of Mexican birth, to the eastern bank of the Salado

near the same spot on which occurred the battle of Rosillo. There they alighted [got down] from their fine horses ... with no other arms than the large, dull machetes which each of those monsters carried hanging from their belts. After having heaped offensive words and insulting epithets [names] upon them [the Spanish prisoners] they beheaded them ... I myself saw the clothing and bloodstained jewels which those tigers carried from their saddle horns, making public festival of their crime and of having divided the spoils. (Dawson, pp. 21-22)

The entire town was shocked at the brutal killings. It was also fearful of Spanish revenge. Soon the Spanish sent a larger army north, and it too met defeat. Finally, a Spanish army of 3,000 arrived and badly defeated the now outnumbered Mexican and American fighters, cutting many down in cold blood as they ran for safety. Leading citizens, such as Navarro's older brothers and his uncle, Francisco Ruiz, were exiled and fled to the United States.

White Dove. With his uncle, Navarro took part in political uprisings against the Spanish. When the rebels were defeated in 1813, he was forced to flee to nearby Louisiana. Navarro remained there for three years before returning to San Antonio, where he became firmly established as a well-known merchant in the community.

In his twenties now, Navarro stood nearly six feet tall. He had a muscular build but walked with a limp due to a horseback riding accident. His peaceful nature—and perhaps the white clothes he favored—prompted his friends to call him the White Dove. Perhaps partly because of the terrible events he had witnessed, Navarro had grown into a quiet, serious young man by 1821, when Mexico finally won independence from Spain.

Participation: Growth of Texas

Moses Austin. Navarro began to concentrate on acquiring more education for himself. Meanwhile, events had occurred that would deeply affect both Navarro's future and that of Texas. In late 1820, during the revolution's final days, an elderly white stranger arrived in San Antonio. He spoke of land and Indians and of farms and settlements. The stranger, Moses Austin, met with Governor Martinez and finally won permission to settle 300 Anglo (white) families on Texas soil. Although Austin died soon after, his dream of settling Texas with land-hungry Americans would be carried on by his son Stephen.

Marriage. With the fight for independence won, Navarro set out to further his education, intending to become a lawyer. For almost five years, he worked hard at his studies. He read as widely as possible to gain general knowledge, afterward devoting himself to whatever law books he could find. He continued to play a role in politics, becoming a member of the Mexican legislature in his province. In 1825, at age thirty, Navarro married a young woman named Margarita de la Garza. The couple had five children in all, four sons and a daughter.

Historic friendship. Navarro was reelected to a second term in the legislature. During this time, he became friends with Moses's son Stephen F. Austin. The two had much in common. Both were self-educated and experienced lawmakers. Both also had calm, easy-going personalities tempered by a strong desire, inherited from their fathers, to see the wilderness replaced by farms and towns. Navarro began buying land and cattle, soon becoming one of San Antonio's largest landowners. Receiving land grants in five Texas counties, Navarro set up his own ranches on them. Meanwhile, he ran a general store, practiced law, and remained active in politics.

Texas fever. Navarro was won over by Austin's argument that since Mexicans were not settling Texas, whites should be given a chance to do so. Austin had been held in a Mexican jail for nearly two years because his plans for settling white farmers in Texas had aroused suspicions that the United States secretly wished to own the region. On his release in 1824, however, the Mexican government had agreed to a much larger white colony than before. Soon other *empresarios,* or land developers, followed Austin's example and obtained similar grants of land for settlement by American families. "Texas fever" began sweeping the southern United States, as pioneers moved west in ever-growing numbers. Navarro lent his support to the development of Texas.

Laws. In the legislature, Navarro worked to aid Austin's plans by introducing a number of laws that encouraged white immigration. One 1829 law, for example, prevented debt-collectors from taking the land or farm tools of settlers, many of whom had borrowed money to make the move and now faced heavy bills. Other laws softened Mexican antislavery edicts to allow settlers to keep their slaves. Still others changed the requirement that all settlers be Roman Catholics.

James Bowie. In 1831 Navarro's niece Ursula married James Bowie, at thirty-five the model of a hard-drinking, hard-gambling frontiersman. Less than two years later at age twenty-one, Ursula Bowie and her two young children died of cholera. Despite their different personalities, Bowie and Navarro got along well. Bowie himself would perish at the Alamo in 1836.

Talk of independence. As the Anglos flooded into Texas in the 1820s, the Tejanos became more and more of a minority. By the early 1830s, around 15,000 whites had arrived, while the original Tejano population numbered about 3,000. Once again the Mexican government grew uneasy. Now it faced not only the possibility of U.S. interest in Texas, but also that of the Texans wishing to govern themselves. Such talk was in the air. A Mexican general named Augustín Terán visited the remote northern province as early as 1828 and suggested that the government send more troops right away. "Either the government occupies Texas *now,* or it is lost forever," he warned (Dawson, p. 49). Suspicion fell on Tejanos like Navarro, who were accused of encouraging a dangerous situation. Stephen Austin, in Mexico City for negotiations, was arrested again in 1833. Navarro was elected senator to the National Congress in Mexico City in 1835, but by that time the situation had worsened so much that he found an excuse for not going. It is likely that he, too, feared arrest.

Declaration, constitution. Shortly after Austin's release in 1835, the Mexican army invaded Texas and the war for Texas independence from President Antonio López de Santa Anna's Mexican government began. If the white Texans had any fears about their Tejano friends' loyalties, they were soon reassured. One by one, influential Tejanos lined up on the side of Texas: José Navarro, Francisco Ruiz, Juan Seguin, Salvador Flores, Lorenzo de Zavala. Though not all Tejanos supported the colonists, the ones who did showed greater unity than the whites, who constantly quarreled among themselves. In November 1835, Navarro was one of three native Texans (along with Ruiz and de Zavala) to sign the Texas

Declaration of Independence from Mexico. He also joined the committee that wrote a constitution for the new Republic of Texas, which was modeled on that of the United States.

Rebuilding. The war ended with Sam Houston's victory at San Jacinto in 1836 (see **Sam Houston**), and shortly after that San Antonians returned to clean up their shattered town, which had been occupied by the huge invading army. Navarro and others had lost their cattle, which were eaten by Mexican troops. In the midst of rebuilding the family store and getting his ranch back on its feet, Navarro was saddened to learn of the death, in 1836, of his friend Stephen Austin, the "Father of Texas." Despite such distractions, Navarro kept on with public service in the Republic of Texas. He served in the Texas Congress through the 1830s.

Ill-fated expedition. In 1841 Texas president Mirabeau Lamar decided to send a large expedition into New Mexico. He thought the citizens of the Santa Fe area could be persuaded to secede from Mexico, which still controlled the Southwest, and join Texas, which claimed New Mexico as its territory. Lamar asked Navarro to be one of the expedition's four commissioners. Though he was reluctant to join the Santa Fe Expedition, Navarro did agree to accompany the 321-man force. The well-armed party left confidently from Austin, Texas's new capital, in June 1841.

Almost immediately, however, things began to go wrong. Bad planning combined with bad luck, and the men became hopelessly lost in the unmapped desert without enough food to sustain them. Bands of Comanche and Kiowa Indians attacked stragglers, and the party also had to deal with the threat of Mexican opposition. Finally, the whole force was captured by the Mexican army. Chained together in small groups, their clothing now in tatters, and surviving on a small piece of bread per day, they were forced to march more than 1,000 miles south to Mexico City. The Mexican govern-

---

Santa Anna Tempts Navarro

"Over and over again was he offered liberty, station and wealth, if he would turn against Texas, or use his influence to bring her back into the Mexican confederacy; but inflexibly pure, the stern and honest patriot spurned every effort with disdain"—American reporter George Wilkins Kendall. (Dawson, p. 73)

Navarro's Answer

"As I fought, so shall I be willing to die. I will never forsake Texas and her cause. I am her son." (Dawson, p. 73)

---

ment, outraged that its one-time province would be so bold as to attempt capturing more Mexican lands for itself, threw the Texas "troublemakers" into prison. As a Mexican, Navarro was singled out for especially harsh treatment. The survivors—perhaps half of the original force—were released after a time, but Navarro was sentenced to be shot as a traitor.

Imprisonment. In response to appeals from men like Sam Houston, who had treated Mexican president Santa Anna fairly after capturing him at San Jacinto, Santa Anna reduced Navarro's sentence to life imprisonment. But he was sent to the worst of Mexican prisons, the infamous castle at San Juan de Ulloa. According to the American reporter George Wilkins Kendall, who had accompanied the expedition, Santa Anna's orders were to shut Navarro up alone "in the darkest, dampest, dreariest dungeon within its walls" (Dawson, p. 75). Santa Anna came to visit Navarro, hoping he would beg for mercy. When the door to his cell was opened, however, Navarro would not move or say a word, angering Santa Anna further.

Santa Anna's harsh treatment of Navarro was punishment for more than the brazen attempt to take New Mexico. In Santa Anna's eyes, Navarro had committed treason against Mexico several years earlier when he signed the Texas Declaration of Independence. Apparently Santa Anna bore a more personal grudge against the prisoner, too. In earlier years the Mexican general sought the hand of Navarro's sister in marriage but was rejected as a man of poor character.

Escape. Only after Santa Anna was overthrown in 1844 did Navarro gain an opportunity to escape. Friendly guards began to let him out for brief walks along the shore of the island prison. An American trader passed by in his boat, spied the lonely figure, and steered the boat to shore. Navarro jumped aboard. The new Mexican president made no attempt to recapture the escaped prisoner.

State constitution. Though Navarro returned to a hero's welcome in Texas, his health had suffered from the disastrous expedition and long imprisonment. His wealth had also diminished. In his absence, his cattle had been driven off or stolen. He barely had time to recover, however, before once more being called upon to serve Texas. The territory was going to become a state. Navarro won election to the convention held to approve statehood and write a state constitution. One of the most heated debates at this convention concerned whether or not the Mexicans should have the right to vote. The only Texas Mexican at the convention was Navarro. In the end, the constitution was modeled on the independent Texas constitution that Navarro had helped write nearly a decade earlier. At the first state elections in the winter of 1845, he was elected state senator from San Antonio. The following year, Navarro County in southern Texas was named for him.

Disappointment. Now members of the twenty-eighth state, many Texans wanted to win more territory for Texas and supported the idea of invading Mexico to take more land. With the recent experience of the messy Santa Fe Expedition fresh in his mind, Navarro opposed the idea. When war broke out between Mexico and the United States in 1846, the Tejanos faced open hostility from Texan whites for the first time. Newer immigrants, who had brought the population to more than 200,000, viewed the Tejanos with prejudice and suspicion. The war ended in 1848, with the United States taking possession of the entire western territories formerly controlled by Mexico. Now in his fifties, Navarro watched with growing disappointment as the divisions deepened between the few remaining Tejanos and the ever-increasing Anglos. Lynchings and killings became more and more common, and some towns passed laws preventing Mexican Americans from living or working there. Disturbed by such events, Navarro retired to private life when his senate term ended in 1849.

Aftermath

Longhorns. Navarro spent the next twenty years living the quiet life of the gentleman rancher. He owned huge areas of ranch land on which he raised longhorn cattle, the famous breed brought by the Spaniards. Beginning in 1850, Navarro lived in a house in San Antonio, spending most of his nights there, while visiting his ranches during the day. All of his sons fought for the South in the Civil War, but he continued to center his life around his business and family. Cattle boomed in Texas with the opening of the Chisholm Trail from San Antonio to Kansas in 1866, and Navarro's sons kept the ranches going as their father grew older. Navarro was asked to

▲ Navarro's home

rejoin the state senate once the war ended but, in failing health, he refused. Navarro died of cancer on January 14, 1871, leaving behind a sizable estate and years of Texas patriotism. He has been publicly recognized, along with Austin, as a cocreator of Texas.

For More Information

Dawson, Joseph Martin. *José Antonio Navarro: Co-Creator of Texas*. Waco: Baylor University Press, 1969.

Meier, Matt S. *Mexican American Biographies: A Historical Dictionary, 1836-1987*. New York: Greenwood Press, 1988.

Montejano, David. *Anglos and Mexicans in the Making of Texas, 1836-1986*. Austin: University of Texas Press, 1986.

Sam Houston

1793-1863

Personal Background

Sam Houston was born in western Virginia's Rockbridge County on March 2, 1793. His mother's family, the Paxtons, was one of the county's wealthiest and best known. Their daughter Elizabeth had married Captain Samuel Houston, veteran of George Washington's Revolutionary Army and descendant of Irish Protestants who had come to America in 1730. Captain Houston continued his army service after the war as an inspector of the Virginia militia. It was between two of his frequent inspection trips that his and Elizabeth's fifth son was born, in the spring of 1793. They named him Samuel, after his father, but he would always be called Sam.

Virginia childhood. The Houstons had another boy and then three daughters in the years following Sam's birth, so that there were nine children in all. Like other "up country" Virginian children of the time, the Houston boys and girls grew up in a land where pioneering and Indian battles were still a memory for their older relatives. They spent their days mostly out of doors, riding horses, swimming in nearby Mill Creek, hunting in the woods, climbing trees, and pretending to fight Indians and Redcoats. Every Sunday, they went to Timber Ridge Church, named after the Houston plantation a few hundred feet away. Houston's father started a school next to the church with his neighbors, but Sam was rarely to be

▲ Sam Houston

Event: Independence, annexation and white settlement of Texas.

Role: Having led the Texans to victory over Mexico in 1836 at the Battle of San Jacinto, Sam Houston went on to serve as president of the Independent Republic of Texas, overseeing its annexation by the United States as the twenty-eighth state in 1845. After statehood, he served as senator and then governor.

found in the simple log building. A poor student, he frequently skipped school, preferring to steal into the woods with a book or explore the shelves of his father's library.

By wagon to Tennessee. When Sam was fourteen, his father died while traveling on an inspection tour. Elizabeth Houston sold what she inherited from her husband and paid off his debts, which were large due to his poor business dealings. She loaded her family and belongings into two sturdy wagons and took them west to the Tennessee frontier. Two cousins of Houston's father had settled there after the Revolutionary War near what became the town of Maryville. They had been among the first white settlers, though more had followed. Still, when Elizabeth and her children arrived, Maryville was little more than a few rough log houses built along the sides of an old Indian trail. Elizabeth bought more than 400 acres of uncleared Tennessee land here. Her older children built a house and went to work clearing the land for farming.

Dreams of glory. Though old enough to assist his brothers, Sam was bored by farming and did little to help out. And he was no more enthusiastic about going to school than he had been in Virginia. Instead of working or studying, he would take his favorite book, *The Iliad,* into the forest and disappear for hours or even days at a time. The ancient Greek story of warfare and heroism seemed a far cry from the dull routine of farm life. Sam dreamed of performing such heroic deeds himself. Thanks to his mother's and brothers' hard work, the farm did well. Soon Elizabeth bought a share in Maryville's general store. She sent Sam to work in the store, so that he could at least learn a useful trade. But the store bored him as much as farming, and he couldn't bring himself to stick with it. He also grew increasingly tired of being bossed around by his hard-working older brothers, who kept trying to get him to do his share of work for the family.

Participation: Growth of Texas

Co-loh-neh: the Raven. Just across the Tennessee River from Maryville lay Indian country—the territory of the Cherokee, who had been pushed west from Georgia by white settlers. Sam's wanderings in the forest had taken him among the Cherokee. Impressed by their way of life, he made friends with them. Here, he thought, was the noble society of *The Iliad*. Prosperous, hospitable, and warlike, the Cherokee had absorbed into their culture many whites who, like Sam, were dissatisfied with white society. As a teenager, Sam began slipping across the river to spend time with his Cherokee friends, who welcomed him. At sixteen, he began living with the Indians and refused to come home when his brothers came for him. Oo-Loo-Te-ka, a powerful tribal chief, adopted Sam as his son, giving him the name Co-loh-neh, or the Raven. Sam lived happily among the Cherokee for most of the next three years. He learned many of their ways and for the rest of his life felt deeply tied to them.

Unusual schoolmaster. Sam returned to Maryville in the spring of 1812, looking for work to pay off debts he had piled up buying gifts for Indian friends over the past few years. Unwilling to take a clerking job, he told his shocked (and highly amused) family that he had decided to open a school! Now fully grown, he stood six-feet two-inches, with brown hair, clear gray eyes, and strong, handsome features. In his habitual "hunting shirt of flowered calico," the rugged nineteen-year-old did not look much like a schoolmaster (Williams, p. 28). He had spent less than a year in school himself. Still, the school he opened attracted students, whom he lectured about *The Iliad* and other favorite Greek classics. He was able to pay off his debts.

During the year that he ran his school, exciting events were taking shape in the outside world. War had been declared against the British, and fighting had broken out in the West between the Americans and Britain's Indian allies, the Creek and the Shawnee. Sam closed his school and on March 1, 1813, a day before his twentieth birthday, joined the army.

Horseshoe Bend (1814). A year later, leading a company of the Thirty-ninth Infantry Regiment, Third Lieutenant Sam Houston arrived at the hastily built outpost of Fort Strother, in present-day Alabama. There General Andrew Jackson was preparing to lead his army against the Creek, who had built a strong fort at nearby Horseshoe Bend, a sharp peninsula in the Tallapoosa River. In the attack that followed, Houston was hit on the inside of the upper thigh by a long arrow. Failing in his attempts to remove the arrow himself, he made a fellow officer pull it out, tearing a deep wound. Then General Jackson called for volunteers to storm the fort. Houston dragged himself to his feet and, limping badly, led the charge. This time he was hit by two bullets at once, one ripping deep into his right shoulder and the other, a few inches lower in his upper arm. He spun to the ground and half-fainted. The army surgeons did not bother to operate, thinking that he would not live. He was lucky. If they had operated, they probably would have amputated his arm. The wounds in his thigh and shoulder never completely healed, but at least he still had use of the arm.

Jackson's Junto. The Battle of Horseshoe Bend broke the power of the Creek, and Houston's bravery during it impressed Jackson. By 1815, with the war over and with Houston nearly recovered from his wounds, Jackson arranged for him to be assigned to Jackson's own staff in Nashville. From the Hermitage, his elegant estate outside of town, Jackson was beginning to build the political machine that would carry him to the White House. Houston became an early member of Jackson's team, which was called the Tennessee Junto. Nashville was a hotbed of political activity, and Houston, still in his early twenties, socialized with governors, congressmen, and future presidents such as James Polk and James Buchanan.

Cherokee service. In 1817 Jackson arranged for Houston to be assigned as government subagent for the Cherokee, whose land the government wanted for white settlement. Houston's job was to persuade the reluctant Cherokee to move farther west, a direction that their traditions linked with death and defeat. It was a tough assignment. Many of the Cherokee resented being repeatedly pushed from land they had been given, supposedly forever, in treaties with the U.S. government. Houston, however, did in fact believe that moving west was in the best interests of the Cherokee and was able to convince Oo-Loo-Te-ka to lead them to the Arkansas Territory.

Lawyer, congressman, governor. Houston got into trouble as an Indian subagent for dressing as he wanted, not as he was expected to dress. He appeared in the office of the powerful secretary of war wearing an Indian outfit—breechclout, blanket, and turkey feathers. The secretary, John C. Calhoun, was outraged and gave him a stern lecture. Soon after, corrupt officials whom he had attacked for cheating the Indians accused him of being dishonest himself. He proved his innocence but felt disgusted with the whole thing. Resigning from the army in 1818, Houston returned to Nashville. He began to practice law, using his growing legal practice as a political springboard and resuming his place among Jackson's Tennessee Junto. In 1823 he was elected to Congress, and he won reelection in 1825. Popular and well respected, in 1827 Houston was elected governor of Tennessee. Here, as in Washington, he also made a few enemies, for Houston generally said and did exactly what he wanted.

The Raven flies west. While preparing his reelection campaign early in 1829, Houston married Eliza Allen, the young daughter of a wealthy and powerful friend. His friend Andrew Jackson had just been elected president, and the young governor's political horizons seemed boundless. At this point, however, personal scandal tainted Houston's political life. A few months after they were married, Eliza left Houston and returned to her parents. The Tennessee voters were shocked, for such a breakup was considered a disgrace. The separation would be permanent and became the greatest mystery about Houston's life. Neither he nor Eliza would ever tell anyone what happened between them.

In April, Houston resigned the governorship under the cloud of this personal scandal. Declaring himself "a ruined man" (Williams, p. 69), he left Nashville secretly and headed west by riverboat. In his time of trouble, he intended to take refuge with the Cherokee. Refuge was not the only thing he had in mind, however. Houston had heard tales of a huge, seemingly unbounded land beyond Arkansas. Always ambitious, he now had vague dreams of carving an empire out of the territory owned by Mexico known as *Tejas,* or Texas.

Wigwam. Houston settled right back into Cherokee life. Although it had been eleven years since he had lived with his adopted family, he still spoke the language well and immediately began dressing Cherokee-style again. The Indians had settled along the banks of the Arkansas River, just a few hundred miles from the Red River, which formed the border with Mexican-owned Texas. In about a year, he opened a trading post he called the Wigwam. In order to avoid paying taxes, he asked Oo-Loo-Te-ka to formally adopt him into the tribe, with "rights, privileges and immunities ... as if he was a native Cherokee" (Williams, p. 81). At the same time, he married a tall, beautiful Cherokee widow named Tiana.

Unofficial representative. For the next few years, Houston ran his trading post and involved himself in Cherokee affairs, acting as the tribe's unofficial representative to the U.S. government. He discovered, for example, that a corrupt army officer was swindling the Cherokee out of the $50,000 that the United States had agreed to give them each year. Dressed in fine buckskin and a decorative Indian blanket, Houston led an Indian delegation to Washington to complain directly to his friend President Jackson. The dishonest officer and four others were fired from their jobs in disgrace, becoming Houston's enemies. He took such trips to Washington often in the next few years, trying to keep the Cherokee from being treated unfairly. He also worked to keep peace between the Cherokee and their new neighbors, the Osage.

"Damn rascal." On one trip to Washington, in 1832, Houston heard that a congressman, William Stanbery, had made a speech accusing Houston of being dishonest in his dealings with the Indians. He was furious. A few days later, while out for a stroll around the capital with his thick walking stick, he happened to encounter the congressman. Houston approached Stanbery and demanded an explanation for his accusations. Faced with the large, wrathful Houston, Stanbery tried to draw a pistol. Crying "damn rascal," Houston began beating the congressman over the shoulders with the hickory stick, badly bruising him. Congress tried Houston and gave him a fine, which President Jackson, though embarrassed by Houston's behavior, said he did not have to pay.

G.T.T. On his trips east, Houston had also been slowly moving forward with his plans for Texas, making arrangements with politicians and possible financial backers. It remains unclear what his exact intentions were. Probably he did not know himself. According

▲ Stephen Austin

to some, he was already planning to revolutionize Texas by turning it into an independent nation, possibly with Indian help, or joining it to the United States. With an ever-increasing population and the resulting land shortage, Americans were heading west in droves. In the 1830s and 1840s, Texas was the most popular destination. Pioneers scrawled "G.T.T.," Gone To Texas, on the doors of the cabins they left behind, joining the others on the dangerous journey west. By the early 1830s, 15,000 Americans had settled in Texas, most within recent years. The 3,000 Mexicans living there, called

Tejanos, were already outnumbered by white settlers. Houston left his wife Tiana and set out for Texas in 1832. (Tiana would later remarry, as would Houston.) At this time, talk of separation from Mexico was already in the Texas air.

Yanqui parties. Houston settled in the town of Nacogdoches, about fifty miles from the Louisiana border, and set up a law practice. Like others, he purchased thousands of acres of land to be sold at a profit later. (It is not clear where he got the money to do so, though probably he had eastern partners.) But political issues would have to be settled first. A new Mexican government came to power in 1833, headed by Antonio López de Santa Anna, who was determined to bring the unruly *Yanquis* (Yankees) in Texas under his control. For their part, the Yanquis had split into two groups. The Peace Party, headed by Texas colonizer Stephen Austin, wanted to negotiate with the Mexicans to gain greater independence. The War Party, made up of leaders like William Travis, were spoiling to fight for complete independence.

War. By 1835 it was clear that war was coming. In October, the Texans elected Houston commander in chief of their small army. Soon after, bands of Texans, disobeying Houston's orders, captured Mexican forts at the Alamo and Goliad. By the end of March 1836, however, both forts had been recaptured by the Mexicans and their Texan defenders wiped out.

The Alamo

Having occupied the fort against Houston's orders, the Texans held it despite his orders to leave and blow it up. Nearly 200— including Davy Crockett and Jim Bowie— died in the Mexican attack.

Fresh from victory at the Alamo, Santa Anna personally led his tough and experienced army deeper into Texas. Houston organized the now frightened Texans in a month-long, eastward retreat known as the Runaway Scrape.

San Jacinto. During the retreat, Houston did his best to train his men and give them courage. April 20th found the two armies facing each other, both camped along the San Jacinto River. Santa Anna commanded an advance guard of about 800 men, the same number as the Texans. Hearing of the Mexicans' low numbers, Houston decided to let his once-again eager troops face their pursuers. During the night, however, reinforcements slipped into the

▲ Siege of the Alamo

Mexican camp, nearly doubling Santa Anna's force. It seemed as if the Texans' chance had slipped away. But the following afternoon, as the tired reinforcements slept, Houston's Texans attacked and completely defeated the overconfident Mexican force. In what remains one of the most lopsided battles in history, nearly half the Mexicans died, with the rest taken prisoner, while the Texans lost only six men. Santa Anna himself was captured, while Houston's ankle was shattered by a bullet.

Republic. Houston's spectacular victory ended the war and assured Texan independence. It also led to the war hero's election as president of the Independent Republic of Texas in the summer of 1836, with over 5,000 votes against Stephen Austin's 587. President Houston's main goal was to arrange for the United States to annex, or add, Texas to the Union as quickly as possible. Unfortunately a business collapse known as the Panic of 1837 temporarily shattered the U.S. economy, and Houston's old friend President Jackson refused to consider annexation, though he did officially recognize the new republic. Meanwhile, a city sprang up near the site of the battle of San Jacinto. Its founders named it Houston, and invited its namesake president to make his capital there. It quickly grew into a flourishing, hard-drinking frontier town.

Marriage and family. Always known for his ability to enjoy a good time, Houston was as hard-drinking as anyone else in town. Yet in 1840, after he ended his term as president, his drinking days became numbered. He even began attending church occasionally. In that year, at age forty-seven, he married a quiet, serious, and intensely religious young woman of twenty named Margaret Lea. Beautiful, dark-haired and very shy, Margaret had fallen in love with Houston at first sight, as he had with her. The love proved lasting, and the couple had eight children between 1843 and 1860.

Second term. Houston was reelected president in late 1841, serving until 1844. During his second term he continued his efforts to win annexation, also defending his country against renewed threats from Mexico. Houston's main weapon in the fight for annexation was the possibility that his state would make alliances with foreign powers such as France or Britain. His skillful diplomacy was rewarded shortly after he retired from the presidency, when annexation finally took place in July of 1845. Texas joined the United States as the twenty-eighth state. Its population had grown to 200,000, with more arriving every day. Many of the newcomers were European immigrants. Germans settled entire towns, giving them German names like New Braunfels, for example. Texas prospered as the hard-working immigrants—mostly farmers and craftsmen—replaced the frontier types of past years.

Aftermath

Senator. From 1846 to 1859, Houston served in Washington as Texas senator, fighting to stop the regional divisions that increasingly pitted North against South. He was the only Southern senator who voted for every part of the Compromise of 1850, which attempted to find a middle ground in the argument over slavery. Part of the compromise gave away Texas land to the government. Houston became increasingly unpopular in Texas for such positions, which put the Union interests before that of his state. Through much of his Senate career, he warned that the course pursued by the South could end only in bloody civil war.

Personal downfall for the Union. Yet in 1859 he was elected governor on a platform that called for the Union's preservation. Two years later, however, after Texans voted for secession, Houston was removed from office when he flatly refused to take an oath of allegiance to the Confederacy.

> **"Margaret, I will never do it!"**
> Governor Houston on his refusal to secede from the Union. (Williams, p. 161)

Houston, now badly troubled by his old wounds, retired quietly to his farm in Huntsville. From there he watched as his predictions about civil war came true. His oldest son, Sam Jr., was wounded and captured by Northern soldiers in 1863. All of his other children were at his bedside when Houston died on July 26, 1863. Reportedly, his final words were "Margaret! Margaret! Texas! Texas!" (Williams, p. 362).

For More Information

James, Bessie Rowlan, and Marquis James. *Six Feet Six: The Heroic Story of Sam Houston*. Indianapolis: Bobbs-Merrill, 1931.

Williams, John Hoyt. *Sam Houston*. New York: Simon and Schuster, 1993.

Zachary Taylor

1784-1850

Personal Background

Family life. Blending plantation life with a military career would be natural for Zachary Taylor in later years. His father, Richard Taylor, was a lieutenant colonel in the Revolutionary War before he turned to farming in Orange County, Virginia. With the help of thirty-two slaves, Taylor ran a successful farm. He married the aristocratic Sarah Dabney Strother, and the two started a family. They had a son named Hancock in 1781, another named William in 1782, and Zachary in 1784. The third of nine children, Zachary was born in a log cabin on the Taylor farm.

In 1783 Zachary's father had received a land grant of 6,000 acres in Kentucky for his service to the country. The family moved to a new plantation on Beargrass Creek near Louisville in 1785. There Zachary grew up among frontier farmers, while his father, by careful management, expanded his landholdings to 11,650 acres and served as a Kentucky legislator.

As a boy, Zachary spent much of his time performing chores and handling farm equipment. He also helped direct the work of the slaves. While opportunities for education were limited, Zachary's father and some of the other frontier parents hired a teacher for a time. Zachary learned to read and write and developed an interest in books, mostly about military subjects.

▲ **Zachary Taylor**

Event: The Mexican War.
Role: A soldier for most of his adult life, Zachary Taylor became a hero when he won a series of battles against more numerous enemy forces in the war between the United States and Mexico in 1846. Taylor's resulting popularity led to his election as U.S. president in 1848.

The mostly unschooled boy grew into a short-legged young man, stocky and powerfully built. He was strong and determined, qualities he demonstrated at age seventeen by swimming across the Ohio River and back. When he was twenty-two, his older brother William became a second lieutenant in the army. The next year, in 1808, Zachary too began a military career.

Military career. Due possibly to his father's political connections, the army commissioned Taylor as a first lieutenant and assigned him to the Seventh Infantry. He was soon ordered to command a small fort near Memphis, Tennessee.

During his early years in the army, Taylor established himself as an unconventional military man who hated to be challenged by other officers about his decisions. He also heartily disliked the standard uniform and often discarded it, instead dressing in "a big straw sombrero, a pair of enlisted men's trousers which were too short for him, a loose linen coat, and a pair of 'soldier's shoes'" (Bauer, p. 165).

By 1810 Taylor's success with his men had led to a promotion to the rank of captain. That same year he married Peggy Mackall Smith. As a wedding gift, his father gave the couple 364 acres of land. Taylor would increase this holding in the coming years, acquiring plantations around the South and hundreds of slaves. He and Peggy would have six children.

War of 1812. Two years after Taylor married, the United States went to war with England. In the first year, Taylor, now a captain, was assigned to command Fort Harrison on the Wabash River in Indiana. Nearby was a federation of Indians who sided with the English.

Taylor and thirty-four of his fifty men fell ill with fever. In September, they were attacked by about 450 Indians who set fire to the fort. Taylor rallied his feverish men to beat off the attack and put out the fire. The Indians then set up a siege to starve out the fort's defenders. Living on green corn, Taylor's men held out for a few days until Kentucky volunteers arrived and broke the siege. This battle was the first of Taylor's victories against a larger enemy force. In his down-to-earth style, he had commanded his men with courage and cool-headedness. His success in holding the fort earned him a brevet, a temporary promotion, to major.

Saukenuk. Taylor saw little action again until 1814. In the late summer of that year, he led a 430-man expedition up the Mississippi River from St. Louis. As punishment for a Sauk Indian attack on three American keelboats, the soldiers wanted to destroy the tribal town of Saukenuk. The British, however, managed to arrive first and reinforce the town, even providing a cannon for its defense. The combined British-Sauk resistance sent the small American force retreating to the Des Moines River. Saukenuk was the only battle Taylor ever lost.

Peace. After the war ended and the army was reduced, Taylor was returned to the rank of captain. He resented the demotion and disliked the inactive army life, so he resigned. But his civilian days were numbered. In 1816 President James Madison reinstated Taylor and assigned him to command Fort Winnebago near Green Bay, Wisconsin. During the next several years, Taylor managed garrisons and recruited soldiers in places such as Fort Slenden, Louisiana, before returning to his life as a plantation owner in 1823.

Black Hawk War. In 1832 war erupted in the upper Mississippi Valley when Black Hawk, a Sauk chief, led a group of his followers from exile in Iowa back into northern Illinois. Serving in the army again, Taylor was ordered to set up a supply base at Dixon's Ferry for troops operating against Black Hawk. Taylor later helped pursue the chief and his followers. At one point, some U.S. militiamen became so frightened they abandoned the battle site. A disappointed Taylor wrote to General Henry Atkinson, "The more I see of the militia, the less confidence I have in their effecting anything of importance" (Bauer, p. 61).

On the upper Mississippi. Taylor stayed in the upper Mississippi River Valley for several years. In 1834 he was appointed Indian agent for the Winnebago and for some of the Sioux Indians. The following year, he persuaded the Sauk, Fox, Menominee, and Winnebago to sign a treaty and stop battling one another. That year he also supervised construction of a road across Wisconsin, which was to become an important westward route for pioneers. He earned a reputation in the area as a capable officer who kept his men well trained, stayed out of military politics, and treated Indian tribes fairly.

Florida. Within five years, Taylor found himself once more in combat. In 1835 Florida's Seminole Indians began armed resistance against the government's efforts to remove them from their homes to Indian Territory (now Oklahoma). American forces made little progress in combating the Seminole army, and in 1867 Taylor was sent to Florida. In December, he led about 1,000 volunteers and regular soldiers into the wilderness to search for the Seminole. He found them near Lake Okeechobee. This time Taylor had the greater numbers, but the Indians were in an excellent defensive position. They were hidden by trees, with the lake on their left and swamps to the right and in front. Despite heavy losses, Taylor's regular soldiers managed to drive back the Indians. The Seminole broke and scattered. In a move that was to become typical of his style of warfare, Taylor chose not to pursue the fleeing Indians. Although incomplete, the victory earned him another temporary promotion to brevet brigadier general. It was in Florida that Taylor earned the nickname "Old Rough and Ready" for his willingness to share the hardships of the campaigns with his men.

The Seminole now reverted to guerrilla tactics. To subdue them, Taylor's men carried out search-and-destroy missions. Several hundred Indians surrendered, but their resistance could not be completely broken. In 1840, discouraged and in ill health, Taylor asked to be transferred.

Participation: Mexican War

In the Southwest. Taylor was reassigned to command troops in the Southwest. He served for two years in Indian Territory, then was stationed in Louisiana. Meanwhile, tensions were rising between the United States and Mexico over the issue of Texas. The Republic of Texas had gained independence from Mexico in 1836 and now wanted to become part of the United States. Mexico, however, refused to recognize Texas's independence and threatened war should the United States try to annex the state. Meanwhile, Mexico controlled lands in the southwestern United States, including what is now Arizona, California, Nevada, New Mexico, Utah, and part of Colorado.

The question of whether to annex Texas set off a great debate in the Senate. Fearing that Mexico might invade the state before anything was decided, Texas's president Sam Houston asked for

U.S. military aid. U.S. President John Tyler sent warships to the Gulf of Mexico and ordered Taylor and 1,150 men to Fort Jesup, Louisiana, near the Texas border, to act as a corps of observation.

In May 1845, Taylor and his troops were alerted to the likelihood of conflict with Mexico. Through a joint resolution of both houses of Congress, the United States finally approved the annexation of Texas to the nation. In July, Texas's government accepted this resolution.

Corpus Christi. Now Secretary of War William L. Marcy ordered Taylor to advance to a position from which he could drive back a Mexican invasion of Texas. Taylor chose Corpus Christi, a small trading post just west of the mouth of the Nueces River. The Nueces had long been recognized by Mexico as the border between the two countries. By land and sea, American troops were soon moving to Corpus Christi. They faced difficult conditions there. Tents leaked, water was bad, and one of every five soldiers was stricken with sickness. Accustomed to such harsh conditions, Taylor seemed indifferent to the problems. He continued to drill his troops, preparing them for war.

Meanwhile, President James Polk sent John Slidell to Mexico to try for a peaceful settlement between the two countries. There was disagreement over whether the border between them was the Nueces River or the Rio Grande River farther west. Slidell's goal was to win acceptance of the Rio Grande as the border and to purchase as much of New Mexico and California as possible. The mission failed. In 1846 Taylor was ordered to the Rio Grande, and his troops began to advance.

Matamoros. On the way to the Rio Grande, the soldiers had their first encounter with Mexican troops at the Arroyo Colorado, a coastal lagoon. The Mexican commander warned Taylor that he had committed an act of war by crossing the Nueces River. Taylor responded with cannon fire, forcing the Mexican troops to retreat. The Americans were soon on the Rio Grande opposite the Mexican city of Matamoros.

The Mexicans continued to warn the Americans that they were committing an act of war. Taylor continued to stress his peaceful intentions. Meanwhile, Mexico, a land of Roman Catholics, tried to persuade the Roman Catholics among the Americans to desert to the Mexican side, dropping leaflets and promising land grants to all deserters. A few Americans decided to switch sides and were shot by their own sentries as they tried to swim across the river.

Taylor began to construct Fort Texas across the river from Matamoros, a clear sign that the Americans were there to stay. On April 11, Mexican General Pedro de Ampudia ordered Taylor to withdraw beyond the Nueces River or be attacked. This threat increased when Ampudia was replaced by General Mariano Arista, who arrived with orders that it was necessary for hostilities to begin. On April 20, shooting finally broke out when some Mexican soldiers ambushed an American patrol.

Palo Alto and Resaca de la Palma. After the fighting began, General Taylor left 500 men to defend Fort Texas and marched the rest of his troops to his supply base at Point Isabel, thirty miles away on the Gulf of Mexico. His purpose was to bring back supplies to the Fort Texas base. After filling their wagons, the men started out for the fort only to find their path barred by about 6,000 Mexican troops.

A battle began, with artillery duels followed by unsuccessful cavalry charges from both sides. The Mexicans then attempted a combined cavalry and infantry charge, but this was driven back by American artillery. Amidst all the warfare, a fire broke out. The heavy smoke stopped the fighting and obscured everything long enough for Taylor's troops to ambush the Mexican soldiers from all sides. In the confusion, the Mexicans were forced to withdraw to the safer grounds of Resaca de la Palma about five miles away. As at Lake Okeechobee, Taylor declined to pursue a retreating enemy. Instead, his men camped on the battlefield.

The next day, Taylor learned that the Mexicans had regrouped along the Resaca de la Palma, a ravine filled with rough brush and small palms. The general held a council of war. His leading officers voted seven to four not to attack the Mexican forces until reinforcements arrived. Yet Taylor directed them to go to their respective commands and be ready to move in thirty minutes. He had decided to attack.

Mexican artillery opened on the Americans as they approached. Small units engaged one another in hand-to-hand combat in the brush. Finally, the Americans worked their way around the Mexican flank. The panicked Mexican soldiers fled for the Rio Grande, and many drowned trying to cross it. Others headed for the safety of Matamoros, several miles south. Once again, Taylor did not pursue a fleeing enemy. This time, 49 Americans and 154 Mexicans died in the battle.

After the victory at Resaca de la Palma, Taylor scheduled a meeting with Navy Commodore David Conner to discuss the strategy for the next American attack. Knowing that Conner was never seen out of uniform, Taylor wore full military dress. Knowing that Taylor hated uniforms, Conner wore street clothes. Despite their embarrassment over the mix-up, the two officers worked well together and quickly drew up a strategy for attacking the Mexicans at Matamoros. By now, however, General Arista had retreated from Matamoros to Linares, 160 miles to the south. His decision to cross a bleak desert without sufficient supplies cost hundreds of Mexican lives. Only 2,368 of Arista's 6,000 men ever reached Linares.

Taylor captured Matamoros on May 18, 1845, and spent several weeks there. While intent on defeating Mexico, he showed compassion for the enemy. He directed his surgeons to attend to the Mexican wounded and contributed several hundred dollars of his own money to their support.

In June, news of the battles of Palo Alto and Resaca de la Palma reached the American newspapers. Taylor received widespread praise and was promoted to major general.

Monterrey. Because communications to Texas depended on horses and sailing ships, it was several weeks before Taylor received further orders from the War Department. However, he assumed that the city of Monterrey would be the next objective and planned accordingly. He established a base upriver at Camargo, and hundreds of volunteers poured into the area.

By September 1846, Taylor's troops had grown to more than 6,000 men, half of whom were volunteers. Taylor began to march the men toward Monterrey. Mexico's leader, Antonio López de Santa Anna, ordered General Pedro de Ampudia to fall south to Saltillo and await more troops before fighting the Americans. Ampudia, eager for glory, defied the order.

When Taylor and his men arrived in Monterrey, they surveyed

the city's defenses. Unfinished fortifications stood on the hills to the west. Taylor sent General William Worth and his men to attack this position. Meanwhile, the other American troops pushed toward a tannery that had been equipped by the Mexicans to protect the center of the town.

Worth's attack was successful. His soldiers took control of the hills and blocked the road to Saltillo. The troops attacking the tannery were also successful, despite heavy losses. Mexican resistance crumbled and Ampudia surrendered. With his regular and volunteer army of 6,000, Taylor had once again defeated more numerous troops. The Mexicans had 10,000 men, 7,000 of whom were regular soldiers. As before, Taylor did not pursue the defeated army, even promising a truce for eight weeks, allowing time for the Mexicans to retreat from the fighting.

Polk. Although Taylor's victory excited the public, the truce angered President Polk, who by this time may have begun to worry about Taylor as a rival for the office of president. Polk canceled the truce and showed his contempt for Taylor by sending a direct order to one of Taylor's officers to proceed to Tampico.

A movement to nominate Taylor for president in the 1848 election was already under way. Polk tried to bolster his own position by appointing Missouri senator Thomas Hart Benton to head the army, but Congress and his own Cabinet rejected the idea. Eventually, the president appointed Winfield Scott to lead the forces in Mexico. Meanwhile Taylor would command American defenses in the war.

Buena Vista. In January 1847, Taylor received an order to transfer 9,000 of his troops to Scott's command for a move on Vera Cruz. Included in these troops were many of Taylor's best officers and soldiers. Their loss was only partly offset by new volunteers, and Taylor soon faced a new threat. Santa Anna was marching northward with 20,000 men.

In February, Scott ordered Taylor to abandon Saltillo and concentrate his forces at Monterrey. Taylor balked at this order since he thought Saltillo would provide the Mexicans with a base from which to attack Monterrey. He told Scott he would pull back only under direct orders from Washington.

As Santa Anna approached, Taylor decided to make a stand at San Juan de Buena Vista, a ranch situated on a plateau below a

▲ **Naval bombardment of Vera Cruz**

mountain pass leading to Saltillo. Early on the morning of February 23, the Mexicans attacked. The outnumbered Americans, now mostly volunteers, were in retreat by mid-morning. Taylor, however, who had been at Saltillo when the battle began, soon appeared on the battlefield riding his familiar horse, Old Whitey. The spirits of the Americans rose, their resistance stiffened, and the Mexican advance stalled. Mexican reserves were called forward to resume the advance, but it stalled again when Americans brought up their own reinforcements. In the evening, Santa Anna retreated from the battlefield. The Americans expected him to renew the attack the next day; instead, his forces retreated to their base at San Luis Potosi. Once more, hundreds of tired and starving Mexican soldiers died on the march. Taylor and his men had defeated a force three times their number.

Attention in the war turned to Vera Cruz and Mexico City. Except for minor engagements with Mexican cavalry, Taylor fought his last battle at Buena Vista. With the signing of the Treaty of Guadalupe Hidalgo in early 1848, the Mexican War ended and so did Taylor's military service. In his final months of battle, he wrote to one of his daughters, "I am heartily tired of this war" (Bauer, p. 211).

Aftermath

Taylor for president. Taylor's victory at Buena Vista strengthened his popularity with the American public. A Taylor-for-president movement began, with "Rough and Ready Clubs" springing up around the country. Taylor was at first uninterested in running. In 1846 he had written to a friend, "I am not and never shall be an aspirant for that honor. My opinion has always been against the elevating of a military chief to that position" (Bauer, p. 217). Still troubled by his wartime difficulties with the administration, however, he began to grow interested. Even before he returned from Mexico, he started to write letters to newspapers sharing his views on various issues. Though he never declared himself a contender, the Whig party chose him as its candidate. Taylor remained on active duty throughout the campaign and thus barely beat the Democrat candidate, John Lewis Cass, in the November election.

The Taylor presidency. Taylor was pro-Union. At the same time, he was a strong supporter of states' rights, or the belief that states should determine certain policies independent of the national government. In a letter to Jefferson Davis, he agreed that Southerners had a right to resist abolitionists with weapons if their behavior went beyond the limits of proper protest. However, Taylor felt it was treason to secede from the Union, and he never pushed for the extension of slavery, even though he was one of the nation's largest slave holders. Taylor actually supported California's admission to the Union as a free state.

Foreign policy. As president, Taylor maintained a strict foreign policy that dealt firmly with other countries. When some Americans tried on their own to invade the Spanish colony of Cuba and were seized by Spain to be tried for piracy, Taylor warned that their execution would mean war. Taylor also warned that Spain's transfer of Cuba to France would mean war, and he warned France not to attempt to take the Hawaiian Islands or more Caribbean territory.

Domestic issues. In 1849 California was being overrun by gold seekers, and local governments began to fall apart under the rapid influx of gold seekers. The crime rate soared, murderers often going unpunished. So Taylor reacted by sending a military governor into California to restore order. He also sent troops to New Mexico when Texas threatened to occupy some land that it claimed there.

During the final months of Taylor's presidency, Congress debated a complex piece of legislation. Taylor called it the Omnibus Bill because it included many parts that he believed should be treated separately. The bill, the Compromise of 1850, admitted California to the Union as a free state, organized the Utah and New Mexico territories, settled the Texas-New Mexico boundary problem by paying Texas $10 million, abolished the slave trade in the District of Columbia, and strengthened the Fugitive Slave Law.

Final days. On July 4, 1850, while the omnibus bill was still being debated in Congress, Taylor attended an Independence Day ceremony in Washington. The weather, he thought, was hotter than he remembered it being in Mexico or Florida. He complained of a headache and dizziness. That evening, after eating cherries and iced milk, he suffered cramps. Over the next several days, his health worsened. Taylor died on July 9, 1850. Although a doctor diagnosed his condition as cholera morbus, now known as gastroenteritis, in 1994 Taylor's body was exhumed because some people thought he was poisoned. No evidence of foul play was found.

Over the years Taylor's family had grown to include four daughters and a son. One of the daughters married Jefferson Davis against her father's wishes. Two months after the wedding, she died. Davis remarried and became president of the Confederate States of America in 1861. Taylor's son, Richard, became a Confederate general in the Civil War.

For More Information

Bauer, K. Jack. *Zachary Taylor.* Baton Rouge: University of Louisiana Press, 1985.

Nichols, Edward J. *Zach Taylor's Little Army.* Garden City, New York: Doubleday, 1963.

Young, Bob, and Jan Young. *Old Rough and Ready.* New York: Julian Messner, 1970.

John Charles Frémont

1813-1890

Jessie Ann Benton Frémont

1824-1902

Personal Background

John Charles Frémont was born John Charles Frémon, Jr., on January 21, 1813, in Savannah, Georgia. He was the eldest child of Anne Beverly Whiting Pryor and John Charles Frémon, Sr., who were married before Anne obtained a divorce from her first husband. John Charles, Jr., called Charley, and later, Charles, was ridiculed during much of his life for his parents' behavior. As a result, he remained somewhat of an outsider.

Name change. When Charley was seven months old, the family moved to Nashville, Tennessee, where his sister, Katherine, was born. Financial hardship soon forced the family to relocate again to Norfolk, Virginia, where Charley's youngest brother, Francis, was born. Upon arrival in Norfolk, their father, who had immigrated from France, changed his name to the more pronounceable Frémont and worked as a French language and dance instructor in town. Anne Frémont took in boarders and raised her three children on a very tight budget.

Early childhood. Charley developed into a very bright child. At age five, he memorized the "Star Spangled Banner" and sang it in front of his Sunday school class at church, earning a reputation as "that incomparable Charley Frémont" (Eyre, p. 13). He also possessed a great memory and an aptitude for mathematics. But his

▲ John Charles Frémont

Event: Mexican War; settlement of California.

Role: John Charles Frémont captured northern California in the Mexican War and obtained the surrender of Mexican General Andrés Pico in southern California, which ended the war and secured the territory for the United States. Jessie Frémont added to her husband's fame and encouraged others to settle in the West by recording and publishing his adventures.

father would not live to see Charley develop his potential. Mr. Frémont died of pneumonia in late 1818 when Charley was not yet six years old. The hardships that followed soon drove Anne and the children to Charleston, South Carolina, where Anne again took in boarders and cared for her family as best she could.

Education. Though she could not afford much, Anne wanted the best education she could get for her eldest son. She sent him to the local school and began inquiring about secondary education. A local minister, who was impressed by the young Frémont's scholastic abilities, advised Anne to find her son a sponsor who could help meet his educational expenses. The sponsor was John W. Mitchell, a Charleston attorney, who took Charley under his wing and hired him as a law clerk. In addition to providing work for Frémont, Mitchell tutored the boy in foreign languages and math in the evenings and enrolled him in Dr. Robertson's Preparatory School when he was about ten. There Frémont easily mastered Greek and Latin and so impressed Robertson that the schoolmaster wrote to Anne:

> "Your son, Charles, has already proven that he has a prodigious memory, also an enthusiastic gift for application, which leaves no doubt of his future progress.... The boy seems to learn by intuition and astonishes me with his progress" (Eyre, p. 18).

Frémont graduated from Robertson's school and entered Charleston College when he turned fourteen. Despite such a promising beginning, his college career would end in dismissal.

Expulsions. Frémont did so well in his classes that he had ample time on his hands to get into trouble. Instead of reporting to study hall on the weekends, he would play in the woods with friends or go sailing on the bay. During the next six years, Frémont's attention turned from his studies to girls and the outside world. Telling his mother "the whole world outdoors is calling me!" Frémont cut his classes, disobeyed his teachers, and much to his mother's dismay soon found himself expelled from school at age twenty, just three months prior to graduation (Eyre, p. 19).

Luckily for Frémont, he had done well enough in his classes to impress a Charleston College trustee who came to his aid. Joel Poinsett, the former minister to Chile (and for whom the flower, poinsettia, is named), offered Frémont a job as a math instructor on

▲ Jessie Ann Benton Frémont

a ship bound for South America. In May 1833, after passing a naval exam with top honors, Frémont set sail out of Charleston aboard the sloop *Natchez,* telling his disappointed mother, "I will make you proud of me or die trying, Mother" (Eyre, p. 18).

Two years later, Frémont returned home a thoroughly inspired and changed man. He had a broader view of the world and a thirst for travel and adventure. However, having gotten quite sea-sick while aboard the *Natchez,* Frémont decided his subsequent ventures would be conducted on land and was offered such a job the following year.

Topographical engineer and officer. Accepting a post in 1836 with the U.S. Corps of Topographical Engineers, Frémont worked as a civil engineer, surveying land for a railroad between South Carolina and Ohio. The following year he ventured farther west for the government, mapping land beyond the Mississippi River deep into Cherokee country. In 1838 Frémont was commissioned second lieutenant in the newly created Military Topographical Corps and was sent to map land west of St. Louis with famed French explorer and astronomer Jean Nicholas Nicollet.

Under the guidance of Nicollet, Frémont grew into an experienced, educated explorer. While they mapped the rivers and valleys of the Midwest by day, Nicollet taught Frémont to chart the stars and sky by night.

Returns home to many changes. In 1839, with his second expedition completed, Frémont returned to Charleston only to learn that his brother, Francis, had been accidentally shot and killed. With his sister, Katherine, having died years earlier, Frémont was now the sole provider for his mother. Determined to take good care of her, he wasted no time in securing a position with a third government expedition.

Participation:
Mexican War and Settlement of California

The Bentons. In preparation for his next venture into the western wilderness, Frémont moved to Washington, D.C. There he met with the expedition's organizers, including Senator Thomas Hart Benton, who was a powerful advocate of western expansion. Benton took an immediate liking to Frémont, and the two began discussing U.S. settlement of California and Frémont's possible role in it. At this time, Mexico controlled California but occupied only small towns along the coast. The interior remained a virtual wilderness, but Benton, among others, feared that Mexico would soon enlist the help of Britain to formally settle the region. It was Benton's hope that the United States would obtain the California territory from Mexico before British ships arrived to claim the land for themselves.

During their weeks together, Frémont was greatly influenced by Benton and adopted his views toward U.S. possession of California. Frémont began to envision, as Benton did, a prosperous and vast United States extending from the Atlantic to the Pacific Ocean. He also began to envision himself as a major force in achieving this and relished the thought of traveling over a part of the world that still remained uncharted. The "opening up of unknown lands; the study without books, learning at first hand from Nature herself," Frémont said, are "becoming a source of never ending delight to me" (Eyre, p. 37). He felt extremely lucky at the prospect of being chosen for such work.

Frémont meets Jessie. While at the senator's house, Frémont met a second Benton who had an even more profound impact on him than had the first. Jessie Ann Benton, the senator's very intelligent, very independent daughter, met Frémont and, according to the young explorer, it was love at first sight. Though more than ten years apart in age, Jessie and John Charles were very similar in character and experience. Jessie was the protégé of her father—well educated and widely traveled. She spoke Spanish and French and spent much of her time studying, among other writings, Thomas Jefferson's personal papers in the Library of Congress. Since she was a young girl, Jessie had accompanied her father on his daily rounds to the state capitol. She was well versed in politics and personally knew most of the leading political figures of the day.

Though somewhat of a tomboy, Jessie at fifteen was an attractive young woman and became smitten with the dashing, soon-to-be-famous Frémont. Being a women in those days prevented Jessie from following in her father's footsteps, but she could marry a man who would. Such a husband would allow her to live out her dreams of exploration and political advancement, goals that were practically unthinkable for women in the 1840s.

Though Frémont called Jessie "the woman of my heart," she was too young and Frémont too poor to gain her parents' permission for marriage yet (Eyre, p. 45). So Frémont left on his expedition, but within seven months returned to Washington a newly commissioned first lieutenant to claim his bride. After attempting to elope three times, Jessie and Charles finally succeeded on the fourth try and were married on October 19, 1841.

California. Meanwhile, Senator Benton's vision of claiming California for the United States was becoming a reality. The new Polk administration granted permission for exploration of California, and Frémont was chosen to lead the historic series of expeditions, which would, among other things, map the region for establishment of rail lines to the West. With Jessie's encouragement, Frémont left for the Rocky Mountains in June 1842 and had great fortune in recruiting men for the journey. While in St. Louis he met and obtained the services of Kit Carson, who soon proved irreplaceable. Carson would accompany Frémont on all of his subsequent travels in the West.

During their first two expeditions, Frémont's crew mapped the West from the highest peak of the Rocky Mountains, named Frémont's Peak, to the West Coast of California. As Benton had thought, Frémont's exploration proved that California was a lush land, highly suitable for occupation and cultivation.

A team effort. When Frémont returned to Washington after the first two expeditions, Jessie helped him compile his findings for a series of government reports. In doing what she called her "most happy life's work," Jessie wrote about her husband's adventures, making his experiences come alive for readers (Eyre, p. 89). Describing Frémont's first sight of the great Salt Lake, Jessie recorded her husband's personal impressions:

> We reached the butte ... and beheld at our feet the object of our anxious search, the waters of the Inland Sea [Salt Lake] stretching in still and solitary grandeur far beyond the limit of our vision. It was one of the great points in our exploration ... I am doubtful if the followers of Balboa felt more enthusiasm when, from the height of the Andes, they saw for the first time the Great Western Ocean [the Pacific Ocean]. (Eyre, p. 104)

The reports sparked the imagination of many would-be pioneers, providing not only scientific detail of the region but also the excitement of frontier life.

The Frémonts' cooperative effort was received with great enthusiasm by Congress. It had 10,000 copies of the report reprinted for the general public to read. In the eyes of one senator, Frémont's exploration had "proved that the country several hundred miles beyond the Missouri [River] was not a desert as formerly marked on the maps, but a fertile prairie with plenty of timber and water" just "waiting to be claimed by emigrants" (Eyre, p. 90).

War. By 1846, U.S. interest in California was reaching its peak, and the country stood on the brink of war with Mexico over the territory. President James Polk sent Frémont to California as a lieutenant colonel in the spring of 1846 to prepare for such an event. In the meantime, two Mexican generals, Andrés Pico and José Castro, were preparing their respective battalions for combat. Pico's troops were to defend southern California, and Castro's troops would protect northern California. Additionally, the Mexicans had enlisted British help and were awaiting Royal Navy ships in Monterey and San Diego.

Upon arrival in the Sacramento Valley in May 1846, Frémont set up camp at Lassen's Ranch (near Sutter's Fort) and worked quickly to recruit American civilians into his battalion. Frémont's California Battalion became a curious mixture of trappers, engineers, adventurers, miners, and ranchers. In the end, they proved to be a highly capable group of more than 400 men.

> ### Letter to the President
>
> In spring 1846, Frémont wrote to Polk, informing him of the Mexican Army's movements in California and vowing his loyalty to the United States in the event of war. He wrote:
>
> "We can see with the glass, Mexican troops mustering at St. John's. I would write you at length if I did not fear my letter would be intercepted. We have in no-wise done wrong to any of the people, and if we are hemmed in and assaulted, we will die, every man of us, under the flag of his country." (Eyre, p. 140)
>
> From accounts such as these, Frémont appears a loyal officer rather than a revolutionary out for his own glory, as some were to later suggest.

Bear Flag Revolt. By early summer, war had been officially declared between the United States and Mexico, but because the mail was so slow, word had not yet reached California. While he waited for instructions, Frémont readied his troops, gathering together needed supplies and ammunition. To further that end, he planned to capture a well-supplied ranch in Sonoma, owned by retired Mexican general Mariano Vallejo. Having heard rumors that Castro was also on his way to the same ranch on a raid for supplies, Frémont determined to get there first. On June 14, 1846, Frémont led thirty-four men into Vallejo's ranch, captured the owner, and took possession of all their horses and military equipment, including nine brass cannons, 250 muskets, and 100 pounds of gunpowder. The prisoners were sent to nearby Sutter's Fort, and the captured ranch was turned into a garrison. Frémont and his men raised the newly created bear flag, a sign that California was now a free republic, over the Sonoma garrison.

Golden Gate

In July 1846, just after the Bear Flag Revolt, while Frémont was on his way to Monterey, he passed through the entrance to San Francisco Bay and seeing its "gilded waves" named it "Golden Gate Harbor." In mapping the area for his government reports, he used this title for the bay. The name proved highly appropriate when the gold rush of 1849 in San Francisco occurred. Today, the entranceway to the San Francisco Bay is still called the Golden Gate.

The Bear Flag Revolt, as it came to be known, touched off the first in a series of controversies surrounding Frémont's actions during the Mexican War. While he won praise from some, he was strongly criticized by others for his unauthorized action. The wife of a prisoner described Frémont's battalion as a sordid group of "horse thieves, trappers and run away sailors" who were unwarranted in their aggression (Herr, p. 144). Thomas Larkin, the U.S. Consul stationed in Monterey, agreed. He insisted that Frémont's actions provoked the Mexicans living in California to resist American occupation "more strongly than if they had been treated diplomatically" (Herr, p. 145). On the other hand, Captain John B. Montgomery of the U.S. warship *Portsmouth,* which was stationed in Yerba Buena (San Francisco) at the time of the attack, was surprised by the Bear Flag Revolt but declared that "the capture of the horses and surprise at Sonoma were master strokes" by Frémont and his "gallant little band" (Herr, p. 145).

Jessie defends her husband. Meanwhile, Jessie, who had been hired by Secretary of State James Buchanan to translate Spanish documents for the U.S. government during the Mexican War, suffered vicious attacks on her husband at home. Some, mostly Whig party members who also disliked her father, gossiped about Frémont's "disreputable" father, who had "run off with another man's wife," and implied that Frémont's character was just as poor (Herr, p. 134). Jessie stood firmly by her husband, however, and wrote to him in California, focusing on his recent promotion rather than on the negative rumors and the Bear Flag Revolt:

> Your merit has advanced you in eight years from an unknown second lieutenant, to the most talked of and admired lieutenant-colonel in the army.... I have heard of no envy except from some of the lower order of Whig papers who only see you as Colonel Benton's son-in-law. (Herr, pp. 138-39)

Soon, popular opinion began to shift toward Jessie's point of view.

In July, after he'd learned that war had been officially declared, Frémont traveled to Monterey to receive orders from Naval Commodore Robert Stockton. There he found the United States in sole possession of Monterey, and he triumphantly declared all of northern California to be U.S. territory. A naval officer published this account of Frémont's arrival, which helped transform him into a national hero:

> Colonel Frémont's party arrived here yesterday. They are the most daring and hardy set of fellows I ever looked upon. They are splendid marksmen.... They never sleep in a house, but on the ground, with a blanket around them, their saddle for a pillow, and a rifle by their side. (Herr, p. 146)

Suddenly Frémont was seen as a heroic, romantic figure, praised by some and envied by others.

War ends. In the following months, Frémont's fame increased as he and Stockton developed a plan to capture Los Angeles. Before the attack, Stockton commissioned Frémont as major in the navy, and Frémont took this lower rank, resigning his lieutenant colonel position in the army to avoid any conflict of interest. This was Frémont's second controversial decision of the war and the one that led directly to his later court-martial. With 220 men, Frémont rode into southern California under Stockton and captured Los Angeles. With this victory, the entire state was declared United States territory. Frémont was appointed temporary governor and sent to Monterey to organize the new state government. This plan soon changed, however, when a U.S. Army commander, General S. W. Kearny, failed to secure Los Angeles after the capture. Frémont was sent back into battle in the south. While he and his battalion set up camp at the San Fernando Mission, Kearny and Stockton regained Los Angeles.

Meanwhile, General Pico, who was routed from Los Angeles a second time, sought out Frémont at the mission in order to surrender to him. As temporary governor, Frémont had pardoned Pico's brother rather than execute him as a prisoner of war. Because he had spared his brother's life, Pico knew Frémont to be a reasonable man and therefore wanted to surrender to him. On January 12, 1847, Pico rode into Frémont's headquarters at the Old Cahuenga Ranch House and the Articles of Capitulation were signed the following day. As Kearny himself declared, Pico's surrender to Frémont ended the Mexican War: "The enemy capitulated to him yesterday … agreeing to lay down their arms, and we have now the prospect of having peace and quietness in this country" (Eyre, p. 180).

Aftermath

Court-martial. But peace and quiet was not to come right away for Frémont. With his fame now at an all-time high because he had obtained Mexican surrender and was now governor of California, he made enemies among political leaders who were jealous of his success and questioned his motives. Kearny was especially judgmental and openly accused Frémont of marrying his wife for her political connections and fighting in California only out of a "thirst for glory" (Herr, p. 155). Even President Polk refused to endorse Frémont's war record and condemned him for taking a lower rank of major in the navy when the president had commissioned him as lieutenant colonel in the army. The president in fact seemed to be less concerned about Frémont's alleged wrongdoing than he was about Frémont gaining all the glory for the conquest of California.

Whatever Kearny's or Polk's motives, they soon forced Frémont to resign as governor of California and had him court-martialed for failing to follow orders. Frémont retained his ardent supporters, however, many of whom went to Washington to defend him. Jessie and her father of course defended him to the president, as did Kit Carson, who rode all the way from San Diego to stand by his former employer. Carson later wrote: "I was with Frémont from

1842 to 1847. The hardships through which we passed, I find it impossible to describe, and the credit which he deserves I am incapable to do him justice" (Eyre, p. 354).

Despite such testimony on his behalf, Frémont was convicted in an 1847 court-martial. He was subsequently pardoned by Polk but resigned his military rank in disgust and moved to California with Jessie and their children to resume work as an engineer for the railroad. There the Frémonts made their home and raised their daughter Elizabeth and sons Frank and Charley (a daughter, Anne, and son, Benton, each died in infancy).

Remaining years. The husband and wife team lived a long and adventure-filled life. Frémont went on to become a California senator, the first Republican presidential candidate in 1856, and a general during the Civil War. Jessie continued to write about western expansion and to publish accounts of her husband's exploits, drawing acclaim even from Henry Wadsworth Longfellow, who wrote: "Frémont has particularly touched my imagination. What a wild life, and what a fresh kind of existence!" (Herr, p. 83). In fact, both of the Frémonts helped inspire a generation to follow in their lead and settle in California.

Frémont died of peritonitis on July 13, 1890, while in Washington, D.C. He was seventy-seven at the time. Jessie continued to write until her death, publishing articles on California for *Century* magazine and writing books on her life with Frémont in the West. She died of natural causes on December 27, 1902, at the age of seventy-eight.

> ### A Far West Sketch
> ### by Jessie Frémont
>
> "The new day brought us into enchanting natural parks of grassy uplands and fir and hemlock growths in varying stages; the layered boughs, tipped with the lighter green of the spring growth, rested in tent-like spread on soft young grass and wild flowers. It was all gracious and open and smiling with, at times, a break in the trees giving us a glimpse, across the valley below, of the near Yosemite range. And in the fresh stir of morning air we laughed and sang and 'were glad we were alive'". (Frémont, pp. 134–35)

For More Information

Eyre, Alice. *The Famous Frémonts and Their America.* New York: Fine Arts Press, 1948.

Frémont, Jessie. *Far West Sketches.* Boston: D. Lothrop Company, 1890.

Herr, Pamela. *Jessie Benton Frémont.* New York: Franklin Watts, 1987.

Transcendental and Romantic Movements

1836
Ralph Waldo Emerson writes *Nature,* a short book that outlines the basic beliefs of the transcendental movement.

1839
Margaret Fuller holds the Conversations, a series of classes for Boston women (and later men).

1843
Nathaniel Hawthorne makes fun of transcendental beliefs in his story "The Celestial Railroad."

1841
Henry David Thoreau builds cabin in the woods near Walden Pond. Communal living experiment begins at Brook Farm.

1840
Fuller edits first issue of the journal *The Dial.*

1844
Fuller becomes the first female journalist hired by the *New York Daily Tribune.*

1845
Fuller publishes *Woman in the Nineteenth Century,* saying women are independent of men, not inferior to them.

1848
First women's rights convention is held at Seneca Falls, New York.

1859
Thoreau prints essay on antislavery rebel John Brown.

1854
Thoreau's book *Walden* is published.

1850
Hawthorne publishes the *Scarlet Letter.*

1849
Thoreau's essay on civil disobedience is printed.

TRANSCENDENTAL AND ROMANTIC MOVEMENTS

People often regard the period before the Civil War as the richest in the literary history of the United States. Two movements related to each other surfaced in America during this period. Beginning in Europe, the romantic movement was a trend in the arts. Related to it was the transcendental movement, which popularized certain ideas, mostly through writings. From 1830 into the 1850s, American writers, influenced by both the romantic and transcendental movements, created a distinctly American body of literature.

Centered in New England, the transcendental movement made popular the ideas of self-reliance and freedom of thought. It urged people to listen to their own intuition rather than public opinion. Transcendentalists believed in basic human goodness and felt that society's ills could be cured if individuals took responsibility for their own self-improvement. Members of the movement supported social causes of the 1800s such as abolition, women's rights, and temperance— a movement to stop Americans from drinking alcohol. Leading transcendentalists brought their ideas to the world through lectures, essays, and poems; it is through these writings that the movement is best remembered.

The guiding member of the transcendental movement was Ralph Waldo Emerson, a Unitarian minister who left the church partly in protest of religious authority. Afterward, Emerson turned his attention to lecturing and writing. In his famous essay *Nature,* Emerson stated basic ideas of the movement: Americans should look inward and to nature for knowledge, and there is a spark of the divine in all people that will lead to social reform. Living in Concord, Massachusetts, Emerson gathered around him like-minded friends with whom he shared and discussed such ideas.

One of Emerson's closest friends, **Henry David Thoreau,** created some of the most powerful writing of the movement. While other members attempted to live together in experimental communities such as Brook Farm in West Roxbury, Massachusetts, Thoreau isolated himself in the woods of Concord to study nature and practice self-reliance. Out of this experience came the book *Walden, or Life in the Woods,* with observations on nature and human existence. Thoreau also was one of the first to use the tactic of nonviolent resistance, later practiced by other reformers in America and abroad. Protesting against the Mexican War, he refused to pay his taxes and then explained why in an essay:

> If a thousand men were not to pay their tax bills this year, that would not be a violent and bloody measure, as it would be to pay them and enable the State to commit violence and shed innocent blood. This is ... a peaceable revolution. (Anne C. Rose, *Transcendentalism as a Social Movement, 1830–1850.* [New Haven: Yale University Press, 1981], pp. 222–23)

Another member of the movement, **Margaret Fuller,** joined Emerson, Thoreau, and the rest in their discussions. A lecturer, writer, and editor, she took steps to advance the cause of women by holding classes. Called "Conversations," these classes challenged women to think for themselves, often for the first time. A few other women of the day were becoming active in social causes, such as abolishing slavery. Along with Fuller's efforts, such activity would lead to the first women's rights convention in 1848, nearly a decade after the Conversations were first held. Besides leading these discussion classes, Fuller also edited the *Dial*, a journal that spread the ideas of the transcendental movement.

The writer **Nathaniel Hawthorne** had strong ties to the movement, though he rejected some of its ideas. His wife, Sophia Peabody, came from a family of firm believers. Also, the Hawthornes lived in Concord, socialized with Emerson, Thoreau, and Fuller, and even stayed for a time at Brook Farm. Hawthorne differed sharply from the others, however, concerning their steadfast belief in basic human goodness. In his view, the transcendentalists failed to acknowledge human evil. Hawthorne's own writings, by contrast, explored the ideas of sin and guilt and drew on America's Puritan past to sketch romantic tales of ordinary people affected by evil.

Hawthorne's tales were part of the romantic movement in literature. Science and reasoning had previously been put on a pedestal in society. Replacing this trend, romantic writers believed in the importance of the individual imagination. They wrote stories about nature and the lives of common folk, sometimes dealing with experiences that helped shape the character of a nation's people. Hawthorne, writing tales about the Puritans of colonial days, helped set the foundation for a distinctly American literature. Other romantic writers of his day—Herman Melville, Emily Dickinson, Edgar Allan Poe, and Walt Whitman—created novels and poems about nature and human nature that began to fill out the body of a national literature. Meanwhile, outside the romantic movement, African Americans such as Frederick Douglass added books of a different sort, writing their life stories to expose the evils of slavery. All of these authors turned to their own instincts and heritage for inspiration, and, in the process, wrote works that would give their country a separate literary identity.

Henry David Thoreau

1817-1862

Personal Background

Early childhood and family. David Henry Thoreau was born
July 12, 1817, in Concord, Massachusetts, the third of four children
born to John and Cynthia Thoreau. Henry, as his family called him,
belonged to the third generation of Thoreaus in America. His paternal grandfather, Jean Thoreau, a French seafarer, had settled in
America after being shipwrecked. The Thoreaus (pronounced
Thórow or *Thorough* in Concord) were a close-knit family. John, a
quiet and serious man, struggled through several trades before
finding success as a maker of lead pencils. Cynthia, a strong-willed,
talkative, warmhearted woman and a fierce abolitionist, kept a
boardinghouse. The family home, filled with boarders and relatives,
was a bustling center of activity and talk.

Henry, nicknamed "Judge" by his schoolmates, was a serious
and somewhat aloof child. He had no interest in childhood games.
In the words of one schoolmate: "He seemed to have no fun in
him.… His quietness was more noticeable, no doubt, from the contrast between him and his brother John, who was as chock full of
fun as an egg is of meat" (Harding, p. 49). The young Thoreau
seemed to take more enjoyment in the frequent long walks the family took through the lush woods of Concord and along the area's
hills and ponds.

▲ **Henry David Thoreau**

Event: Transcendental writings.
Role: A major transcendental writer, Henry David Thoreau captured nature's rich beauty in words. He is perhaps best known for his book *Walden*, which discusses simple, self-reliant living. Thoreau also wrote essays, such as "Civil Disobedience," a protest to the Mexican War and the Fugitive Slave Act.

Concord. Concord lies about 16 miles west of Boston, and during Thoreau's time, the town held about 2,000 citizens. Though farming was the main occupation, the manufacture of clocks, hats, pencils, bricks, and soap was becoming increasingly important and profitable during the mid-1800s. Concord was, in fact, a thriving center because it sat at a major crossroads leading to Boston, New Hampshire, western Massachusetts, and southern New England. The town was a stopping place for travelers and wagon drivers. Politics and scholarly talk were part of the atmosphere in Concord; many of its citizens were Harvard graduates, and the townsfolk took pride in Concord's part in the American Revolution.

Thoreau later considered it his good fortune to have been born in Concord. Shortly after his birth, his family moved to nearby Chelmsford and, later, Boston, and did not return to Concord until 1823. When he was five, Thoreau visited Walden Pond in Concord with his grandmother. In spite of his young age, Thoreau remembered the visit vividly. Years later, he wrote that seeing the pond at this time became "one of the most ancient scenes stamped on the tablets of my memory.... That woodland vision for a long time made the drapery of my dreams" (Canby, p. 33).

Education. Thoreau and his older brother were educated at Concord Academy, a private school for boys that taught subjects such as classical literature and languages. Because Thoreau proved to be the stronger student and his parents could only afford to send one son to college, they decided to send their younger son, now sixteen, to Harvard.

Thoreau barely passed his entrance exams but managed to do so well in his first year that he was granted a twenty-five-dollar scholarship, about half the full tuition. As he had as a boy in Concord, Thoreau remained rather aloof from his Harvard classmates and did not seem to have been particularly popular. One classmate later wrote:

> He was cold and unimpressible. The touch of his hand was moist and indifferent, as if he had taken up something when he saw your hand coming, and caught your grasp upon it. How the prominent, gray-blue eyes seemed to rove down the path, just in advance of his feet, as his grave Indian stride carried him down the University Hall! (Canby, pp. 45-46)

Thoreau himself did not think too highly of his college education. He did grant that at Harvard he learned to express himself in writing. After college, he began keeping a journal of his thoughts on the world around him and the human spirit.

Schoolmaster for a fortnight. After graduating, Thoreau returned to Concord, having had the good luck to land one of the two main teaching posts in town for a $500 annual salary. He was responsible for fifty to one hundred boys, all cramped together in one stuffy classroom. The school committee required that teachers punish the students with regular floggings, but Thoreau ignored this requirement and announced "that he should not flog, but would talk morals as punishment instead" (Canby, p. 67). When school administrators insisted that he follow their rules, Thoreau resigned after only two weeks on the job. It wouldn't be the last time Thoreau ignored rules that clashed with his personal beliefs.

After this, he applied for teaching positions throughout New England and as far away as Virginia. While he looked for jobs, he helped his father in the pencil-making business. During this time, he changed the order of his names from David Henry to Henry David, apparently preferring the sound.

When no job offers came his way, Thoreau opened his own school in Concord. His first class included four students, whom "he read a little Greek or English [to], or for variety, [took for] a stroll in the fields" (Richardson, p. 38).

First, and only, love. In the summer of 1839, when Thoreau was twenty-two, a girl named Ellen Sewall visited Concord. The beautiful, bright, lively seventeen-year-old had come, along with her eleven-year-old brother, for a two-week visit with an aunt, who boarded with the Thoreaus.

Both Thoreau and his brother, John, were quite taken with the young woman. The three spent many hours together, going on long walks through the woods and sailing on the Concord River. At first, it seems, Ellen was more attracted to the talkative and outgoing John. Thoreau could only stand back and watch as his brother courted the girl whom he also loved. The following summer, John proposed marriage to Ellen, and though she at first accepted, she

97

very quickly broke the engagement because her family did not approve.

Now the field was clear for Thoreau to make his move. But the young man apparently had great difficulty in expressing his emotions, especially feelings of love. He expected Ellen to know that he loved her without his showing it. He later wrote, "Love is the profoundest of secrets. Divulged, even to the beloved, it is no longer Love" (Canby, p. 117). Thoreau may not have stated his love for Ellen, but in November of 1840, he did write her at her home in Scituate, proposing marriage. Ellen refused, again under the guidance of her father, who did not think it would be a good match. She wrote to her aunt: "I do feel so sorry H[enry] wrote me. It was such a pity.... But it is all over now" (Canby, p. 121).

For Thoreau, however, it was not over; the rejection crushed him. After receiving Ellen's refusal, he wrote in his journal, "I did not think so bright a day would issue in so dark a night" (Richardson, p. 85). Thoreau never forgot Ellen Sewall, and on his deathbed, he spoke of his love for her.

A second tragedy. Fortunately, the thwarted romance did not result in hard feelings between the two brothers. But, soon afterward, in January 1842, Henry was devastated by the tragic death of his brother. John cut his finger while sharpening his razor and the cut became badly infected. A week later, John got lockjaw, a stiffening of the jaws often coupled with violent spasms, and two days later he died. Occurring just a year after Ellen's rejection, this second trauma crushed Thoreau.

> He mourned deeply for this beloved brother. He laid aside his flute and for years refused to speak his name. A friend told to me that twelve years later Thoreau started, turned pale, and could hardly overcome his emotion when some reference to John was made. (Harding, p. 149)

For a time, Thoreau did not write at all; when he again took up his pen, it was with a new burst of creative energy.

How others saw Thoreau. Physically, Thoreau was on the short side and sturdily built. He had a plain face, with a prominent nose, large, clear gray-blue eyes, full lips, and a serious expression.

His personality was powerful. The following observations of Thoreau reveal how others saw him:

> He always reminded me of an eagle, ready to soar to great heights or to swoop down on anything he considered evil. (Anonymous–Harding, p. 102)

> He was a queer kind of duck. Always used to wear a gray shirt and tramp through the woods every day. (Frank Pierce-Harding, p. 154)

> Yet, hermit ... as he was, he ... threw himself heartily and child-like into the company of young people whom he loved. (Ralph Waldo Emerson—Thomas, p. 267)

Participation: *Walden* and "Civil Disobedience"

Ralph Waldo Emerson. Soon after graduating from Harvard and returning to Concord, Thoreau began a friendship with Ralph Waldo Emerson that would last his lifetime. By the time he met Thoreau, who was fourteen years his junior, Emerson already had established himself as an important writer and lecturer and was popular in America and abroad. The relationship between the two was in many ways one between teacher and student; in the early years, Emerson called Thoreau "the boy" and Thoreau considered Emerson a master in his field.

Thoreau was writing essays and some poetry at the time he met Emerson. As Thoreau refined his writings, Emerson read and commented on them. Thoreau appreciated Emerson's insights and in many ways idolized him. Some say Thoreau took his hero worship to an extreme. Observers who knew both men claimed that Thoreau took on Emerson's way of speaking, his mannerisms, and

Musical Thoreau

A serious man, Thoreau was at the same time quite musical. He played the flute, sang a little, and loved to dance. The following account gives an interesting glimpse into a rarely seen side of Thoreau:

"Once, after a day so stormy that he had not taken his customary outdoor exercise, Henry came flying down from his study ... and soon began to dance, all by himself, spinning airily round, displaying remarkable litheness and agility; growing more and more inspired, he finally sprang over the center-table, alighting like a feather on the other side. Then, not in the least out of breath, continued his waltz until his enthusiasm abated." (Harding, p. 95)

his expressions, so that with closed eyes, one could not tell the difference between the two men. But Thoreau was more a man of action; Emerson, a man of ideas.

As the friendship grew, Thoreau became more involved in the older man's family life. When Emerson traveled on lecture tours, often for long stretches at a time, Thoreau lived at the Emerson house and took on responsibilities there. The children took to calling him "father." Over time, Thoreau began to disapprove of Emerson's long and frequent absences and the resulting neglect of his family. This strained the friendship as Emerson and Thoreau grew older.

Thoreau, the Lecturer

In time, Thoreau, like Emerson, would lecture to audiences, but Thoreau never felt comfortable at it. He would stand on the platform and eye the audience distrustfully, afraid that he would end up trying to please his listeners rather than himself.

The transcendentalists. Nonetheless, the friendship was extremely significant in setting the tone for Thoreau's writing and intellectual life. Through Emerson, he met a brilliant group of thinkers and writers, including Margaret Fuller, Nathaniel Hawthorne, and Amos Bronson Alcott (see **Margaret Fuller** and **Nathaniel Hawthorne**). The group believed in a style of life that called for plain living and lofty thinking. Its members promoted social reform, freedom of ideas, and a spiritual way of searching for truth. *Transcend* means "to go beyond," and members of the group were known as transcendentalists because they believed that to find the truth people must look beyond what they have been taught to believe and rely instead on their intuition, or instinct. The transcendentalists encouraged people to know themselves and nature well, promising that this path would lead to social reform of morally wrong practices such as slavery.

Emerson was a leading force in shaping and defining the transcendental movement. He believed in social and religious reform and most of all, in self-reliance. Emerson frowned on the tendency of people to conform to a given way of doing things in society, believing the best way to know oneself was to separate from society. Although he preached these ideas, Thoreau would live them.

Early career. In his early and mid-twenties, Thoreau focused on developing his craft as a writer. He strove for perfection in his writing, believing that "nothing goes by luck in composition ... it allows no trick." (Richardson, p. 96). By now, he was regularly publishing poems and some essays. As always, he continued to write in his journal.

In 1843 Thoreau moved to New York to live with Emerson's brother William and serve as a tutor for William's son. This gave Thoreau the opportunity to investigate New York's writing market. His intention was to break into the city's literary scene so that he could make a steady income from his writing. He encountered stiff competition, however, and realized that getting his work published might not be that easy. During his stay in New York, he met notable writers of the period, including Walt Whitman and Henry James, Sr.

Walden Pond. About a year after Thoreau returned from New York, one of its gentlemen, Ellery Channing, wrote to Thoreau, suggesting he build a hut in the woods near Walden Pond. Channing knew that Thoreau planned to write a book about a river trip he had taken with his brother John and suggested he do so there. That spring of 1845, Thoreau borrowed an axe and set out to act on the suggestion. On a plot of land that his friend Emerson owned, he built a one-room cabin and moved in on July 4, a day that symbolized for him a move toward greater freedom and independence. His purpose was twofold: first, he wanted to study nature, and second, he wanted to devote himself to his writing. Also, he wanted to be self-sufficient and, to this end, plowed a two-and-a-half acre field and planted white beans, corn, and potatoes.

Thoreau described his decision to move to the woods in dramatic terms:

> I went to the woods because I wished to live deliberately, to front only the essential facts of life, and see if I could not learn what it had to teach, and not, when I came to die, discover that I had not lived. (Schneider, p. 13).

During his stay at Walden Pond, Thoreau was by no means a hermit. Nearly every week, he walked to his family's home to enjoy his favorite meal, Sunday dinner. He often went into town to pick up supplies and sometimes to perform odd jobs, such as painting and carpentry, to help support himself. Friends also visited him fre-

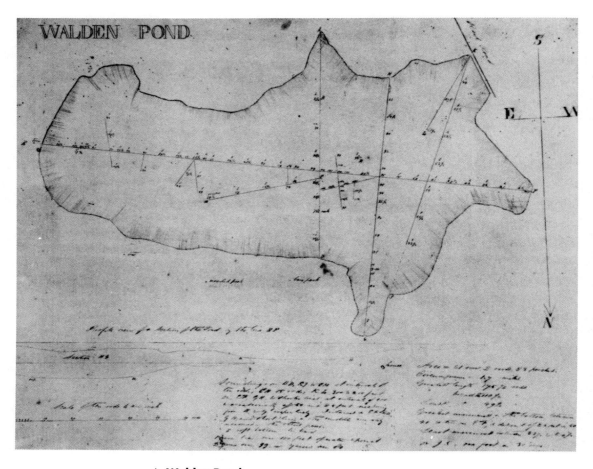

▲ **Walden Pond**

quently at the tiny wilderness cabin. Once he reported having twenty-five to thirty guests at one time. Otherwise he wrote, walked for hours through the woods, and labored with the food crops he had planted.

Mostly he spent his days working toward his goals of studying nature and writing. His two years at Walden Pond were a time of powerful creative output. Before returning to life in Concord, Thoreau completed drafts of two of his greatest works, *A Week on the Concord and Merrimack,* and *Walden, or Life in the Woods. Walden,* perhaps his most famous work, is a series of essays, mostly about nature but also about human nature, with titles like "Economy" and "The Bean Field." The book was written in response to some friends, who kept asking why he, a Harvard graduate, wanted to live in a woodland hut. In the opening chapter, Thoreau sees his neighbors as prisoners of their farms and shops.

> The greater part of what my neighbors call good, I believe in my soul to be bad.
>
> Most of the luxuries, and many of the so-called comforts of life, are ... postive [obstacles] to the elevation of mankind.
>
> My purpose in going to Walden Pond was not to live cheaply ... but to transact some private business with the fewest obstacles. (Thomas, pp. 6, 9, 13).

Thoreau lived simply in the woods with little cost to himself, except for the six weeks a year he spent raising crops and the odd jobs he performed. He proved it possible for a man to live in New England with little effort if all he desired were the basics in food, clothing, and shelter.

"Civil Disobedience." One of the famous incidents of Thoreau's life was the night in 1841 that he spent in the Concord jail for his refusal to pay taxes. For years, he had chosen not to pay the "poll" tax, a tax levied on all men older than twenty. This decision not to pay was Thoreau's way of protesting slavery, which the government allowed. One evening while still living at Walden Pond, he encountered the local tax collector on his way into the village. When the tax man warned him that his refusal to pay could one day land him in jail, Thoreau volunteered to be arrested. As the story goes, Emerson had joined with Thoreau in not paying taxes, and when he visited him in jail, he said, "Henry, why are you here?" And Thoreau retorted, "Waldo, why are you *not* here?" (Harding, p. 191).

Thoreau was soon released after his aunt paid his bail and his sister and mother collected money to pay his back taxes. Later, outraged by the Mexican War, which he saw as greed for other people's land, and by the Fugitive Slave Act, which aided owners in capturing escaped slaves, he wrote an essay titled "Resistance to Civil Government." The essay argued that a person's main duty was to his own conscience, even if it called for breaking the law of the land.

Why has every man a conscience then? I think we should be men first and subjects afterward … The only obligation which I have … is to do at any time what I think right. (Thomas, p. 225)

The essay, later called "Civil Disobedience," objected to any government at all. Thoreau supported anarchy, for he insisted that people misuse government. "Witness the present Mexican War," he argued, started by a few people who used the government as a tool (Thomas, p. 224). Thoreau preferred not to wait until unjust laws were corrected by the majority in society. Instead he immediately withdrew from his partnership with the government and acted as he believed was right.

Thoreau admired John Brown, who staged a violent revolt against slavery in 1859. Brown led the revolt because he believed slavery had to be stopped right away. In fact, Thoreau thought of Brown as a member of the transcendental movement, a man who followed the voice inside even though it went against government policy. Thoreau's essay "The Last Days of John Brown" spoke of the change in public opinion in the North after Brown's death sentence. Many Northerners were until then unconvinced that slavery must be totally abolished. After Brown's death, however, they recognized that, whatever the law said, true justice would only be served by ending slavery in the nation altogether. Thoreau, it is true, believed in peaceful or nonviolent resistance to the government, and Brown committed murder. It was not the method that Thoreau admired, but Brown's taking immediate action on his belief that no one should be a slave.

Thoreau's Influence

Of all Thoreau's writings, "Civil Disobedience" probably affected the most lives. Mahatma Gandhi read it early in his fight against Great Britain for independence in India. In the United States, Martin Luther King, Jr., practiced the same philosophy of peaceful resistance to promote black equality in the mid-twentieth century South.

Aftermath

Final Years. Thoreau ended his retreat in the fall of 1847, after which he published "Civil Disobedience," in 1849; *Walden,* in 1854; and "The Last Days of John Brown," in 1859. He left the woods for as good a reason as he had come: "It seemed to me that I had several more lives to live, and could not spare any more time for that one" (Thomas, p. 213).

For the most part, Thoreau was a vegetarian. This along with his regular long walks in the fresh country air should have kept him healthy and strong. However, he often suffered from poor health and was sometimes plagued by sleeping sickness. In spite of his ill health, he continued to write and travel throughout most of his life.

After recovering from a long illness in 1855, Thoreau lived rather energetically for five years before declining again into poor health in the beginning of 1862.

Thoreau's last days were peaceful and serene; he was not at all worried about or afraid of death. When his aunt asked him if he had made his peace with God, he replied, "I did not know we had quarrelled" (Harding, p. 140). Thoreau died quietly on May 6, 1862, of tuberculosis.

For More Information

Blair, Walter, ed., et al. *The Literature of the United States.* Glenview, Illinois: Scott, Foresman and Company, 1971.

Canby, Henry Seidfel. *Thoreau: The Biography of a Man Who Believed in What He Wanted.* Boston: Houghton Mifflin, 1939.

Harding, Walter, ed. *Thoreau: Man of Concord.* New York: Holt, Rinehart, and Winston, 1960.

Richardson, Robert. *Henry Thoreau: A Life of the Mind.* Berkeley and Los Angeles: University of California Press, 1986.

Schneider, Richard. *Henry David Thoreau.* Boston: Twayne Publishers, 1987.

Thomas, Owen, ed. *Walden and Civil Disobedience.* New York: W. W. Norton, 1966.

Margaret Fuller

1810-1850

Personal Background

The Fighting Fullers. On May 23, 1810, Sarah Margaret Fuller was born in Cambridgeport, Massachusetts, a short distance from Harvard University. She was the first of nine children born to Timothy and Margaret Fuller, and because their second child died in infancy, Margaret, as she preferred to be called, was an only child until she was five.

Timothy Fuller had wanted his first child to be a boy. Nevertheless, he loved Margaret and was determined to instill in her a zeal for learning, excellence, and perfection. His family, who for generations had lived in New England, were called the "Fighting Fullers" because of their rebellious and ambitious natures. Timothy, a lawyer and politician, placed first in his class at Harvard but was not awarded the position because he had taken part in a student rebellion. Free-thinking and fiercely strong-willed, Timothy strongly influenced his daughter's life. Margaret's mother was a much softer, gentler, and more spiritual person than Timothy; fortunately, Margaret had the calming influence of her mother to balance out her father's forceful and ambitious nature.

Early education. From the time she was a toddler, Margaret focused on learning and thinking. Her father, she wrote, aimed to bring "forward the intellect as early as possible" (Chevigny, p. 37).

▲ Margaret Fuller

Event: "Conversations" and the *Dial*.
Role: Margaret Fuller was one of the foremost writers and thinkers of her time. Despite public criticism, she pioneered the involvement of women in public discussions about subjects formerly closed to them. As editor of the *Dial*, a journal of the transcendental movement, she helped promote its ideals.

Her days were filled with reading, studying, and reciting lessons. By age four she could read; at six, she was reading in Latin, and by eight, she was reading volumes of Shakespeare.

Though Margaret was mainly educated by her father at home, she attended the grammar school in Cambridge for a time. As a woman, however, she would not be admitted into Harvard University with the boys who were her schoolmates earlier in life.

When Margaret reached adulthood, she appreciated the purpose of her father's strict training. "Very early," she wrote, "I knew that the only object in life was to grow" (Brown, p. 17). At the same time, though, she felt as though she really had not had a childhood. As a young girl, she had few friends. Her greatest pleasure was relaxing in the garden behind the house and gazing out at the field that lay beyond. Margaret often escaped from the daily grind of her studies to this garden, which was fragrant and bright with the flowers that her mother lovingly tended.

As she told it, her constant reading and studying kept her mind overly excited. She developed a habit of staying up past a normal bedtime because she was so wound up from being "too active and too intense" (Chevigny, p. 37). Her sleeplessness and her excess nervous energy caused her to suffer from nightmares, sleepwalking, and severe headaches. Later in life, she expressed the wish that she had been allowed to grow at a more normal pace, without so great an emphasis on developing her intellect. She wrote: "I am confident I should have been much superior to myself had sense, intellect, affection, passion been brought out in natural order" (Brown, p. 17).

Young adulthood and new friends. By the time Fuller was a teenager, she developed a passion for learning and a sense of discipline. A typical day began at 5:00 in the morning with an hour's walk, which was followed by a practice session at the piano, and then a full day of lessons and reading in French, philosophy, Greek, Italian, and more. Often she did not go to bed until near midnight, and only after she had written in her journal. In a letter to a teacher penned when she was fifteen, Fuller explained why she followed such a rigid schedule: "I have learned to believe that nothing, no!

not perfection, is unattainable" (Chevigny, p. 56). She was caught up in a search for perfection.

Cambridge was a lively center of learning and culture, and, as she matured, Fuller began to make valuable and lasting friendships. Her circle of friends included such noteworthy young minds as writers Oliver Wendell Holmes and Richard Henry Dana, as well as Frederic Henry Hedge, the son of a well-known Harvard professor. Hedge described Fuller as a "blooming girl" with a healthy complexion and a tendency to be overweight that bothered her; her dresses were often too tight.

> With no pretensions to beauty then, or at any time, her face was one that attracted, that awakened a lively interest, that made one desirous of a nearer acquaintance. It was a face that fascinated, without satisfying.... You saw the evidence of a mighty force, but what direction that force would assume ... it was impossible to divine. (Chevigny, p. 30)

In addition to her brilliant mind and vibrant energy, Fuller also attracted others with her engaging conversation. Often, new acquaintances, especially men, were at first put off by Fuller's forceful personality, but she soon won them over with her charm and her interesting and animated talk.

As Fuller was perfecting her mind and talent for conversation, she also was widening her social circle. Her father had risen in Massachusetts politics, first as a representative to Congress and, in 1825, as speaker of the Massachusetts House of Representatives. Because of this, she increasingly found herself in the company of some of the city's most accomplished people.

Farm life in Groton. This lively whirl of culture, society, and discussion temporarily came to an end in 1833, when the family moved to a farm in Groton, a country town about forty miles northwest of Boston. With this sudden loss of a way of life that had become very important to her, Fuller was lonely and bored. She managed to make the most of the situation, however, and threw herself into her new life with her characteristic energy. Because her mother was ill and bedridden during much of this time, Fuller handled most of the daily chores. She also took it upon herself to educate one sister, Ellen, and three of her brothers, Arthur, Richard, and Lloyd. For five to eight hours a day, Margaret taught them languages, geography, and history. "I'll tell you how I pass my time without society or exercise," she wrote to a friend. "Even till two o'clock, sometimes later, I pour ideas into the heads of the little Fullers." (Anthony, p. 41).

Two years after moving to Groton, Timothy died of cholera, leaving his family with a meager estate. As the oldest and only adult child, Fuller was faced with the responsibility of heading a large family.

Participation: Conversations and the *Dial*

Emerson and the transcendental movement. At twenty-five, Fuller began to make her true mark in the world. Her interest in philosophy and writing led her to seek an introduction to Ralph Waldo Emerson, the leader of a movement that promoted self-reliance and moral and spiritual excellence.

Fuller seemed to be looking for a mentor, someone to help give her direction in life. She developed a strong and intimate friendship with Emerson, as well as with his wife, Lidian, and often visited them at their home in Concord. Fuller later admitted to a friend that Emerson had a greater influence on her than any other American. Like Henry David Thoreau, Fuller met many like-minded intellectuals through Emerson (see **Henry David Thoreau**). The circle of thinkers who gathered regularly to share their ideas were called transcendentalists. A more appropriate name for the group, however, might have been idealists. Their philosophy centered around social reform, self-truth, self-reliance, and personal excellence. Such ideas had long been important to Fuller's own thinking.

In the Transcendental Club, she found a community of peers. There were more than a dozen men in the club, plus three women from Emerson's family, and Margaret.

Teacher. In her late twenties, Fuller earned a living as a schoolteacher. She worked for a little more than a year at the Temple

School in Boston, run by transcendentalist Amos Bronson Alcott. After this, she moved to Providence, Rhode Island, where she worked at the Green Street School for an annual salary of $1,000. She spent two years in Providence, but found the heavy workload was taking too much time away from her writing. She resigned her post and returned to Groton to help her mother move from the farm to Jamaica Plain, a residential section of Boston.

The Conversations. Now the twenty-nine-year-old Fuller set about to find another way to earn an income. She decided to blend her gift for conversation, her long-standing interest in women and their intellectual growth and independence, and her teaching skills into a career choice. With the help of friends, she set up classes for Bostonian women, at which she spoke on a series of subjects such as ethics, ideals, art, and women's roles. The purpose of these classes, she wrote, was "to supply a point of union to well-educated and thinking women" (Anthony, p. 62). True to her transcendentalist philosophy, Fuller hoped to instill in the women an intellectual self-reliance and a sense of their inner worth.

At the first meeting of the Conversations, on November 6, 1839, Fuller spoke on Greek mythology and, when she had finished her lecture, encouraged the women to share their thoughts and ask questions. When they proved reluctant to speak out, however, she had them write their ideas down on paper. She then read these notes aloud at the second meeting, inspiring most of the women to abandon their initial shyness and participate in the discussions. Ednah Cheney, a woman who attended the Conversations, wrote of the experience:

> I found myself in a new world of thought; a flood of light irradiated all that I had seen in nature, observed in life, or read in books. Whatever [Fuller] spoke of revealed a hidden meaning, and everything seemed to be put into true relation. Perhaps I could best express it by saying that I was no longer the limitation of myself, but I felt that the whole wealth of the universe was open to me. (Chevigny, p. 230)

The Conversations quickly grew to be a popular forum for women to share their ideas and beliefs. Soon the classes attracted so much interest around town that Fuller expanded them to include men. She offered two classes a week, one for women only and one for both men and women.

The Conversations, which continued for about five years, received their share of criticism from the press and others. Throughout much of her adult life, as she became more and more of a public figure, Fuller endured a great deal of scorn and ridicule. Poet James Russell Lowell, for example, wrote a satirical poem about her, and Sophia Hawthorne, wife to the novelist, wrote that "if she were married truly, she would no longer be puzzled about the rights of women" (Chevigny, p. 231). Many people were threatened by this forceful, brilliant, and independent woman. Practicing self-reliance, Fuller ignored her critics and continued to speak her truth to the world.

> ### Some Conventions That Fuller Broke
>
> - First woman to set foot in the library at Harvard University.
> - First woman to work as a journalist for the American press.
> - Author of the first book in America advocating equal rights for women.

The *Dial*. During this time, Fuller embarked on a second monumental project. She agreed to serve as editor on the *Dial,* a literary magazine put out by members of the Transcendental Club and other like-minded intellectuals. Working for almost no money, Fuller struggled to produce the groundbreaking journal, whose idealistic purpose she described in a letter to a friend:

> A perfectly free organ is to be offered for the expression of individual thought and character ... I hope ... that this periodical will not aim at leading public opinion, but at stimulating each man to think for himself, to think more deeply and more nobly by letting them see how some minds are kept alive by a wise self-trust. (Brown, p. 57)

The first issue of the quarterly journal came out in July 1840. Like later issues, it included poetry, artistic and literary criticism, fiction, and essays. Fuller worked tirelessly to meet the strong demands of the job. Her many duties included convincing writers to work without pay, reading and editing all the articles, writing to fill empty pages, and enlisting the help of friends. To Henry Hedge, she wrote at a particularly desperate time, "Henry, I adjure [urge] you in the name of all the Genii, Muses, Pegasus, Apollo, Pollio, [and] Apollyon to send me something good for this journal, before the first of May" (Anthony, p. 98).

In spite of the difficulties, Fuller accomplished a great deal as editor of the *Dial*. She encouraged new talent, inspired some lazy thinkers to write down their ideas, and, most important, offered a platform for the sharing of transcendentalist ideas and philosophies.

Small though it was, with a readership of barely 300, the *Dial* caused quite a stir in literary circles around the country. It received attention, usually negative, from some of the nation's leading newspapers. The *Philadelphia Gazette* labeled its editors "zanies" and "Bedlamites" and the *New York Knickerbocker* wrote parodies of the journal's articles. Even some transcendentalists complained about the journal, claiming that it was too feminine and needed a "beard." As always, however, Fuller ignored her critics and continued working doggedly at producing the journal.

After two years, Fuller began to feel the strain of the demands of working on the Conversations and the *Dial* at the same time. She resigned her post as editor and asked Emerson to take over her duties at the journal.

Woman in the Nineteenth Century. In the fall of 1843, Fuller wrote about women's roles in a book titled *Woman in the Nineteenth Century.* In this long essay, based on transcendentalist ideas of self-reliance, she urged women to strive for dependence on themselves rather than on men, to expand their intellect, and to realize their full power as women. She wrote:

> I would have Woman lay aside all thought, such as she habitually cherishes, of being taught and led by men. I would have her, like the Indian girl, dedicate herself to the Sun, the Sun of Truth, and go nowhere if his beams did not make clear the path. I would have her free from compromise, from complaisance, from helplessness, because I would have her good enough and strong enough to love one and all beings, from the fulness, not the poverty of being. (Chevigny, p. 264)

Many women involved in the right-to-vote movement would echo Fuller's words from this ground-breaking book.

The *Daily-Tribune*. Toward the end of 1844, Fuller entered an entirely new and exciting chapter of her life. Horace Greeley, the editor of the *New York Daily-Tribune,* offered her a job as a literary critic for his newspaper. Greeley had been impressed by Fuller's writing but may have also been prodded to hire her by his wife, who had long admired Fuller. When Fuller accepted the job, Mary Greeley invited her to live at their country estate in Turtle Bay, on the East River across from New York City.

As the first female member of the American press, Fuller wrote three articles per week—two on literary topics and one on social issues. A brief list of the articles she wrote includes "Our City Charities," "On the Narrative of Frederic Douglass," and "The Irish Character." In New York, Fuller came into contact with some of the leading literary figures of her time, including Edgar Allen Poe. As a valued member of the city's literary circles, Fuller continued to grow intellectually and develop her critical skills.

Also during this time, Fuller grew more committed to social reform. She became increasingly sympathetic to women abandoned by society, such as prostitutes, as well as other oppressed groups, including Indians, blacks, the poor, and the physically and mentally disabled. While living in New York, she spent Christmas Eve and other holidays visiting women in prisons and houses of correction, offering them guidance and hope. She wrote about some of her ideas and experiences in her column.

As busy as she was, Fuller also managed to fall in love for the first time during this hectic and active period. Although she had several crushes in her younger years and some light romances, she did not experience a mature love until she met James Nathan in the early months of 1845. Nathan, a Jewish businessman who played the guitar and wrote poetry, was attractive, romantic, and had, Fuller said, a "feminine sweetness and sensibility" (Anthony, p. 113). Their romance was sincere and passionate, but it did not last long. In April, Nathan left New York on an extended trip for Europe, and although the two continued to write after he left, Fuller knew that the relationship was over.

Aftermath

Europe. Fuller spent two productive years working in New York. When she left in 1846, it was to fulfill her lifelong dream of traveling abroad. Greeley agreed to let her continue writing for the

Tribune from overseas, and she left for Europe in August 1846. Upon her arrival, Fuller's spreading fame led to meetings with some of the most famous and important thinkers of the day. Among many others, she met, in England, writers William Wordsworth and Thomas Carlyle; in Paris, writer George Sands and her lover, composer Frederic Chopin; and in Italy, poets Robert Browning and Elizabeth Barrett Browning.

Fuller delighted in her busy and stimulating new life in Europe. But still she felt the sting of betrayal when Nathan wrote to tell her he had become engaged to a German girl. Proud and hurt, she asked his agent in England to communicate to Nathan that she "was too much involved in the routine of visiting and receiving visitors to allow her mind a moment's repose to reply to [his letter]" (Brown, p. 93). Little did she know that true love was about to transform her life.

Giovanni Angelo Ossoli. By early 1847 Fuller was living in Rome, where she was actively involved in the cause of the revolutionaries fighting to unify Italy. One day, while visiting St. Peter's Cathedral during Holy Week, she became separated from her friends and began searching for them. A young Italian man noticed her distress and tried to help her, and when they could not find her friends, he offered to walk her home. Although he spoke no English, and her Italian was still rough, the two sparked an instant friendship.

Giovanni Ossoli was a marquis from a poor, noble Italian family. About ten years younger than Fuller, who was now thirty-seven, Ossoli was a tall, quiet, and reserved man with handsome looks and a melancholy air. Although he was not highly educated or extremely intellectual, Fuller found in him a kindred spirit. Under her guidance, Ossoli began to take a greater role in the cause to unite Italy, fighting as an officer in the revolution.

That autumn, Fuller wrote her mother that she had "not been so well since she was a child, nor so happy ever, as during the last six weeks" (Brown, p. 102). Just as suddenly, however, her high spirits turned to despair when she learned she was pregnant. Ossoli already had proposed to her before this discovery, but she had refused, feeling that they were far too different to make a workable match. Now she agreed to marry him, but they would have to keep the marriage a secret because his family would not approve of their son marrying an American Protestant woman of Fuller's bent. It is unknown exactly when the couple married, but their son, Angelo Eugene Philip Ossoli, was born on September 5, 1848.

Wife, mother, and revolutionary. Marriage seemed to agree with Fuller. She and Ossoli were devoted to each other. However, the war to unite Italy was being fought all around them, and danger and hardship threatened their contentment. Fuller became increasingly involved in the Italian cause. She wrote columns about the revolution for the *Tribune* and, meanwhile, worked at a hospital helping the sick and wounded and comforting the dying. So powerful was Fuller's soothing nature that the suffering men cried out for her when she was away from the wards.

Back to America. In the summer of 1850, the Ossolis booked passage on a merchant ship bound for America, embarking upon a journey that, from the outset, was marked by difficulty. The captain of the ship, the *Elizabeth,* died of smallpox before they left Europe, leaving the first mate in charge. Meanwhile, young Angelo caught smallpox and became very ill, but he recovered during the voyage.

Just near their journey's end, tragedy struck. A sudden storm blew the ship off course and ran it aground just a few hundred yards off the coast of New Jersey. The ship's cargo of marble slabs broke a hole through the ship's bottom, and the pounding waves tore at the vessel. As the storm raged, onlookers gathered onshore, but could only watch helplessly as the ship and its passengers tossed and turned. The Ossolis managed to stay safely on the boat for more than day, but the storm finally broke the ship to pieces and threw all remaining passengers overboard. Fuller drowned, along with her husband and son, on July 19, 1850. Though Angelo's young body was washed ashore, Margaret and her husband were never seen again.

For More Information

Anthony, Katharine. *Margaret Fuller: A Psychological Biography.* New York: Harcourt, Brace, and Howe, 1920.

Brown, Arthur W. *Margaret Fuller.* New York: Twayne Publishers, 1964.

Chevigny, Bell Gale. *The Woman and the Myth: Margaret Fuller's Life and Writings.* Old Westbury, New York: Feminist Press, 1976.

James, Laurie. *Men, Women, and Margaret Fuller.* New York: Golden Heritage Press, 1990.

Nathaniel Hawthorne

1804-1864

Personal Background

Salem, Massachusetts. By the time Nathaniel Hawthorne was born, on July 4, 1804, the Hathorne family had been settled for almost two centuries on American soil. Generations of Hathornes (Nathaniel changed the spelling of the name to Hawthorne) had lived and died in Salem. In the late 1700s, during the Salem witch trials, John Hathorne was one of the three judges who ruled on cases involving townspeople accused of witchery. Family tradition claimed that one accused witch had cursed the Hathorne name, which many, including Nathaniel himself, believed to have led to the Hathorne family's decline. Once a prosperous and powerful family in the small seaside town, by the early 1800s the Hathornes had lost most of their money. Nathaniel grew up as a member of one of Salem's most noted families, whose income did not match its social standing.

In the early 1800s Salem, about thirty miles up the north shore from Boston, was slowly losing its status as a thriving seaport. Still, many of its citizens, including Nathaniel's father, Captain Nathaniel Hathorne, made their living at sea. Captain Hathorne died in 1808 of yellow fever while away at sea, leaving his widow, Elizabeth, nearly penniless. She took four-year-old Nathaniel, his older sister, Elizabeth, and younger sister, Louise, to live at her family home with her four brothers and four sisters, all unmarried.

▲ **Nathaniel Hawthorne**

Event: The romantic movement.
Role: Nathaniel Hawthorne drew on the rich history of his native New England to write short stories, novels, and other pieces, many of which centered around the themes of sin and punishment, and good versus evil.

Reading and storytelling. When he was nine, Nathaniel severely injured his foot during a ball game. The injury, which was slow to heal, temporarily crippled him. For nearly two years, he walked with crutches, did not attend school, and spent most of his time indoors reading books. The habit of constant reading that he developed during this period stayed with him throughout his life. During his confinement, he also learned to amuse himself, as well as his sisters, by making up stories or retelling the stories he had read, adding his own fantastic variations to the tales. His two sisters listened with delight to their imaginative brother's yarns.

Education. His uncle, Robert Manning, financed most of Nathaniel's education. As a boy, he attended private schools and also was tutored at home. Nathaniel was not the most ambitious student, but his love for writing showed itself early. At fifteen, he started his own newspaper, *The Spectator,* which he published, edited, and wrote. Distributed among his family and friends and lasting all of two issues, the handwritten newspaper contained essays with titles such as "On Wealth," "On Benevolence," and "On Industry."

When he was seventeen, Hawthorne moved north to Brunswick, Maine, to attend Bowdoin College. Describing himself as "an idle student, negligent of college rules" (Young, p. 16), he paid numerous fines for such offenses as drinking and gambling and for missing classes and church services. Not surprisingly, his grades at Bowdoin were unremarkable—he graduated eighteenth in a class of thirty-eight. But at the same time Hawthorne had earned the reputation of being the best writer in his class, and it was during these years that he chose his career.

His college years also proved valuable in the friendships he formed. At Bowdoin, Hawthorne met future United States President Franklin Pierce, poet Henry Wadsworth Longfellow, and lawyer and businessman Horatio Bridge. Longfellow remembered Hawthorne as being shy, quiet, and thoughtful. After Hawthorne's death, the poet spoke at Bowdoin in a room where he and other literary types had gathered during his college years:

Hawthorne often came into this room, and sometimes he would go there, behind the window curtains, and remain in silent revery

▲ **Hawthorne's birthplace**

the whole evening. No one disturbed him; he came and went as he liked. He was a mysterious man. (Dauber, p. 5)

Twelve years of solitude. After college, Hawthorne returned to Salem and entered the strangest and most mysterious period of his life—a period he called his "dismal years" (Dauber, p. 7). Living at home, he spent twelve years in almost complete isolation. He remained in his room most of the time, reading and writing, going out only occasionally. He guessed that only about twenty people in town knew of his existence. Later, he described this isolation:

[My] natural tendency … toward seclusion, I now indulged to the utmost, so that for months together, I scarcely held human intercourse outside my own family; seldom going out except at twilight, or only to take the nearest way to the most convenient solitude, which was oftenest the seashore. (Young, p. 18)

This yen for solitude seems to have run in Hawthorne's immediate family. He, his mother, and sisters kept their distance from the outside world and, sometimes, from each other. Elizabeth Hathorne, after her husband's death, spent much of her time in seclusion, away even from her own children. They claimed she ate most of her meals in her room, and Hawthorne said that weeks sometimes went by without seeing his mother. Hawthorne's wife, Sophia, described her mother-in-law's room as "the mysterious chamber into which no mortal ever peeped" (Turner, p. 12). Sophia also reported that when her sister-in-law Elizabeth lived with her and Nathaniel for two years, Sophia saw the strikingly beautiful but reclusive woman only once.

Thus Hawthorne learned early this tendency toward isolation. From his early twenties to mid-thirties, he spent most of his time holed away in his room in the small, dark New England house. During his twelve years in this "haunted chamber," his daily routine varied little. He read, wrote, often daydreamed, and stopped only for meals. At sunset, he left his house for a long walk, and at night, after supper, he visited and talked with his sisters.

Records from the Salem library show that Hawthorne withdrew nearly 1,200 books in these years. Many were histories of early New England, Massachusetts, and Salem, describing the Puritans, colonial politics, witch trials, and other timely subjects. His literary output was as impressive as his reading. He regularly submitted stories, essays, and articles to various periodicals. Also, he published on his own a romantic novel called *Fanshawe,* which he later so disliked that he burned all his own copies and any copy he came across. Altogether, during this time Hawthorne wrote one novel and forty-four sketches and tales, many of which he published in a collection called *Twice-Told Tales.*

Hawthorne's isolation was not total, of course. He took occasional trips to various parts of New England, including Martha's Vineyard, New Hampshire, western Massachusetts, and Connecticut. At home, he regularly went for long walks around Salem along the shore, by the railroad tracks, and to nearby villages. Like Henry David Thoreau, Hawthorne seemed to depend on these walking excursions not only because they were healthful and energizing but also because they gave him a chance to reflect on his work (see **Henry David Thoreau**).

Hawthorne's isolation finally ended in about 1837. The publication of *Twice-Told Tales* that year brought him public recognition, which drew him back out into the world. He later wrote to his fiancée, Sophia Peabody, describing his experience of self-imposed isolation in the room "under the eaves":

> This deserves to be called a haunted chamber; for thousands upon thousands of visions have appeared to me in it.... If ever I should have a biographer, he ought to make great mention of this chamber in my memoirs, because so much of my lonely youth was wasted here, and here my mind and character were formed; and here I have been glad and hopeful, and here I have been despondent [deeply depressed]; and here I sat a long, long time, waiting patiently for the world to know me. (Martin, p. 27)

Sophia Peabody. In 1838, soon after rejoining the world, Hawthorne met and fell in love with Sophia Peabody, a neighbor in Salem. The Peabodys were an intellectual and social family who believed in many transcendentalist ideas, including social reform. Sophia's sister Elizabeth had arranged a meeting with the author, whose *Twice-Told Tales* had made him well known in literary circles. The first time he visited, Sophia stayed in her room, even after her sister ran excitedly upstairs to tell her that she must come and meet the author for he was "handsomer than Lord Byron!" (Young, p. 28). Sophia, an artist who was physically fragile and plagued by frequent piercing headaches, spent most of her time in her room, which she also used as an art studio.

Eventually, the two did meet, and they immediately fell in love, in spite of their very opposite personalities. Whereas Hawthorne had a tendency to be antisocial, dark, and brooding, Sophia was bright, friendly, and talkative. Their romance progressed quickly, but their courtship was long. Hawthorne did not have the funds to support a wife. In 1839, to earn money, he took on a job measuring salt and coal at the Boston Custom House. Meanwhile, he and Sophia shared their thoughts and feelings in letters that strengthened the bond between them. Intelligent and expressive, Sophia showered her love on Hawthorne, and he returned it in full. He called her his "Dove," and she adored him. To Sophia, Hawthorne gratefully wrote: "It is a miracle worthy even of thee to have converted a life of shadows into the deepest truth, by thy magic touch" (Young, pp. 29-30).

Brook Farm and the transcendentalists. After working for two years at the Custom House, Hawthorne decided to take part in an experimental community led by George Ripley. The community was begun by transcendentalists, people who believed in plain living and deep thinking. Brook Farm was a community in which transcendentalist followers shared food, living quarters, and farm and household chores, as well as beliefs. On this dairy farm in the Boston suburb of West Roxbury, Ripley hoped to shape an ideal community of laborers and intellectuals. His goal was "to insure a more natural union between intellectual and manual labor than now exists; to combine the thinker and the worker, as far as possible, in the same individual" (Mellow, p. 178).

The move to Brook Farm was not a typical one for Hawthorne, who objected to some of the transcendental beliefs and who treasured his privacy. However, in 1841 he joined the community, investing $1,000 of his savings in the effort. His motive stemmed in part from his eagerness to marry Sophia. He saw Brook Farm as a possible place for them to live affordably as man and wife. When he first arrived, he embraced the hardy life on the farm, planting peas and potatoes, milking cows, and shoveling manure. But he grew tired from the workload, too tired to write. After just six months his enthusiasm had changed to distaste: "It is my opinion that a man's soul may be buried and perish under a dung-heap or in a furrow of the field just as well as under a pile of money" (Stewart, p. 60).

Marriage. Hawthorne married Sophia five days after his thirty-eighth birthday, on July 9, 1842. The couple set up their home at an old parsonage in Concord called the Old Manse. Their neighbors in town included Ralph Waldo Emerson, Thoreau, and Amos Bronson Alcott.

Happy in his new home and with his beloved wife, Hawthorne found little time to write. In fact, he had hardly written anything but love letters to Sophia since their courtship had begun nearly five years before. In a journal that the newlyweds shared, Hawthorne wrote:

A rainy day—a rainy day. I do verily believe there is no sunshine in this world, except what beams from my wife's eyes. At present, she has laid her strict command on me to take pen in hand.... And what is there to write about at all? Happiness has no succession of events. (Mellow, pp. 205-206)

Eventually, of course, Hawthorne did find something to write about. He was on his way to becoming one of America's most important authors.

Participation: The Romantic Movement

Good vs. evil. The philosophy at Brook Farm placed great faith in the essential good in human nature. There was faith that if a person lived in a certain way and relied on instinct and intuition more than experience or reason, improvement of the individual and the world would follow. Hawthorne objected greatly to what he saw as too much credit to the good and too little recognition of human evil. He poked fun at such beliefs in his story "The Celestial Railroad," or heavenly railroad, which includes a monster, Giant Transcendentalism. In his more serious storytelling, Hawthorne included symbols of evil that brought out the darker side of human nature. His use of symbols and his tales of ordinary people were features of a movement in literature at the time. Called the romantic movement, it had begun in Europe and spread to America in the fictional tales of Edgar Allen Poe and Hawthorne. Romantic writers stressed feelings and instinct in their stories more than reason and logic.

Magnificent Appearance

Hawthorne was incredibly handsome. Tall, with thick black hair, penetrating blue eyes, and fine features, most who knew him commented on his magnificent looks. When he walked down the street, passersby often turned to stare. Once, an old lady stopped him to inquire whether she was speaking to a man or an angel. At Hawthorne's wedding, the preacher was momentarily taken aback when he first beheld the handsome face looking at him from the altar.

Hawthorne's role. With a keen and lyrical sense of detail, Hawthorne drew upon his New England past, especially the harsh, judgmental Puritan society of his ancestors. Many of his themes center around guilt, sin and remorse, and good versus evil. Often he wrapped his messages in allegory, stories that used symbols, settings, and characters to represent deeper truths. He believed that

125

some readers were put off by his symbolic style and confessed that he sometimes did not know his own meaning: "Upon my honor, I am not quite sure that I entirely comprehend my own meaning, in some of those blasted allegories" (Turner, p. 69).

Always, however, at the heart of Hawthorne's work is a sense of human kindness, and the demand for it in a cold and unfriendly world. His tales are often full of eerie mystery, with, for example, images of characters wandering alone on moonless nights down dark country roads or crooked city streets. Henry James, another American novelist, observed, "In no American writer is there to be found the same predominance of weird imagination as in Hawthorne" (Hawthorne, p. v).

Hawthorne's tales. Hawthorne wrote more than 100 tales and sketches, most of which he published in *Twice-Told Tales* (1837), *Mosses from an Old Manse* (1846), and *The Snow Image and Other Twice-Told Tales* (1851). Some of the better-known tales include "Rappaccini's Daughter," "My Kinsman, Major Molineux," "The Artist of the Beautiful," and "The Maypole of Merry Mount."

In one of his stories, "The Gentle Boy," Hawthorne presents the bitter irony of the hateful prejudice the Puritans, who themselves had been persecuted in England, felt toward Quaker refugees. Interestingly, Hawthorne's own ancestor, William Hathorne, had been an Indian fighter and a persecutor of Quakers. In the story, a young boy named Ilbrahim is left an orphan after his father, a Quaker, is executed and his mother is imprisoned. A kindly and childless Puritan couple, Tobias and Dorothy Pearson, open their home to the boy. Ilbrahim is sweet, loving, gentle, and trusting, yet the fact that he is a Quaker makes him hated by all the townspeople, including the children. The villagers also shun the Pearsons for taking the boy in. At school one day, other children brutally beat Ilbrahmin. He survives the attack but his gentle spirit is crushed. Soon after, he dies.

Another story about Puritan New England is "Young Goodman Brown." The theme revolves around good versus evil, with evil winning. Goodman Brown witnesses an eerie nighttime scene of devil worshipers at a witches' sabbath. They are gathered in the deepest part of the forest around a dancing, blazing fire. A dark figure addresses the crowd, saying, "Evil is the nature of mankind. Evil must be your only happiness" (Cowley, p. 66). Whether real or imagined, the vision ruins the young man for life, leaving him "a stern, a sad, a darkly meditative, a distrustful, if not a desperate man" (Cowley, p. 68).

The Scarlet Letter. Hawthorne's most famous and lasting work, which was published in 1850, is *The Scarlet Letter.* Most critics consider it among the greatest of American novels. Set in Puritan Boston in the 1640s, *The Scarlet Letter* blends many of Hawthorne's earlier themes of guilt, sin, and remorse.

The plot revolves around the relationships between Hester Prynne, her husband, Roger Chillingworth, and her lover, a minister named Arthur Dimmesdale. The darkly beautiful Hester Prynne is found guilty of adultery and condemned to wearing a scarlet *A* sewn on the chest of her dress.

With her sin made public, Hester lives with the open scorn of the townspeople. As time passes, however, her able work as a seamstress and her charity toward the poor earn her a certain respect. Dimmesdale, on the other hand, is considered almost a saint but is tortured by the secret of his sin. Meanwhile, Chillingworth, who is not known by the town to be Hester's husband, searches out the man who wronged him and becomes increasingly evil in his torment of Dimmesdale.

In the end, the novel leaves many questions unanswered. Does *A* stand for "adultery" or "angel"? Is Chillingworth, who did not participate in the sin of adultery, more guilty than Hester and Dimmesdale, who did? A section from *The Scarlet Letter,* in which Hester suddenly takes off the scarlet *A* she has worn for seven years, shows how the author hints at deeper meanings through his storytelling:

> The mystic token alighted on the hither verge of the stream … there lay the embroidered letter, glittering like a lost jewel, which some ill-fated wanderer might pick up, and thenceforth be haunted by strange phantoms of guilt, sinkings of the heart, and unaccountable misfortune.

> The stigma gone, Hester heaved a long, deep sigh, in which the burden of shame and anguish departed from her spirit. O exquisite relief! She had not known the weight until she had felt the freedom! (Cowley, p. 487)

In *The Scarlet Letter,* Hawthorne deals not only with individual evil but with the American past. He takes a searching look at the nation's history through story, beginning a tradition in American novel writing.

Aftermath

Other writings. *The Scarlet Letter* is considered Hawthorne's greatest work. Other novels include *The House of the Seven Gabels* (1851), *The Marble Faun* (1852), and *The Blithedale Romance* (1852). Later, he published *Our Old Home* (1863), describing his travels through England. Printed after his death were mostly notebooks and journals that he kept during the early years of his marriage and his years in Europe.

On the continent. In 1853 Hawthorne's old friend Franklin Pierce, now president, sent him to England to serve as a consul to Liverpool. Now, having grown accustomed to being a public figure, Hawthorne enjoyed the social and cultural life in England. Because his reputation as a writer was widespread, he frequently spoke at public dinners. At the same time, he took his position very seriously and worked hard at performing his duties. He resigned in 1857 to spend two years in Italy with his family before returning to the United States.

Family. After nearly a decade in Europe, Hawthorne went home with his family to Concord. His love for Sophia had grown deeper with the years. They had three children: Una, born in 1844; Julian, born 1846; and Rose, born 1851. Though Hawthorne had been fortunate to have excellent health throughout his life, in his last few years he suffered increasing ailments. On May 19, 1864 while traveling through New England with Franklin Pierce, Nathaniel Hawthorne died in his sleep, alone in a hotel room in New Hampshire.

For More Information

Cowley, Malcolm. *The Portable Hawthorne.* New York: Penguin Books, 1948.

Dauber, Kenneth. *Nathaniel Hawthorne: Life, Work, and Criticism.* Fredericton, Canada: York Press, 1986.

Martin, Terence. *Nathaniel Hawthorne.* Boston: Twayne Publishers, 1965.

Mellow, James R. *Nathaniel Hawthorne in His Times.* Boston: Houghton Mifflin, 1980.

Stewart, Randall. *Nathaniel Hawthorne, a Biography.* New Haven, Connecticut: Yale University Press, 1948.

Turner, Arlin. *Nathaniel Hawthorne: An Introduction and Interpretation.* New York: Barnes and Noble, 1961.

Young, Philip. *Hawthorne's Secret: An Un-Told Tale.* Boston: David R. Godine, 1984.

Pre-Civil War Controversies

1820
Missouri Compromise admits Missouri into the union as a slave state and Maine as a free state; bans slavery in Louisiana Purchase north of latitude 36°30'.

1846
Dred Scott sues for freedom.

1854
Stephen A. Douglas's Kansas-Nebraska Act overturns Missouri Compromise. Republican party forms, aims to keep slavery out of the western territories.

1850
Compromise of 1850 allows Utah and New Mexico to decide issue of slavery for themselves and includes Fugitive Slave Act, which aids owners in capturing escaped slaves.

1848
Free-Soil party forms, promises to abolish slavery in District of Columbia.

1856
John Brown leads raid that kills five men at Pottawatomie Creek, Kansas.

1857
Supreme Court reverses lower court decision; rules against Scott.

1858
Abraham Lincoln debates Douglas in Illinois.

1861
South secedes from Union; Civil War begins.

1860
Lincoln elected president.

1859
Brown conducts raid at Harpers Ferry, Virginia.

PRE-CIVIL WAR CONTROVERSIES

Sharp differences distinguished life in the North and South during the early 1800s. Built on slavery and farming, the South had few cities, and individuals there operated more independently of one another than in the North. The North, by contrast, had little slavery, but it did have many factories, cities, and railroads and was far more group-oriented than the South.

The westward movement, and winning of western lands after the Mexican War, raised the question of whether Northern or Southern ways would reign in the new territories. So far, slave states and free states had kept a balance of power in the nation. The new territories threatened to upset the balance. Feelings ran high on both sides. Southern slaveholders saw that unless at least some of the territories became slave states, the South would soon be outvoted in Congress. With a two-thirds majority, antislavery forces might be able to outlaw slavery forever. Northerners likewise feared the South gaining more territory and then winning more seats in Congress and perhaps on the Supreme Court. The two sides became locked in a bitter race to claim the new lands. It was a contest that drew in the entire nation.

Congress struggled to find solutions that would satisfy both sides. One early attempt, the Missouri Compromise, dealt with the Louisiana Purchase, a huge area from the Mississippi River to the Rocky Mountains purchased from France in 1803. Missouri, the first state west of the Mississippi, was admitted as a slave state and Maine as a free state, making the count thirteen slave and thirteen free states in the Union. Also, slavery was banned in the new territory north of latitude 36°30' but permitted south of it.

Legislation Regarding Slavery

- **The Missouri Compromise (1820–21)** Admitted Missouri to the Union as a slave state; Maine as a free state. Prohibited slavery north of latitude 36°30' in Louisiana Purchase.

- **Compromise of 1850** Allowed New Mexico and Utah to decide issue of slavery for themselves. Admitted California as a free state. Abolished slave trade in District of Columbia. Included Fugitive Slave Act to promote the capture of runaways.

- **Kansas-Nebraska Act (1854)** Created the territories of Kansas and Nebraska. Repealed the Missouri Compromise. Declared that all territories should settle the question of slavery for themselves.

A promoter of compromise between North and South in the 1840s and 1850s was **Stephen A. Douglas,** known as "the Little Giant." He was determined that the country should expand and tried to skirt the slavery issue by leaving it up to the new territories to decide for themselves. As senator from Illinois, Douglas helped write the Compromise of 1850, which let Utah and New Mexico settle the slavery question on their own. The tactic, called popular sovereignty, left the central government out of the slavery question altogether.

Douglas also proposed the Kansas-Nebraska Act, another compromise approved by Congress in 1854. The act established within the Louisiana Purchase two separate territories, Kansas and Nebraska, and left it up to their voters to decide whether to allow slavery or not. The act also overturned the Missouri Compromise's ban on slavery north of 36°30'.

Both proslavery and antislavery whites moved into Kansas in 1854 to settle the question there, and a series of bloody conflicts erupted that would plague the area for six years.

John Brown became an antislavery settler in Kansas. An abolitionist, Brown moved to Kansas from New York with his five sons in 1855. After proslavery raiders burned

Lawrence, Kansas, he led a raid on Pottawatomie Creek, killing five proslavery men in revenge. The violence in Kansas—"Bleeding Kansas," as newspapers and politicians called it—was watched closely by a horrified public. As it came to a climax in 1857, the Supreme Court added to the tension with its pro-Southern ruling in the case of *Dred Scott* v. *Sanford*.

Purchased by an army doctor in St. Louis, Missouri, **Dred Scott,** a slave, had moved with the doctor to Illinois and Wisconsin Territory. They lived for several years in these areas, which were covered under the Missouri Compromise's ban on slavery. Scott sued for his freedom in 1846, after being brought back to the slave state of Missouri. He argued that since slavery was outlawed in Illinois, he became free when taken there. Earlier court rulings had freed slaves who had been taken to free territory and been brought back, and a Missouri court ruled in Scott's favor. That ruling was overturned by the Missouri Supreme Court. In overturning the ruling, the court made a proslavery statement and ignored the facts and legal aspects of the case. When Scott's lawyers appealed to the United States Supreme Court, that court's Southern majority also ruled against Scott, for similar reasons.

By that time, the case was famous and both sides, proslavery and antislavery, were tensely awaiting the decision. In the end, the court went beyond the issues raised by the case, answering questions of even greater importance. Did Congress have the right to ban slavery in territories? Did blacks, slave or not, have the right to sue for freedom? Did they, in fact, have the right to become citizens at all? The answer was a loud "no." According to the court, no black man had rights that a white man must respect. The decision heightened tensions between the regions, comforting the South but enraging the North. The Dred Scott decision became the most criticized action ever taken by the Supreme Court.

The result of these controversies was the emergence of the antislavery Republican party, founded in 1854, as a strong political force in favor of taking political action to keep slavery out of the western territories.

▲ Harpers Ferry, Virginia

The failure of political action to solve the heated problem became painfully obvious in 1859, when John Brown and nineteen followers captured a government arsenal, or warehouse for army weapons, at Harpers Ferry, Virginia. Seventeen men, both blacks and whites, were killed as a result of Brown's raid. He had expected slaves throughout the South to join the uprising, but instead he himself was hanged for treason, murder, and inspiring a slave revolt.

Brown's raid remains a controversial moment in history. Was he insane, or was he a martyr who sacrificed himself to the antislavery cause? He apparently had no careful plan for his uprising, but afterwards he acted with sober dignity. Moreover, Brown had been convincing enough to get funding for his uprising from six well-established Northerners, and he also won the respect of major personalities of his day, such as Henry David Thoreau and Frederick Douglass. Brown's raid polarized the nation to the boiling point. The incident raised sympathy in the North and fears in the South, riveting attention on the possibility of destroying slavery, not just limiting its expansion.

Meanwhile, the Republican party, which had been formed to stop the spread of slavery in the nation, grew steadily stronger. In 1860 Republican candidate Abraham Lincoln defeated a divided Democratic Party, winning all Northern states but New Jersey and taking the free states of California and Oregon as well. Lincoln's victory set the stage for Southern secession, or withdrawal from the Union, and Civil War. Southerners saw his election as a threat to the survival of slavery and their own well being. In leaving the United States to form an independent country of their own, they moved to protect the Southern way of life.

Stephen A. Douglas

1813-1861

Personal Background

Early life. Stephen A. Douglas was born at Brandon, Vermont, on April 23, 1813. His father, a medical doctor for whom Stephen was named, died when the boy was three months old. Although a successful doctor, he left the family with financial problems. Stephen's mother, Sarah, found herself too poor to care for her daughter and new baby son alone. So she moved to a small farm her father had left her, which lay next door to another small farm owned by her bachelor brother. Sarah merged her land with her brother's, and the kind uncle raised Stephen in strict Christian style.

When the boy was fourteen, Stephen's uncle married, and the new family seemed to have no place for him. So Stephen decided to find an occupation. He signed on as an apprentice with a cabinetmaker. For the next two years, he worked at this trade, first in Middlebury with Nathan Parker, then at home with the local cabinetmaker.

Stephen's little early formal education came from attendance for a short time at Brandon Academy after his cabinetmaking experience. He gained a reputation as a speaker on the school's debating society but left the academy after only two years. By that time, Stephen's mother had remarried and he went to live with her in Canandaigua, New York. There was a fine school at Canandaigua,

▲ **Stephen A. Douglas**

Event: The Kansas-Nebraska Act and the Lincoln-Douglas Debates.

Role: A powerful political leader, Stephen A. Douglas battled for two goals in Congress and as a candidate for president: (1) upholding the rights of people in the western territories to make their own governing decisions, particularly in relation to slavery, and (2) managing the spread of slavery to maintain balance in the Union. He was above all devoted to the nation and its growth and favored compromise for this reason. Although he had long opposed Abraham Lincoln, he strongly supported Lincoln at the onset of the Civil War.

and Stephen completed his basic education and began to study law. His political interests also started to show; he produced posters in support of presidential candidate Andrew Jackson, who was running against John Quincy Adams.

The West and the law. At the age of twenty, Douglas decided he wanted to become a lawyer but could not afford the price of a law school education required in the East. New York required aspiring lawyers to take law classes for four years and study under a lawyer for three more years. Even if he could have afforded the luxury of so much time, Douglas was too impatient to spend that many years preparing for a career.

Out west in Illinois, requirements to practice law were less demanding. Douglas would need only to secure the approval of a few already-practicing lawyers. Heading west with his life savings of $300, Douglas studied first in Cleveland, then in St. Louis, and finally in Jacksonville, Illinois, where he set up a practice.

Politics. Within months, his private law practice had given way to political ambition. In Illinois, he found the Democrats divided among themselves. There were the "whole hog" Jacksonians, who believed strongly in state and local governments, and the "milk, and cider" Jacksonians, who were willing to give up some states' rights to the federal government. Douglas joined the "whole hoggers" and through his work for them became at age twenty-two a district attorney in one of the most important districts of Illinois. It was the beginning of a long career in politics.

Just one year after becoming district attorney, Douglas resigned to become a public prosecutor. In and out of court, he was an impressive figure. Full of energy and an able speaker, Douglas drew attention with his enthusiasm and climbed quickly through the political ranks. In 1836 he became a state assemblyman and introduced bills into the legislature that would allow the people of Illinois to elect their own state attorney general. Soon they elected him to that office. It was the beginning of a steady rise, finally ending in his election to the United States Senate.

Douglas sat in Congress for much of the time that slavery was a major issue among the legislators.

First wife. Shortly after becoming a congressman, Douglas became a friend of David S. Reid and while visiting him met the two Reid daughters. Three years later, in 1847, Stephen Douglas married Martha Reid. The two would live happily for six years before Martha died giving birth to a daughter who lived only briefly.

The Missouri Compromise. As the nation expanded, a struggle developed between the states allowing slavery and those who opposed it. Neither free states nor slave states wanted to be outnumbered by the other, so lawmakers struggled for a way to keep the numbers equal. In 1820 Henry Clay had led a compromise action that allowed Missouri to become a slave state while Maine became a free state. The Missouri Compromise also established that no part of the Louisiana Purchase above 36° 30' would allow slavery. No one fully accepted setting such strict limits on freedom and slavery. The compromise only furthered the separation between the North and South.

The Rise of Stephen Douglas	
1837	Illinois attorney general
1838	Registrar of the Federal Land Office, Springfield
1840	Secretary of State for Illinois
1841	Illinois Supreme Court Justice
1843	United States Congressman
1847	United States Senator

The issue of balancing out slave and free states gained importance again in 1850. The war with Mexico had opened up a vast new land in the West, and the discovery of gold in California made it important to consider that territory for statehood. A new battle for and against slavery brewed.

Experience with slavery. Douglas had had some experience with slavery. His first wife was the daughter of a slave owner. Yet Douglas did not come out for or against slavery. He had moved to Illinois to build a career and had, above all, become a western man; his interest was in expanding the United States westward. He had begun to purchase farmland in many places in the West and to take an active interest in seeing a railroad constructed in Illinois. By 1835, he was a staunch supporter of Andrew Jackson's politics. Like Jackson, he believed that strong states rights should be the focus of the Democratic party.

In Congress, Douglas worked for United States expansion west and north, the building of transcontinental railroads, and the freedom of the people in each state to establish their own rules. As chairman of the congressional Committee on Territories, he was a constant champion for establishing local governments in the new areas and for placing as few federal restrictions on them as possible. Douglas felt strongly that the federal government did not have the right to restrict slavery in the territories.

The Compromise of 1850. In 1850 California was to be admitted as a state just as a new and young batch of congressmen from the North were becoming more militant about abolishing slavery. William Seward, who would later run for president against Abraham Lincoln and then become his secretary of state, was a leader of these new Northern rebels. Struggling to keep them in line so as not to break up the Union were the aging Henry Clay and Daniel Webster and the younger Stephen Douglas. His fellow legislators watched the "Little Giant," as Douglas was called, pace back and forth behind the congressional seats, rehearsing his attacks and his proposals. With neither the South nor the North interested in compromise, Clay, Webster, and Douglas prepared a package of bills aimed at appeasing both sides: California would become a free state; slave trading in the District of Columbia would stop, but slaves would still be allowed there; the new territories of New Mexico and Utah would be established and allowed to determine for themselves whether or not to allow slavery; some lands claimed by Texas would be transferred to New Mexico; and a strong Fugitive Slave Law would encourage white bounty hunters to capture blacks, free or slave, and return them to the south (the bounty hunters would be paid for capturing slaves and paid double if the slave status was upheld in court—of course, blacks were not allowed to speak for themselves in a federal court). There was much debate over the package of bills. Another compromise, it was finally forced through Congress, but few in the North or South really approved.

Douglas's goals. As a senator, Douglas continued to press for his favorite goals. He helped organize surveying parties to find the best railroad routes to the West. His personal ties to Illinois made him a champion of a central route. But even before he was elected to Congress, he had become interested in the Oregon Territory. He participated in the fight to establish the United States boundary at 54° 40' (the present tip of Alaska). In his early speeches, Douglas clearly stated his views on expansion of the United States: "We must not only go to 54° 40', but we have got to exclude Great Britain from the coast in toto" (Johannsen, *Stephen A. Douglas,* p. 176). Although his proposals lost to agreements that established the northern border at the 49th parallel, Douglas continued to champion the development of the Oregon Territory. In Congress he also agreed to survey for a northern rail route and a southern one. Eventually all three routes would span the continent, but during his time in Congress, Douglas succeeded in establishing a route only through his home state.

The South in the West. The war with Mexico had shown an ideal route for a railroad between Houston and Los Angeles that would cut into Mexican territory. This problem had been solved by the purchase of a section of Mexico below Arizona, the Gadsden Purchase. Now the South was in a strong position to send migrants from the southeast to the southwest and to unite the South and West. Slavery would, in the process, spread to new territories. Douglas saw this as another swing in the balance between slave and free states, a threat, he felt, that hindered his goal of developing the West. By the end of 1850, Utah and New Mexico had been established as territories that could decide the issue of slavery for themselves. The nation's attention turned to the Midwest.

Position on slavery. By now, Douglas was thinking about becoming a presidential candidate and he began a speaking tour of the East. His fiery speeches gained considerable attention, and newspapers began to report that he had changed his mind and was becoming an abolitionist. Douglas quickly set the matter straight:

> I have never deemed it my duty, as a citizen of a non-slaveholding State, to discuss the domestic institutions of sister States, with which, under the Constitution and laws of the land, I have no right to interfere, and for the consequences of which I am in no wise responsible. (Johannsen, *Stephen A. Douglas,* p. 481)

In 1856 he introduced resolutions in Congress that declared that the United States was a political contract between the people of the various states and territories, and that Congress had no right to establish, abolish, or prohibit slavery in the states or territories. In his speeches he declared that the Fugitive Slave Act had been a wise and just measure that should remain undisturbed in order to preserve national peace. Toward this end, he proposed a solution for the "Kansas problem."

Second wife. In 1857 Douglas married again. This time the bride was Adele Cutts, the pretty and lively grand niece of the former First Lady of the nation Dolley Madison. In 1859 the couple looked forward to their first child, a daughter. Tragedy struck once more in the Douglas family, however, when this daughter died at the age of ten weeks.

Participation: Kansas-Nebraska Act and Lincoln-Douglas Debates

Views of Douglas and Lincoln

Lincoln's early statement "that by the terms of the Declaration of Independence and natural rights the Negro was the equal of the white man became a major target of Douglas' rhetoric [in political speeches]." In Contrast, Douglas declared "I do not believe that the Almighty ever intended the negro to be the equal of the white man." (Johannsen, *Stephen A. Douglas,* pp. 672-73)

Stephen Douglas had always wanted to open the West to settlement that would help spread the United States from sea to sea. Railroads west would further this cause, and Douglas wanted his home state's largest city, Chicago, to be a railroad hub.

The problem was that the territory lay north of parallel 36° 30', the line above which slavery was not to be allowed under the Missouri Compromise. Douglas could, as Southerners urged him to do, push Congress to pass a law that would abolish the Missouri Compromise and allow the new area to decide the issue of slavery for itself. The South had so far blocked the creation of Nebraska into an official territory because it lay above the Missouri Compromise line and therefore would be free rather than slave territory. Douglas prepared a bill to create the Nebraska Territory, allowing the people there to make their own decision about slavery.

However, Douglas needed support from both North and South to pass the act. At the last minute, and without asking his congressional committee, he rewrote the bill adding much more land north of Nebraska Territory, then dividing the territory into two separate regions, Kansas and Nebraska, that would be ready to write state constitutions and become states. The idea was to make the South feel that Kansas could become a slave state to balance the future free state of Nebraska. Early on Monday, January 23, he called a meeting of his Committee on Territories and told them of the changes, then sent it to the Senate as a committee recommendation.

There was joy in the South since the slave owners now had an opportunity to expand slave territory. After all, settlers from Missouri had already started taking their slaves into the new territory. There was rage in the North, where many were opposed to overturning the Missouri Compromise and breaking the old boundary between slave and free states.

Reaction of the press. The repeal of the Missouri Compromise drew immediate wrath from some newspapers. On January 24, the Washington *National Post* accused Douglas of deliberately violating a sacred trust and betraying the precious rights of the people. The act, it said, would turn the United States from a nation of free laborers into a land of despotism filled with masters and slaves. On January 30, Douglas rose to defend his bill from the complaints of opponents in the news and the senate. He argued that the principles of democracy demanded that the people of the area be given free choice. He maintained that because the geography of the area did not lend itself to plantation agriculture anyway, allowing states to choose for themselves would not result in universal slavery.

Senate action. Other senators argued for a delay in order to have more time to study the bill. They wanted to stall until the public could be aroused against it. One opponent of the bill was quite frank about this strategy.

> The great object is delay. The bill must be kept in the Senate as long as possible. Meantime hell must be raised in the North. The ear of Congress is open. It must be deafened with a roar of condemnation. (Johannsen, *Stephen A. Douglas,* p. 422)

Many senators wavered, as did President Franklin Pierce and his cabinet. Some objected to the bill itself. Others feared that it would make Douglas famous enough to become president. Douglas's ownership of slaves in Mississippi was used against him. Charges and countercharges went on through February.

By March 3, 1854, Douglas apparently had had enough. He had listened to the opposing arguments with his usual impatience. Now he attacked his opponents with sneering and vulgar statements. Some called his speech coarse and ungentlemanly. He even accused two of his most ardent critics of obtaining their senate seats by corrupt bargaining. The debate continued till five o'clock in the morning. Even Sam Houston made a final plea to hold to the Missouri Compromise. However, when the vote was taken, the Kansas-Nebraska Act passed by a vote of thirty-seven to fourteen.

House of Representatives. Now the debate passed to the House of Representatives. Senator Douglas attended nearly every meeting, trying to convince the members to vote for his bill. On May 25, the Kansas-Nebraska Act passed in the House, and five days later, President Pierce signed it into law. Douglas claimed that he had passed the bill himself, marshaling and directing the men of Congress. The real problem, however, was that Douglas's act left the issue of slavery to be decided by state governments.

The passage of the Kansas-Nebraska Act did not end the controversy. Although Southerners had little reaction, Northern Democrats split over it. Stephen Douglas's popularity declined and his opposition to a bill that would help shipping on the Great Lakes (and thus slow the construction of railroads) caused his popularity in Illinois to fall even more. He returned home to regain his popularity. Having accomplished this with a series of speeches around the state, he

---

To Abraham Lincoln

Bement, Piatt Col. Ill.
July 30th, 1858

Dear Sir:
Your letter, dated yesterday, accepting my proposition for a joint discussion at one prominent point in each Congressional district ... was received this morning.

The times and places designed are as follows:

Ottawa	August	21st,	1858
Freeport	"	27th,	"
Jonesboro'	September	15,	"
Charleston	"	18,	"
Galesburg	October	7,	"
Quincy	"	13,	"
Alton	"	15,	"

I agree to your suggestion that we shall alternately open and close the discussion. I will speak [first] at Ottawa.... At Freeport you shall open the discussion.... We will alternate in like manner at each successive place. Very resp'y Y'r ob't serv't,

S.A. Douglas

(Johannsen, *The Letters of Stephen A. Douglas*, pp. 424-25)

was again in Washington when President James Buchanan recommended that Kansas be admitted to the Union as a slave state even though the people of Kansas had voted for a free state. Douglas felt that the Kansas people should be heard and broke with the president. The two began a long hard battle that was not resolved until Kansas was admitted as a free state in 1861.

The Lincoln-Douglas debates. By 1858 Douglas had completed two terms as senator from Illinois and was facing another election. His opponent, Abraham Lincoln, was unknown outside of his home state (see **Abraham Lincoln**). Douglas campaigned as usual for states' rights. He believed that slave states and free states could exist together in the Union. Lincoln made his position clear: "A house divided against itself cannot stand.... It will become all one thing or all the other." (Boorstin and Kelley, p. 265). The two agreed to a series of seven debates in different cities around the state. In one debate at Freeport, Illinois, Lincoln trapped Douglas into dealing with a contradiction. The Dred Scott decision (see **Dred Scott**) meant that a slave did not become free by moving into a free territory. Yet Douglas held that local laws were supreme; once in a new territory, a slave who lived there was subject to its laws. Douglas ended up saying that slavery would not exist if local governments did not pass laws to protect it. He admitted also to not caring whether an area allowed slavery. His listeners did care greatly. Yet Douglas was reelected to the Illinois legislature. The debates, however, had made Lincoln a nationally known figure. He would face Douglas again in the 1860 election for president.

Aftermath

Presidential candidate. Douglas, nominated for president in 1860, began to travel the campaign route. While in New York, he stopped long enough to visit his mother. The press took the opportunity to poke fun at his physical appearance. Typical of the news reports was this ad:

BOY LOST

Left Washington, D.C. sometime in July to go home to his mother in New York.... He is about five feet nothing in height, and about the same in diameter the other way. He has a red face, short legs, and a large belly. Answers to the name of "Little Giant." Talks a great deal, and very loud; always about himself. (*New York Herald,* Dec. 13, 1860)

Douglas's opponents in the Senate saw an opportunity to repay him for past remarks. They stripped him of his committee chairmanship, even though some felt that this action would make him a martyr and add to his chances of being elected. He was encouraged to withdraw as a candidate in favor of Jefferson Davis, who some thought might make a more acceptable president. In the end, the Democratic party split, backing several candidates. Douglas received 1,365,976 votes for president, one-half million more than another Democratic candidate, John Breckinridge. Still another candidate, John Bell, won 515,973 votes from the slave states. The split vote for Democratic candidates gave the presidency to the Republican candidate, Abraham Lincoln.

Support for President Lincoln. Immediately, some Southern states planned to secede. Douglas opposed breaking up the Union as passionately as he had worked for states' rights and westward expansion. He and his wife were among the first to welcome Lincoln to Washington and entertained and lobbied vigorously for Lincoln's stand to preserve the Union. The war with the South was, in Douglas's view, a war to preserve the Union; he did not live to see the Emancipation Act throw the focus of war onto slavery.

Death. In June 1861, Douglas became seriously ill due to the effects of rheumatism and a continually hectic schedule. He was perhaps also suffering from his heavy drinking and the always worrisome state of his finances. Five doctors were called in to attend him, but to no avail. With his wife, Adele, at his side, Douglas died June 3, 1861. In his last breath, he answered his wife's query as to whether he had any message for his two sons. Douglas answered, "Tell them to obey the laws and support the Constitution of the United States" (*New York Herald,* June 7, 1861).

For More Information

Boorstin, Daniel J. and Brooks Mather Kelley. *The History of the United States.* Lexington, Massachusetts: Ginn and Company, 1983.

Johannsen, Robert W., ed. *The Letters of Stephen A. Douglas.* Urbana: University of Illinois Press, 1961.

Johannsen, Robert W. *Stephen A. Douglas.* New York: Oxford University Press, 1973.

Milton, George Fort. *The Eve of Conflict: Stephen A. Douglas and the Needless War.* New York: Houghton Mifflin, 1934.

Dred Scott

c. 1795-1858

Personal Background

For a case that became so famous, the Dred Scott decision's central character—Scott himself—remains a shadowy figure. The case was so complicated and so important to the growing quarrel between North and South that many stories arose about it, and about him. Though few of these stories can be proved, and often they contradict each other, a rough outline of Scott's life can be drawn.

Unrecorded birth in Virginia. Dred Scott was born in Virginia, sometime between 1795 and 1809. Because his parents were slaves, no records were kept of his birth, as they would have been for the birth of a free white child. Probably sometime during his childhood he was sold to a Virginia family named Blow. Peter Blow, a soldier in the War of 1812, and his wife, Elizabeth, had eleven children. Times were hard after the war ended, and Blow took his family and several slaves west to Alabama in 1818. There he tried to make a success of raising cotton but, after twelve years, was forced to move again, this time to St. Louis, Missouri.

Henry and Taylor. The move to St. Louis came in 1830. By this time Scott, who of course moved with the family, was probably in his twenties. Having been with the family since his childhood, he naturally would have been close to the Blow children. He seems to have been especially good friends with two of the younger boys,

▲ Dred Scott

Event: *Scott* v. *Sanford* (the Dred Scott decision).

Role: Dred Scott, a slave, was taken by his master to live for three years in free territory, where slavery was prohibited by law. After returning to the slave state of Missouri, Scott sued for freedom in 1846, claiming that living in free territory had made him free. In the most criticized decision of its history, the Supreme Court ruled against Scott in 1857.

Henry and Taylor, both in their early teens when the family moved to St. Louis. As Scott explained years later in a newspaper interview, he was "raised" with the two boys (Ehrlich, p. 11). Henry and Taylor grew up to become the most successful of the Blow children. Both were businessmen and Henry was also a congressman. Their friendship with Scott would prove important to later events.

Dr. Emerson. St. Louis held tragedy as well as promise for the Blows. Peter and Elizabeth both fell ill and died within a few years of the move, leaving the Blow children orphaned. Several of the family slaves were sold, among them Scott, whose new owner was a St. Louis doctor named John Emerson. Emerson was born in Pennsylvania and had moved to St. Louis in 1831. About the same age as Scott, he decided to make a career out of serving as an army doctor. A restless but friendly man, for the next nine years he sent a steady stream of letters to his superiors asking for better assignments. Usually, his requests included descriptions of illnesses he was afflicted with. These maladies, he argued, were made worse by his present assignment, but would probably disappear if he received the posting he wanted.

Fort Armstrong. In 1833 Emerson won a posting to Fort Armstrong, on the Mississippi River in the free (non-slave) state of Illinois. The fort was in Indian country, where there were few luxuries available. Life at Fort Armstrong was not what Emerson had imagined. Within a few months, he began writing his superiors for another transfer. He complained of having a "syphiloid disease" that needed treatment desperately; when this attempt failed, Emerson claimed he had a "slight disease" of the left foot that might need surgery and that kept him from wearing a shoe (Fehrenbacher, p. 243). Busy despite his "diseases," Emerson invested in a piece of land on the Mississippi. Most likely, Scott did much of the work on the cabin Emerson had built there, chopping trees and shaping them into squared-off logs.

Fort Snelling. The army closed Fort Armstrong in 1836. Emerson finally got his transfer, but not back to the comfort of St. Louis. He was sent farther up the Mississippi to Fort Snelling, near what is now St. Paul, Minnesota. The fort was within the boundaries of the Louisiana Purchase, where the Missouri Compromise, passed by Congress in 1820, had forbidden slavery.

While Emerson wrote letters complaining of the cold weather, which worsened his rheumatism, Scott met a young slave girl named Harriet Robinson, and the two fell in love. About half Scott's age, Harriet belonged to a Major Taliaferro, who either sold or gave her to Emerson. Acting as justice of the peace, Taliaferro performed the marriage ceremony for the two. Scott and Harriet remained happily married until his death in 1858. They had four children: two boys, who died in infancy, and two girls, who later were involved in the legal battle.

Fort Jesup. Once again, Emerson's complaints won him a transfer, and once again the new post was worse than before, this time at Fort Jesup in western Louisiana. Emerson now reported in his letters that he preferred Fort Snelling to Fort Jesup, as Louisiana's wet climate aggravated an old liver problem and attacked his "muscles of respiration, [lungs]" making it hard for him to breath (Fehrenbacher, p. 245). The Scotts had stayed on at Fort Snelling, hired out to other army officers there. Meanwhile, Emerson suffered at Fort Jesup, though his ailments did not prevent him from courting and marrying a young woman, Eliza Sanford. In early 1838, Emerson sent for the Scotts, who made the trip by steamboat down the Mississippi.

Back to Fort Snelling. Emerson's never-ending letters to his superiors resulted in still another transfer, this time back to Fort Snelling, in late 1838. On the steamboat trip back up the Mississippi, Harriet gave birth to a daughter, whom they named Eliza, after Emerson's young bride. According to the testimony of other passengers, Eliza was born after the boat had steamed past the Missouri border; in other words, Eliza was born in territory in which, under the Missouri Compromise, slavery was banned. The Emersons and the Scotts remained at Fort Snelling until spring 1840, when Emerson was again transferred to Florida, where he complained of fevers. During Emerson's two-year assignment there, the Scotts remained with Emerson's wife in St. Louis.

Death of Emerson. Emerson's letters finally exhausted his superiors' patience, and in 1842 he was honorably dismissed from the army. Shortly afterward, he died in St. Louis. He left everything—including his slaves, who were considered property—to his wife. Emerson's wife then loaned the Scotts to her brother-in-law, a

Captain Bainbridge. Evidence suggests that the Scotts went with Bainbridge when he was assigned to Texas in 1844 and 1845.

Participation: Pre-Civil War Controversies

Suing for freedom. Soon after returning to St. Louis in the spring of 1846, Scott apparently tried to buy his and his family's freedom from Eliza Emerson, but she refused. On April 6, he and Harriet both filed suits in the Missouri circuit court in St. Louis. They claimed that because they had lived with Emerson on free soil, they were both free, and that Eliza Emerson had thus held them in slavery against the law. They also claimed that she had "beat, bruised and ill-treated" them both (Fehrenbacher, p. 250), and they requested ten dollars in damages. Such suits were not uncommon. Legal precedent—the custom as decided by previous cases—was heavily in the Scotts' favor, for many court decisions had recognized that residence on free soil was enough to allow a slave to claim freedom.

Old friends. In starting the lawsuits, Scott had the support of his old friends Henry and Taylor Blow, now successful St. Louis businessmen. Scott had had plenty of time to renew his friendship with the brothers over the years, as his trips up and down the Mississippi meant many stopovers in St. Louis. Possibly, the Blows had informed Scott about his chances of winning freedom in court. Since he could not read and had no education, the argument goes, he could not have known enough to start the fight himself.

Yet it seems equally possible that, in his wide travels, Scott had become perfectly aware of the legal situation favoring him. Slaves talked of such lawsuits constantly. Whether or not the idea was his own, he must have valued the Blows' support, for court documents reveal that Henry Blow, Taylor Blow, and several of their brothers-in-law paid the Scott's legal fees.

Brief victory. The Scotts had continued to work for a couple named Russell, to whom they had been hired out by Eliza Emerson. Sometime around 1847 Harriet gave birth to their second daughter, named Lizzie. Their case did not go to court until June 1847, when a mistake by the Scotts' lawyers resulted in quick defeat. Aided by the Blows, the Scotts hired new lawyers and started over, since the case remained strong despite the defeat over a technicality. After a number of delays, due to a bad fire in St. Louis and an outbreak of cholera, the case was finally heard in January 1850. The court decided in the Scotts' favor. Scott, Harriet, and their children were free.

Political motives. By that time, Eliza Emerson had moved to Massachusetts, leaving her stake in the trial's outcome to her brother, John Sanford. Sanford appealed the decision, exercising his right to have a higher court review it. Until the appeal was decided, the Scotts' newfound freedom would have to wait. The appeal would be decided by the Missouri State Supreme Court, which like the rest of the country was becoming more and more caught up in stormy political debates over slavery and its future. Up to this point, arguments by lawyers on both sides had dealt simply with the facts of the case. The judges had done the same. From this point on, however, regional and national politics dominated the case. Scott and his family became pawns in the increasingly bitter struggle between North and South.

Missouri Supreme Court. During the late 1840s, as slavery became the leading national issue, attitudes hardened on both sides of the question. Court rulings in Missouri, formerly reflecting a more liberal Southern outlook, adopted a harsher tone against blacks. By 1850 new judges on the Missouri Supreme Court were looking for a case they could use to overrule the more liberal court rulings of the past. In 1852 the Missouri Supreme Court overturned the lower court decision that had been made in Scott's favor, ruling instead that Scott was still a slave. "Times are not now as they were when the former decisions on this subject were made," the court said in ruling on *Dred Scott* v. *Emerson* (Fehrenbacher, p. 264). The judges openly admitted that political motives were behind their decision, and that it was meant to oppose antislavery forces.

Scott v. ***Sanford.*** The Scotts had begun working for one of the Blows' brothers-in-law, Charles LaBeaume, who gave their wages to a sheriff for safekeeping. If the Scotts were finally found to be free, they would get the wages; if not, the money would go to their owner. Exactly who claimed to own the Scotts at this time is unclear, although it seems to have been Eliza Emerson's brother, John Sanford. With Taylor Blow, LaBeaume hired a new lawyer in 1853. On behalf of Scott, this lawyer filed suit against Sanford in the U.S. Circuit Court for the District of Missouri in 1854.

Loyalty. Something in Scott's personality had inspired loyalty in the Blows, who were actually proslavery. They later supported the South in the Civil War. Despite their beliefs, they generously gave their time and money to help their old friend and companion gain his freedom. Their brother-in-law clearly felt the same affection. He had gotten to know Scott by employing him, and now he helped take the cause to a new arena: the federal courts of the United States.

United States Supreme Court. The jury in the U.S. Circuit Court decided against Scott quickly, in May 1854. Scott's lawyer immediately filed an appeal. This meant that the decision, once again, would be reviewed by a higher court, in this case, the Supreme Court of the United States. There, *Dred Scott* v. *Sanford* waited for almost two years, a period in which Congress and the American people continued to grow ever more divided over slavery. Violence between proslavery and antislavery forces was reaching a climax in Kansas during these years. Neither the president nor Congress could effectively resolve the issue, so some began looking toward the Supreme Court for a solution.

National questions. While the busy Supreme Court worked its way through the many cases demanding its attention, Scott and Harriet continued to work for LaBeaume in St. Louis. Meanwhile, newspapers brought *Dred Scott* v. *Sanford* to the attention of the American public. Here was a case that could settle many of the complex questions pitting North against South: Was the Missouri Compromise valid? Did Congress in fact have the power to make laws prohibiting slavery? Did blacks have the right to sue in court?

"No rights." This last question, involving issues of citizenship, had been introduced into the case by the judge in the U.S. Circuit Court decision against Scott. On March 6, 1857, Supreme

▲ Roger Brooke Taney

Court Chief Justice Roger Brooke Taney gave the court's decision. In ruling against Scott, Taney declared not only that the Missouri Compromise was invalid and that Congress had no power to outlaw slavery in the states, but also that blacks, as "beings of an inferior order … had no rights which the white man was bound to respect" (Bell, p. 6). "No rights" meant no right to be a citizen and no right to sue. Thus, Scott's fate was decided not just because he was a slave, but because he was black. Taney gave race as a justification for slavery, and as a reason why even free blacks could not enjoy the fruits of citizenship.

Aftermath

Outcry. The decision, the most controversial in the Court's history, provoked an immediate outcry in the North. Some believed that it hastened the outbreak of the Civil War. Taney himself was a Southerner, as were four other members of the nine-member court, making a Southern majority. One major effect of the decision was to strengthen the Republican party in the North, as Northerners against slavery reacted to the Court's Southern bias. Abraham Lincoln, the Republican presidential candidate, skillfully used the case in his famous debates with Democrat Stephen Douglas (see **Stephen A. Douglas**).

Taney's Words

Taney justified his Dred Scott opinion by arguing that the writers of the Constitution never considered blacks as citizens of the new nation: "We have come to the conclusion that the African race who came to this country, whether free or slave, were not intended to be included in the constitution for the enjoyment of any personal rights or benefits" (Ehrlich, p. 145).

National fame. Dred Scott's name had become one of the most famous of his time. He still worked for LaBeaume, though it is not known exactly what he did for him. Many newspaper stories were written about Scott, but none present a clear picture of the man. Proslavery newspapers invariably portrayed Scott as lazy and ignorant, while antislavery papers described him as intelligent, hardworking, and responsible. Whatever the truth, Scott possessed qualities that made men who knew him willing to sacrifice time and money on his behalf. The quiet way he conducted his eleven-year legal battle suggests that he was a humble person. Yet the battle also called for strength, determination, stubbornness, and a certain modest but unmistakable pride.

Freedom. Sanford died soon after the decision in his favor, and ownership of the Scotts passed to Eliza Emerson's second husband, Dr. Calvin Chaffee. Ironically, Chaffee was an antislavery Republican congressman from Massachusetts. Since only a Missouri citizen could free a slave in Missouri, Chaffee hastily transferred his ownership to Taylor Blow, who wasted no time in freeing Scott, Harriet, and their two girls on May 26, 1857. After winning his freedom, Scott apparently carried clothes for Harriet, who ran a laundry service, and worked as a porter at Barnum's, a well-known St. Louis hotel, where his fame made him something of an attraction. On September 17, 1858, a little more than a year after being freed, Scott died of tuberculosis. His death was noted in news stories across America.

Devotion Beyond the Grave

A few years after Scott's burial in St. Louis, city expansion overtook the cemetery. The bodies were dug up and put elsewhere, and Taylor Blow arranged for Scott to be reburied at his own church. On March 6, 1957, 100 years after the Dred Scott decision, St. Louis citizens attended a ceremony that marked the grave with a granite headstone. On the headstone is carved a brief account of Scott's role in history. It was paid for by a Mrs. Charles Harrison of Villa Nova, Pennsylvania—a descendant of Taylor Blow.

For More Information

Bell, Derrick A. *Civil Rights: Leading Cases.* New York: Little, Brown & Co., 1980.

Ehrlich, Walter. *They Have No Rights: Dred Scott's Struggle for Freedom.* Westport, Connecticut: Greenwood Press, 1979.

Fehrenbacher, Don E. *The Dred Scott Case: Its Significance in American Law and Politics.* New York: Oxford University Press, 1978.

John Brown

1800-1859

Personal Background

Family and professional life. John Brown was born on May 9, 1800, in Torrington, Connecticut, one of sixteen children born to Owen and Ruth Brown. In 1805 the family moved to the Western Reserve district of Ohio. Owen Brown, who worked as a cobbler and leather tanner, taught his children to believe that God was a stern judge whose commandments must always be obeyed. He also taught them that slavery was evil and that it must be opposed at every opportunity. (Owen, like his son John later, helped runaway slaves escape via the Underground Railroad.) John Brown took his father's teachings to heart. He committed the entire Bible to memory, attempted to train for the ministry, and became a life-long opponent of slavery.

Brown married twice. His first wife, Dianthe Lusk, bore seven children; after she died, he married sixteen-year-old Anne Day, and with her had thirteen more children. Brown moved his family about frequently, living at various times in Ohio, Pennsylvania, and Massachusetts. He practiced many trades, working as a cattle driver, leather tanner, stock grower, wool merchant and farmer.

Almost from the beginning, Brown's life was marked by tragedy. His mother died when he was just eight years old, leaving him grief-stricken for many years. His first wife suffered emotional problems and died young; seven of the thirteen children from his

▲ John Brown

Event: Pottawatomie massacre and raid on Harpers Ferry.

Role: John Brown was a radical abolitionist who believed that he was chosen by God to destroy slavery in the United States. In October 1859, Brown and a raiding party seized the federal arsenal at Harpers Ferry, Virginia. He hoped to spark a slave revolt and create in the South a free-soil area, a place where slavery was prohibited. The raid ended in failure, and Brown was wounded, captured, tried, and hanged. The courage he displayed at his trial made him a martyr in the eyes of antislavery Northerners, which hastened the nation's progress toward civil war.

second marriage died in childhood. All of his business ventures ended in failure. He was completely wiped out in the Panic of 1837 and was forced to declare bankruptcy in 1842. All subsequent efforts to recover his fortunes also failed.

Character traits. There were contradictions in Brown's character. Though he was "extremely religious, he could also be dictatorial and self-righteous, with an imperious [commanding] manner that made him intolerant and unappreciative of others, especially his own sons" (Oates, "God's Angry Man," p. 10). He could become obsessed with a single idea and pursue it with unswerving zeal.

At the same time, Brown could be kind and extremely gentle. He exhausted himself staying up night after night caring for his sick children or his ailing first wife. He wept over the graves of his children who died, and worried about the souls of those who lived to question the stern religious ideals he taught them. Perhaps his most admirable trait, in an age when prejudice was rampant in all sections of the country, was his ability to treat African Americans as equals. He developed an extreme bitterness toward slavery and those who defended it.

Antislavery activities. As he grew older, Brown became something of a fanatic on the subject of slavery. He worked on the Underground Railroad, tried to integrate the Congregational Church he attended (he was expelled for his efforts), and grew more and more extreme in his views on slavery and slave owners. He told a friend that he would be willing to die for the destruction of slavery.

Brown criticized blacks for not resisting their enslavement more vigorously and came up with a plan to help large numbers of runaway slaves escape to freedom through an underground pass way. He told renowned black abolitionist Frederick Douglass that he planned to arm the slaves he led to freedom because violent resistance would give them a sense of their own manhood. In 1851 he urged blacks to kill any official who tried to enforce the Fugitive Slave Act.

Participation: Antislavery Raids

Crisis in Kansas. Brown was stirred to action when Congress passed the Kansas-Nebraska Bill in 1854. This bill, sponsored by Senator Stephen A. Douglas of Illinois, repealed the old Missouri Compromise, which prohibited slavery north of the latitude line 36° 30', by introducing the principle of popular sovereignty (see **Stephen A. Douglas**). This meant that the citizens of these territories could, if they so desired, allow slavery into territories where it had previously been forbidden. Brown and other Northern abolitionists attacked the Kansas-Nebraska Act as a Southern conspiracy to win over the territories to slavery. They vowed to prevent this by flooding the territories with free-soil, or antislavery, pioneers.

Among the hundreds of free-soil pioneers who set out for Kansas were five of John Brown's sons. They witnessed the invasion, in 1855, of Kansas by Missouri border ruffians who voted illegally to establish Kansas as a slave state and promised to kill any abolitionist who attempted to settle in the territory. Brown's sons wrote him that a war between freedom and slavery was ready to break out in Kansas and implored him to join them and to bring as many weapons as he could. Brown responded by collecting an arsenal of guns and swords and hurried to Kansas to help save it from proslavery zealots.

Pottawatomie massacre. Violence broke out in Kansas not long after Brown arrived. Raiders from Missouri reentered the state and killed a number of antislavery settlers. An outraged Brown vowed to strike back. He was especially enraged when the free-state town of Lawrence was sacked (its inhabitants offered no resistance) and when news arrived in Kansas of the vicious beating of abolitionist Senator Charles Sumner as he sat at his Senate desk.

Brown apparently believed that God wanted him to avenge these wrongs. On the nights of May 24 and 25, 1856, he led four of his sons and three other men to the homes of proslavery settlers along Pottawatomie Creek. He told his followers that it was time to "fight fire with fire" and to "strike terror in the hearts of the proslavery people" (Oates, *To Purge This Land with Blood,* p. 133). In his view, it was better for a score of bad men to die than for anyone who came to make Kansas a free state to be driven out. Brown and his band dragged five men, all associated with proslavery forces although none was a slave owner, out of their cabins and hacked them to death with swords.

161

The raids by proslavery Missourians and the murders committed by Brown and his men along Pottawatomie Creek led to open civil war in Kansas. Brown's own son Frederick was killed near Ossawatomie by a proslavery leader. This event weighed heavily on Brown, who was heard to say after Frederick's death that God had appointed him "a special angel of death" to destroy slavery through violence (Oates, *To Purge This Land with Blood,* p. 133). This mission would not be accomplished in Kansas; Brown looked east, to New England, where he hoped to gather money and arms, and to Virginia, where he hoped to strike a direct blow at slavery.

Building a following. Brown believed that he would need the support of wealthy, influential men to accomplish his mission. He left Kansas, where federal forces and a newly appointed governor managed to impose an uneasy peace, to try to raise funds in the Northeast. During a fund-raising campaign that resembled a religious revival, Brown told audiences (that included such respected figures as writers Ralph Waldo Emerson and Henry David Thoreau) about the vicious deeds committed by Missouri border ruffians and other proslavery forces in Kansas. He recounted the murders of the free-state settlers and his son Frederick and asked for money to continue the fight in Kansas, vowing that he and his sons would not quit until victory was won.

In fact, Brown had no intention of continuing the fight to keep slavery out of Kansas. He hinted at his larger goals in a brief conversation with Emerson. He told the author that he fervently believed in two things—the Bible and the Declaration of Independence—and he asserted that it would be better for a whole generation of men, women, and children to die violent deaths than for either the Bible or the Declaration to be violated in America. Emerson knew that both were violated daily and agreed with Brown, assuming that he was speaking symbolically. Emerson would later discover that Brown meant every word literally.

Brown used a part of the money he had raised in the Northeast to order a thousand metal pikes from a Connecticut forge-master. He returned briefly to Kansas, but only to recruit men, not to reopen the battle there. He asked the men to meet him in Tabor, Iowa. There he revealed to them that the ultimate target of his planned assault against slavery was in Virginia.

In 1858 Brown visited a wealthy businessman and abolitionist named Gerrit Smith at his mansion in Peterboro, New York. He told Smith why he believed that the slavery issue could never be settled peacefully. Brown cited the following to illustrate the failure of peaceful tactics: the South's defense of slavery as a positive good; the policies of the Buchanan presidency, which attempted to admit Kansas as a slave state even though the majority of the territory's citizens were free-staters; and the Supreme Court's Dred Scott decision (see **Dred Scott**). The only alternative was to incite a massive slave rebellion and to make slave owners pay a bloody price for their sin of holding men in bondage. He admitted his solution was a terrible one, but slavery, he argued, was the same as murder, and slave owners must be violently punished. Brown proposed to march on Virginia, incite a slave insurrection, and even if his scheme failed, to provoke a crisis—even a civil war—that would result in the death of slavery.

Brown succeeded in winning the support of Smith and five other well-known reformers. These men formed a committee called the Secret Six, raised money to support Brown's enterprise, and hoped, even if the scheme fa iled, that it might provoke a civil war that would lead to the destruction of slavery.

After winning their support, Brown went to Chatham, Canada, where he met secretly in a schoolhouse with thirty-four blacks and eleven whites. He told the gathering that blacks all over the South were ready to rise up and that he was prepared to lead that uprising. He planned to invade Virginia and march into Tennessee and northern Alabama with this encouragement. The slaves, he believed, would rise up and wage war to win their freedom. Brown dismissed any suggestion that armed troops might be able to squash his force. He believed that his guerrilla tactics, mountain strongholds, and, most important, a general slave uprising supported by free blacks from every corner of the country would ensure success. He read to the assembly a constitution he had written to govern the new state that would be set up once the slaves were freed. Its preamble declared war against the institution of slavery and its defenders. Brown was proclaimed commander in chief of the armed forces of the new state. The group assembled at Chatham endorsed Brown's plans and the constitution. Most, however, made no plans to accompany his band when it invaded enemy territory.

Back in Kansas. Brown's attack on Virginia was delayed when a disgruntled drillmaster he had hired revealed Brown's plans to some politicians. The Secret Six urged Brown to leave for Kansas until it was safe to return. He went back to Kansas grudgingly. While there, he conducted a daring and bloody raid into Missouri, freeing a number of slaves, killing one slave holder, almost inciting another outbreak of war, and provoking President James Buchanan to put a price of $250 on his head (Brown responded by putting a price of $2.50 on the president's head).

Harpers Ferry raid. As he had after the Pottawatomie massacre, Brown eluded capture after the Missouri raid. He made his way back east and prepared for his attack on Harpers Ferry, Virginia, the site of the federal arsenal and armory. Brown rented a farm on the Maryland side of the Potomac River, only seven miles from Harpers Ferry, and gathered his weapons and recruits there. He finally revealed his plans to his men. They were to attack the town of Harpers Ferry, seize the guns in the federal armory, and wait for the slaves from the surrounding area to rise up and join them. The slaves would be armed, and the entire force would move southward, spreading terror and violence throughout the South. Many of the men thought the scheme was suicidal, but Brown managed to keep their loyalty. Brown believed that the arrival of more recruits, money, and the pikes he had ordered long before were signs that God wanted them to proceed. At 8:00 p.m. on Sunday, October 16, 1859, Brown and his tiny army of sixteen whites and five blacks set out for Harpers Ferry.

Brown left three of his men behind to guard his base of operations at the Maryland farmhouse and led his remaining eighteen men into the darkened town of Harpers Ferry. They quickly seized the armory complex, which was guarded only by a single watchman. A patrol was sent into the surrounding countryside to arouse the nearby slaves and to take hostages. Brown then simply waited for these slaves to join him. None did, except a few that had been forcibly brought in by his patrol. Ironically, the first person to die as a result of the raid was a free black man mistakenly shot by one of the rebels Brown had left to guard a bridge into the town. Brown himself stopped an eastbound train for several hours. In what turned out to be a foolish decision, he finally allowed it to proceed and spread the alarm to alert others of the raid.

By morning of the next day, the townspeople of Harpers Ferry were firing at Brown's men. At the same time, militiamen from towns in nearby Virginia and Maryland were arriving in response to the rumors of a slave insurrection. During the afternoon fighting, eight of the raiders (including two of Brown's sons) and three citizens of the town were killed. Seven of Brown's men, two of whom were later caught, managed to escape. Brown offered to exchange his hostages for a safe passage out of town, but the messengers he sent with the offer were shot by the angry townspeople, even though the messengers carried a white flag. Brown retreated and took refuge with his hostages and surviving men in the thick-walled fire-engine house.

During the night, a detachment of marines under the command of Colonel Robert E. Lee and Lieutenant J.E.B. (Jeb) Stuart arrived. In the morning, Stuart met with Brown and asked him to surrender. When Brown refused, Stuart jumped back and gave the signal to attack. The marines quickly stormed the engine-house with battering rams and bayonets, not wanting to fire a shot for fear of hitting the hostages. They lost one man, killed two of the raiders, and captured John Brown. Brown's bizarre raid on Harpers Ferry was over barely thirty-six hours after it had begun.

Aftermath

Consequences. Brown's raid on Harpers Ferry ended in hopeless failure. No slaves had risen up anywhere in Virginia or Maryland because they had been given no advanced warning of Brown's plans, and, knowing white strength, they were unwilling to risk certain death in a futile uprising. Seventeen people died as a result of the raid: two slaves, three townspeople, one slave owner, one marine, and ten of Brown's men. Brown and six of his men were captured, indicted, tried, and convicted of treason, murder, and inciting slave insurrection. All were sentenced to be hanged.

Brown's preparation for the raid had, in hindsight, been poor. Ignoring the advice of many, including Frederick Douglass, Brown had led his men into a trap. He tried to incite a slave rebellion without telling the slaves about it. He took along no food for his men. (At one almost comical moment, he ordered forty-five breakfasts to be sent over from the local inn.) He also left behind at the Maryland farm a large collection of letters and plans implicating his supporters. Four members of the Secret Six left the country to avoid arrest. Only one, Thomas Wentworth Higginson, courageously stood his ground. The last member of the secret committee, Gerrit Smith, burned all papers linking him to Brown and had himself committed to a mental institution to avoid prosecution.

Brown's finest hour. Brown's finest performance came between his capture and his execution. He won the admiration of his captors with the unflinching courage he displayed in facing certain death. Virginia Governor Henry Wise praised Brown's courage and rejected, as Brown wanted him to, any suggestion that Brown might be insane. During his trial, Brown was always composed and dignified, though he lay wounded on a cot. He wrote his wife a note expressing his belief that his death would only further his cause. His statement on being sentenced to death was a bravely worded defense of his conduct:

> I believe that to have interfered as I have done ... in behalf of [God's] despised poor [the slaves], is no wrong, but right. Now, if it is deemed necessary that I should forfeit my life for the furtherance of the ends of justice, and mingle my blood further with the blood of my children and with the blood of millions in this slave country whose rights are disregarded by wicked, cruel, and unjust enactments, I say, let it be done. (Potter, *The Impending Crisis,* p. 377)

On his way to the gallows, Brown slipped a note to one of his guards. It contained his last message to his countrymen: "I John Brown am now quite certain that the crimes of this guilty land; will never be purged *away;* but with Blood. I had *as I now think;* vainly flattered myself that without *very much* bloodshed; it might be done" (Oates, "God's Angry Man," p. 21).

Death. Brown's body was brought back to his home in the black community of North Elba, New York, in the Adirondack Mountains. He was buried near the Brown farmhouse as four members of a black family sang "Blow Ye the Trumpet, Blow," Brown's favorite hymn.

In the North, Brown's death aroused great emotional sympathy for his cause. Emerson wrote that his hanging would "make the

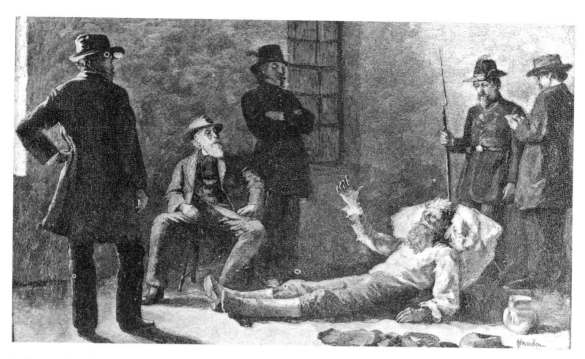

▲ Brown in prison

gallows as glorious as the cross" (Potter, *The Impending Crisis,* p. 379). Thoreau compared Brown to Jesus and called him an angel of light. The Southern reaction to Harpers Ferry was a call for secession. One Southern newspaper argued that the region ought to separate from the Union rather than live under a government where so many citizens regard John Brown as a martyr and a Christian hero rather than a murderer and robber. The raid on Harpers Ferry and Brown's death further polarized the nation.

For More Information

Oates, Stephen B. "God's Angry Man." *American History Illustrated,* Vol. 20. January 1986, pp. 10-21.

Oates, Stephen B. *To Purge This Land with Blood: A Biography of John Brown.* New York: Harper & Row, 1970.

Potter, David M. *The Impending Crisis, 1848-1861.* New York: Harper and Row, 1963.

Potter, David M. *John Brown: A Cry for Freedom.* New York: Crowell, 1980.

Civil War

1860
▼
Abraham Lincoln elected president. South Carolina secedes.

1860
▼
Senate defeats compromise proposed by John Crittenden in hopes of avoiding war.

1861
▼
Ten more states secede. Confederate States of America formed. Fort Sumter taken by Confederacy; war begins.

1862
▼
Mathew B. Brady photographs Battle of Fredericksburg; **Walt Whitman** locates his wounded brother on the battlefield.

1862
▼
Anna Ella Carroll advises Lincoln on how to capture key areas on the western front.

1862
▼
Robert E. Lee promoted to military adviser to Confederate president Jefferson Davis.

1861
▼
Four border states (all slave states) remain in the Union.

1862
▼
Slave trade ends in Washington, D.C.

1863
▼
Lincoln delivers Emancipation Proclamation.

1863
▼
Martin Robinson Delany becomes first black field officer in Union army.

1863
▼
Draft riots in New York result in more than 70 deaths.

1865
▼
Lincoln gets Congress to approve Thirteenth Amendment, ending slavery in the nation.

1865
▼
Lee surrenders to Grant at Appomattox. War ends.

1864
▼
William Tecumseh Sherman burns Atlanta and sets out on March to the Sea.

1863
▼
Lee invades the North, loses at Gettysburg. Lincoln defines the purpose of Civil War in his Gettysburg Address.

1863
▼
Lincoln puts Ulysses S. Grant in charge of Union troops.

CIVIL WAR

Fought from 1861 until 1865, the war between the states was an armed conflict between the North and South. The North entered the war to preserve the Union while Southern states dropped out of the Union and fought to confirm their independence from it. Beginning in 1860, eleven states seceded to form the Confederate States of America: South Carolina, Georgia, Florida, Alabama, Mississippi, Louisiana, Texas, Virginia, Tennessee, North Carolina, and Arkansas.

There were a few slave states bordering the North: Delaware, Maryland, Virginia, Kentucky, and Missouri. None of these border states seceded except Virginia, and northwest Virginia remained loyal to the Union, forming the new state of West Virginia in 1863. Yet all the border states except Delaware sent soldiers to fight for the Confederate army.

Within months the Union, or the North, and the Confederate States of America, or the South, were engaged in a civil war. When the conflict began in April 1861, many Americans expected a quick end to the hostilities. But both sides had advantages that drew out the conflict. Though the North had more money, industry, and manpower, it lacked strong generals. The South, on the other hand, had **Robert E. Lee,** considered by most to be the finest general of the war. It also would be fighting a mostly defensive war on

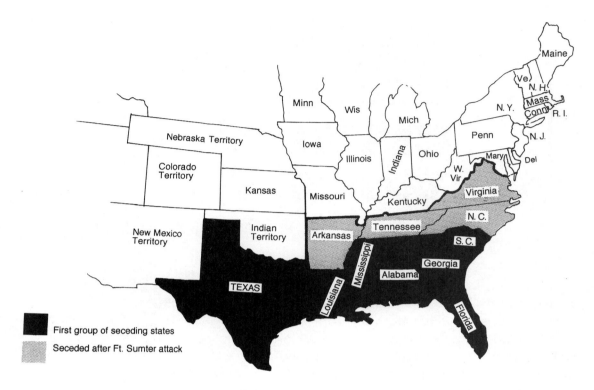

▲ **Seceding states**

Civil War Odds

The Civil War pitted 23 states and 22 million people on the Union side against 11 states and 9 million on the Confederate side (including 3.5 million slaves). Yet numbers do not tell the whole story, as there were sympathizers in both regions for the other side. Southerners insisted they had the right to secede. Some Northerners agreed, and many of them hesitated at having to fight in the Union army.

home territory that its soldiers knew well. In the end, neither side was prepared for the draining conflict that became America's first modern war. The killing was more distant and less personal than ever before, and civilians as well as soldiers were swept into the destruction.

The first two years of fighting dragged on without decisive victories for either the North or South. Generals on both sides had been educated at West Point, where they learned the same battle tactic—pinpoint and break through weak spots in enemy lines. Using the recently developed telegraph and observation balloons, armies worked to collect information, exploring the geography of areas before battle. New rifles, produced for the war, extended a marksman's range by five hundred yards and allowed for quick loading and firing at the advancing enemy. With such inventions came fresh methods of warfare. Since cannon and rifle fire could mow down troops in the open, it became common for enemies to dig trenches and shoot from behind the earthworks. Also the North introduced a new battle tactic called total warfare. Shocking for its time, it extended the fighting beyond the battle-field. Troops were no longer the only targets; roads, factories, and crops were destroyed as well.

With few victories on either side in 1861 and 1862, President **Abraham Lincoln** faced hard choices. Exasperated at the string of weak Union generals in charge at the beginning of the war and willing to experiment to win, the president took command of the Northern troops himself.

On the western front, a battle plan created by **Anna Ella Carroll,** a female adviser to Lincoln, captured two key forts for the Union in 1862. Still neither side was winning. Lincoln decided he had to introduce a drastic change or lose the war, so he announced that he would emancipate, or free, all slaves in Confederate territory on January 1, 1863. The Emancipation Proclamation increased support for the North by adding a moral purpose to its side beyond keeping the Union together. Other countries, such as England, which was strongly opposed to slavery, now could not possibly come out in favor of the South. Overjoyed at the turn of events, **Martin Robinson Delany** rushed to Washington to build a black army and became the first black officer in the regular army.

After Lincoln announced that he would emancipate the slaves, the deadlock broke in the fighting. The Union began

Some Civil War Battles— Which Side Won?

Year	Location	Victor
1861	First Battle of Bull Run	South
1862	Battle of Antietam	North
1862	Battle of Fredericksburg	South
1862	Battle of Shiloh	North
1862	Capture of Forts Henry and Donelson	North
1863	Battle of Chancellorsville	South
1863	Battle of Gettysburg	North
1863	Siege of Vicksburg	North
1864	Capture of Atlanta	North
1865	Surrender at Appomattox	North

winning in the East with a victory at Gettysburg, Pennsylvania, and in the West with Vicksburg, Mississippi. Strong leadership finally surfaced in the Union army. Lincoln happily transferred direct command of the troops from himself to Ulysses S. Grant while **William Tecumseh Sherman** took charge of Union forces in the West. Together they bore down on the two main wings of the Confederate army. Grant's troops squared off to fight Lee's Army of Northern Virginia; Sherman's, to defeat the Army of Tennessee led by Joseph E. Johnston. Sherman captured and burned Atlanta, then marched to the sea (the Atlantic Ocean), his troops destroying livestock, homes, and railroad tracks along the way. The strategy worked. With the South ravaged and its troops tired and shrunken, both Lee and Johnston surrendered.

Draft Riots

The first draft laws in American history were passed during the Civil War. Resentment against the draft led to riots in the North. Angering poor whites, escape clauses in the 1863 law allowed Northerners to hire substitutes or pay $300 to be excused from service. Rioters also felt they would be risking their lives to free slaves who would then compete for their jobs. The worst riot erupted in New York City, where buildings were burned, stores looted, and blacks murdered. The riot resulted in more than 70 deaths and $1.5 million in property damage. Other, smaller riots erupted in Vermont, Ohio, Massachusetts, and New Hampshire.

Mathew B. Brady, the first battlefield photographer, documented the horror of it all. His pictures captured the death, the destruction, and the ghastly prison camps. The South had severe shortages of food and other necessities, and hundreds of wounded on both sides received little or no care. Nursing the stricken on the battlefields and behind the lines, poet **Walt Whitman** also wrote about their pains.

While the South suffered great losses, Northern industry grew rapidly during the war to meet needs for wool, weaponry, and petroleum. Women took factory jobs, and over four hundred were hired as government clerks, a position many of them would retain after the war. Southern women worked as clerks, too, and often took over management of the family farm. Also thousands of women on both sides, such as Clara Barton and Elizabeth Blackwell, came forward to tend the wounded.

Among the nurses were black men and women. In fact, blacks worked for the armies as bakers, smiths, cooks, carpenters, and scouts. Black soldiers in the North, almost always led by white officers, served in segregated regiments and earned less pay than white soldiers. By war's end there were about 200,000 blacks in the Union army. The South too launched a program to train (and free) black soldiers, but the timing was so late that Southern black soldiers never saw action. Indians, on the other hand, fought in both armies. From the Choctaw, Chickasaw, Creek, Seminole, and Cherokee came Confederate soldiers. A tribal split led some Cherokee, under Chief John Ross, to fight for the Union, as did most of the tribes on the Great Plains.

The Southerners, always outnumbered and outgunned, fought valiantly but, in the end, were defeated by a larger, better supplied enemy and the daring tactic of total warfare. Some 640,000 soldiers—whites, blacks, and Indians—died in a war whose outcome forever changed American society. Slavery was abolished and the wealthy Southern planter class destroyed. Lincoln took a few steps toward Reconstruction—bringing the South back into the Union—before the end of the war. Now that it was over, the whole nation would begin the journey down the long and bitter road to recovery in earnest and without Lincoln.

Abraham Lincoln

1809-1865

Personal Background

Family background. Abraham Lincoln was born February 12, 1809, in a log cabin in Hardin County, Kentucky. His father, Thomas Lincoln, was a wandering laborer and farmer. His mother, Nancy Hanks, was a very spiritual woman. Neither parent could read or write. The family moved to southwest Indiana, where they lived as "squatters," claiming the right to settle and farm on public land. Abraham had an older sister and a brother who would die in infancy. When asked about this period of his life at a later date, he recalled the extreme poverty and the grief he experienced when his mother died in 1818. Abraham was only nine years old at the time. Fortunately for his children, Thomas Lincoln soon took a new wife, marrying Sarah Bush Johnston, a widow with three children of her own. An ideal stepmother, she treated both sets of children as if they were hers. She was especially fond of Abraham, as he was of her.

Abraham had to work hard on the family farm and thus received very little formal education. He attended school off and on, but his total schooling amounted to about one year's attendance. Nevertheless, he became an avid reader; his friends and neighbors later remembered how he would walk miles to borrow books. Later in life, Lincoln would reveal a fondness for the English language and its sounds. He wrote poetry as well as his own political

▲ Abraham Lincoln

Event: The Civil War.
Role: Abraham Lincoln rose from extreme poverty to become president of the United States in 1860. His election led to the secession of Southern states, the formation of the Confederacy, and the Civil War (1861-65). Lincoln outlined the strategy and chose the generals who led the Union forces to victory in the war. He issued the Emancipation Proclamation, which freed slaves in the South. Before being assassinated, he also prodded Congress into passing the Thirteenth Amendment, which outlawed slavery throughout the nation.

speeches, pronouncing words in Midwest style (*kin* instead of *can,* for example).

Lawyer and husband. About the time Lincoln turned twenty-one, his family moved to Illinois. He was six feet four inches tall, lanky, and strong—his ability as a wrestler won him many friends. After working as a flatboatman and journeying to New Orleans (where he saw the evils of the slave system close-up), he settled apart from his family in the village of New Salem, Illinois. He worked at various times as a storekeeper, postmaster, and surveyor. When the Black Hawk War broke out in 1832, Lincoln joined the militia and was elected captain of his company. He later joked that he never encountered any live, fighting Indians but that he had done mighty battle with the mosquitoes.

> **Lincoln's Sense of Humor**
>
> Lincoln, who was often depressed and melancholy, had at the same time a great love for storytelling and humor. He thought of humor as therapy: "I laugh because I must not weep ... a funny story ... puts new life into me." (Oates, p. 47)

After his brief military service, Lincoln decided to try his hand at politics. He was defeated the first time he ran for office, but thereafter he was elected (and reelected many times) to the Illinois state legislature. He ran as a member of the Whig party. At the same time, he made his other lasting career choice: he studied law, passed the bar exam, and entered into the first of several law partnerships.

In 1842 Lincoln, against the wishes of her family, married Mary Todd, a union that would last twenty-two years. Together the couple had four sons. Their first-born, Robert, survived, but the other three died before adulthood: Eddie, in 1850; Willie, in 1862; and Tad, in 1870.

State legislator. Lincoln had great success both as a lawyer and a state legislator. He won some dramatic criminal cases (gaining acquittal for one client accused of murder by using an almanac to prove that the night had been too dark for the accusing witness to identify any attacker) and appeared often before the Illinois Supreme Court. In the Illinois State Legislature he became a real power in the Whig party and was instrumental in relocating the state capital to Springfield. In 1846 Lincoln was elected to his only term in Congress, where he introduced his famous "spot resolu-

▲ **Mary Todd Lincoln**

tion," challenging President Polk, who had declared that Mexico started the Mexican War with the United States on American soil, to point out the spot where Americans were attacked. He also voted for Congressman David Wilmot's proposal that slavery be excluded from territory taken from Mexico.

Lincoln on slavery. While in Congress, Lincoln proposed a bill for gradually abolishing slavery in Washington, D.C. (with compensation to be paid to slave owners for the loss of their property), and he sided with those who criticized the war with Mexico as a

177

conspiracy to spread slavery. These stands were unpopular with voters in his district, and he was not returned to Congress. Only forty years old, a frustrated Abraham Lincoln appeared to be finished in American politics.

For about five years, Lincoln took very little interest in political matters. A new sectional crisis, provoked by his old foe, Stephen A. Douglas, finally brought him back into the political arena. Douglas pushed the Kansas-Nebraska Act through Congress, repealing the Missouri Compromise, which prohibited slavery in those parts of the Louisiana Purchase north of the latitude line 36° 30'. The new law (of 1854) allowed settlers in the territories of Kansas and Nebraska to decide for themselves whether or not to permit slavery.

The Kansas-Nebraska Act raised a storm of protest in the Old Northwest (including Illinois). In addition, the Whig party began to die out and the Republican Party, dedicated to keeping slavery out of the territories, was born. Abraham Lincoln was energized by these events. He became one of the founders of the Republican party in Illinois. He believed the spread of slavery must be halted because new free states were the best hope for poor people searching for ways to improve their lives. In Lincoln's eyes, the issue was made even more critical by the Dred Scott decision of the Supreme Court, which decreed that blacks were inferior beings who never would be American citizens and that neither the Declaration of Independence nor the Constitution applied to them. Lincoln was shocked; he believed that a slaveholder's conspiracy was at work, and that the Supreme Court would next declare that free states could not keep slavery out because that would violate Southern property rights guaranteed by the Fifth Amendment.

Lincoln thought that the Kansas-Nebraska Act and the Dred Scott decision had led the country to a critical point in its history and that responses to these acts would tend to divide the nation. He believed that it was his and the Republican Party's duty to preserve freedom in America by ensuring that slavery be excluded from the territories. In 1858 he challenged Stephen Douglas for his Senate seat. Lincoln proclaimed his hatred for slavery, calling the institution an evil that degraded both blacks and whites and violated the central ideas upon which the United States had been founded—the notions of equality and the opportunity to improve one's position. He believed it was morally wrong. Yet Lincoln was willing, at this point, to tolerate it where it already existed. He promised that the Republican party would not interfere with slavery in those states where it was legal but would oppose the expansion of slavery with all its strength.

Lincoln-Douglas debates. Early in the campaign for senator, Lincoln followed Douglas around the state until the senator agreed to a series of seven debates. The two men argued before large crowds of between 10,000 and 20,000 people. Douglas, who realized his political career was at risk, called Lincoln and his party Black Republicans and radical abolitionists, warning that if they got their way, hordes of blacks would pour into Illinois and take away the jobs of whites. He accused Lincoln of favoring black equality and interracial marriage. Faced with this attack, Lincoln was forced to take a stand for race discrimination or face certain defeat in the election. He still opposed slavery but was cornered into declaring support for the Illinois law that denied equal rights to blacks. Lincoln said that he did not believe they should be allowed to vote, serve on juries, hold public office, or intermarry with whites. He stated, reluctantly, that whites were superior and should be in a superior position of power and influence. Because of this statement, some scholars have labeled Lincoln a racist. But others maintain that compared to most whites of his time, "Lincoln was an enlightened man in the matter of race relations," who held that blacks were equal to all men "in their right to liberty, equality of opportunity and the fruits of their own labor" (Oates, p. 73).

Douglas's shameless race-baiting probably helped him keep his senate seat. On January 5, 1859, the state legislature reelected him as senator by a vote of 54 to 46.

Lincoln for president. Ironically, it was Lincoln, not Douglas, who emerged from the Senate campaign in the strongest political position. He was mentioned as a possible Republican candidate for president in 1860 and was much sought after as a speaker throughout the Northeast. When the Republican Convention met in May 1860, the delegates gave the nomination to Lincoln on the third ballot.

Lincoln's chances for victory in the election were greatly enhanced by the breakup of the Democratic party. Northern

Democrats nominated Douglas, Lincoln's old foe. Southern Democrats nominated John C. Breckinridge. John Bell was nominated by a group calling itself the Constitutional Union party, whose campaign ignored the slavery issue. Receiving 180 of the 303 electoral votes and 40 percent of the popular vote, Lincoln won the election. A month later, South Carolina, unconvinced by Republican pledges not to interfere with slavery, seceded from the Union. Within two months, six more states—Mississippi, Florida, Alabama, Georgia, Louisiana, and Texas—followed. President James Buchanan left it up to incoming President Lincoln to handle the crisis.

Prewar politics. Between his election and his inauguration, Lincoln visited his stepmother for the last time, worked on choosing his cabinet and writing his inaugural address, grew a beard (a little girl had suggested in a letter that he'd look good in one), and, most importantly, refused to consider any compromise that might permit the expansion of slavery. He left Illinois by train for Washington, D.C., finishing the journey in secret, at night, because of rumors that he might be assassinated.

The great issues of the war. Lincoln rejected Southerners' claim that they were following in the footsteps of the nation's revolutionary heroes. Revolution, he argued, can only be justified for a just cause. Secession was an unjust counterrevolution, a wicked attempt to overturn his own election. The South, which had controlled the national government for most of the nation's history, left the Union simply because it had lost an election. The American democracy was a fragile experiment in a world of kings and dictators. If secession succeeded, that experiment would fail. A fatal pattern would be set by which a minority could secede whenever it did not like the policy favored by the majority. Lincoln believed that the issue at stake in the Civil War involved more than the United States: it presented to humankind the question of whether a democratic, constitutional republic could survive.

Lincoln tried to reassure Southerners in his inaugural address. He repeated his promise that he did not mean to threaten slavery in the South. But at the same time, he spoke about the supremacy of the national government, asserting that the Union was eternal and secession was illegal. He pledged to enforce the Union in *all* the states and to defend and preserve it. But he also promised to shed no blood unless forced to do so. He appealed to his dissatisfied fellow countrymen in the South not to begin a war.

Lincoln's plea fell on deaf ears. He had indicated in his speech his determination to hold and occupy those forts in the South still under Union control. One of those forts was situated in Charleston Harbor. Trying to avoid an armed clash, Lincoln notified South Carolina's authorities of his intention to send a supply ship carrying no weapons or ammunition to the fort. Confederate artillery opened fire on the fort rather than permit it to be resupplied. Fighting began April 12, 1861. Two days later the federal garrison at Fort Sumter surrendered. The incident sparked a civil war that would be longer and more deadly than anyone imagined.

Participation: The Civil War

Lincoln's military strategy. Lincoln wanted peace, but accepted war as a way to preserve the Union and the democratic principle that a free people have the right to choose their leaders and that the losers in an election must accept the result. After Fort Sumter was fired upon, he called for 75,000 troops to defend the Union. This led to the secession of four more Southern states, Arkansas, North Carolina, Tennessee, and Virginia, bringing the total number of states in the Confederacy to eleven.

When the war began, Lincoln surrounded himself with books on military strategy. He was a working commander in chief, whose overall strategy would eventually help win the war. Plagued by loneliness and self-doubt, the president had many obstacles to overcome: an out-of-date military command system, a Congress that sometimes tried to wrest control of the war effort away from him, and widespread public opposition to the war. Most importantly, he had to find military commanders capable of carrying out the aggressive, coordinated strategy he believed was necessary to break the Southern people and win the war.

In the East, Lincoln was at first forced to rely on General George B. McClellan. (Lincoln originally wanted Robert E. Lee [see **Robert E. Lee**] to lead the Union army, but Lee decided to fight for his home state of Virginia when it decided to secede.) McClellan performed one great service for the Union cause: he trained and molded the Army of the Potomac into a great fighting force. He was, however, overly cautious and always overestimated the enemy's strength. He was also reluctant to fight, causing Lincoln to remark once that "McClellan has got the slows" (Williams, p. iii). Lincoln tolerated his delays and rudeness for as long as he could.

McClellan's failure to pursue Robert E. Lee's Army of Northern Virginia as it retreated from battle at Antietam (in Virginia), however, caused Lincoln to dismiss him. His replacement, Ambrose Burnside, proved to be weak as well; he was replaced by Joseph Hooker after a disastrous defeat at the Battle of Fredericksburg in Virginia, where the lives of thousands of Union soldiers were sacrificed in a series of suicidal assaults against Confederate lines (see **Walt Whitman**). During his command, Hooker suffered a loss of nerve in the midst of the 1863 Battle of Chancellorsville, Virginia, bringing on another devastating Union defeat. Lincoln dismissed Hooker and named General George Gordon Meade as his successor just prior to the Battle of Gettysburg, in southern Pennsylvania. In an important victory for the North, Union forces managed to beat back successive Confederate assaults against their lines in three incredibly bloody days of fighting, beginning on July 1, 1863. Lee led his badly mauled force back to the South (never to invade the North again); Meade, like McClellan before him, failed to follow up on the advantage his army had gained, despite repeated prodding by Lincoln. Lee's army was allowed to escape and the war was prolonged.

Lincoln and the Union cause had much better luck in the West, where Union armies were led by outstanding commanders and won important battles from the outset. After a lengthy siege, Ulysses S. Grant captured Vicksburg, Mississippi, bringing the entire length of the Mississippi River under Union control. Grant became Lincoln's favorite general. He was called to the East, where Lincoln appointed him as commander of all Union forces.

Grand Plan. Lincoln realized that victory would come only by applying constant pressure on the Confederacy, carrying the war into their homeland, and destroying the South's capacity to continue fighting. He found in Grant and William Tecumseh Sherman

▲ Lincoln and George B. McClellan and company at the front

(who replaced Grant as commander in the West—see **William Tecumseh Sherman**) the generals to carry out these policies.

Lincoln and Grant devised a Grand Plan, calling for simultaneous assaults on all battlefronts, to end the war. Grant was to try to destroy Lee's Army of Northern Virginia while in the west Sherman would strike into Georgia, seize Atlanta, a rail center, and destroy rebel resources.

Union forces suffered huge losses carrying out this plan in 1864 and 1865, but Lincoln never considered abandoning it. He instructed Grant, whose army was conducting a prolonged siege of

Petersburg, Virginia, to "hold on with bull-dog grip, and chew and choke as much as possible" (Oates, p. 135). While this was going on, Sherman captured Atlanta, and set out on his march to the sea, (through the South to the Atlantic Ocean), hastening the end of the war not simply by defeating enemy armies, but by wrecking railroads, burning fields, and wiping out other economic resources to cripple their ability to survive and fight. With the help of Grant and Sherman, Lincoln had adopted the strategy of total war, using the superior manpower and resources of the North to carry the fighting close to the Southern people and break their will to continue. It paid off. Only five months after Sherman's army began its march, in April 1865, Lee surrendered to Grant at Appomattox Courthouse, Virginia, and the war was over. Lincoln, who cared deeply about human suffering, nevertheless had pounded Southern civilians and soldiers into surrender, convinced that it was the only way to win the war quickly.

> ## Walt Whitman on Abraham Lincoln
>
> "His poise, his simple, loftiest ability to make an emergency sacred, meet every occasion—never shrinking, never failing, never hurrying—these are the things to be remembered." (Lowenfels, p. 252)

A strong leader. Throughout the war, Lincoln underwent continual crises that might have broken a weaker man. He received vicious hate mail and endured countless attacks on his fitness to be the president of the United States. At one point, a Southern newspaper offered a $100,000 reward for his head. In the midst of it all, he grieved over close friends killed in battle. In spite of these troubles, he managed to define the issues of the war in a way that inspired defenders of the Union to carry on despite repeated setbacks.

The road to emancipation. Early in the war, Lincoln repeated over and over that his first goal was to preserve the Union, not to save or to abolish slavery. The time to attack the institution of slavery would come later. At the outset of the war, Lincoln resisted all calls for an open attack on slavery, keeping a promise made by the Republican party. He wanted the four border slave states—Delaware, Maryland, Kentucky, and Missouri—to stay loyal to the Union. He also wanted to maintain unity in the North; emancipation might upset Northern Democrats and create disharmony in the region, which could lead to defeat.

A little more than a year after the fighting began, Lincoln abandoned his hands-off policy and decided to strike a blow at slavery in the rebel states. A number of factors influenced his change of heart. A group of Republican senators, including Charles Sumner, Zachariah Chandler, and Benjamin F. Wade, begged him to use his emergency war powers to abolish slavery. Such a move would rob the rebels of their labor force and bring the war closer to an end. It would be absurd, they argued, to fight a war in part caused by slavery without eliminating that one cause.

Sumner, who had become Lincoln's friend and a major adviser on foreign policy, told Lincoln that Britain might extend diplomatic recognition to the Confederacy and perhaps even intervene on the side of the South. Britain and most European powers would favor a weak and divided American republic. Turning the war into a crusade against slavery would make it impossible for the British government, whose citizens were strongly opposed to slavery, to extend aid to the rebels. Also, emancipation would finally bring America into line with its own democratic ideals. A growing manpower shortage in Union ranks, was, as black abolitionist Frederick Douglass argued, another powerful reason for emancipation: the freed slaves could be recruited into Union armed forces.

Lincoln agreed with all of these arguments; he had always hated slavery. He hesitated only because he feared a loss of support from Northern Democrats and the border states. He moved carefully on the issue, proposing a plan for gradual, compensated emancipation. Representatives from the border states, summoned to the White House, rejected the proposal out of hand. That very evening an angry Lincoln decided to issue the preliminary emancipation proclamation.

When Lincoln presented his proclamation to his cabinet in July 1862, he was persuaded by Secretary of State William Seward to delay making a public announcement. Union forces had suffered crushing defeats; a proclamation under those circumstances would be seen in Europe as a desperate act, a rash attempt to incite a slave rebellion to make up for battlefield losses. Better to wait until Union forces won a victory, Seward counseled, when a proclamation would be much more well received. Lincoln reluctantly waited until McClellan's forces drove back Lee's army at Antietam. Though he failed to pursue the Confederate force, McClellan had provided enough of a victory for Lincoln. The president declared in September of 1862 that if the war had not ceased by January 1, 1863, all slaves in rebel territory were free.

Lincoln's proclamation was a risky move and angered many. Radical abolitionists were unhappy that he had freed only those slaves in rebel states, not those in the four border slave states. Northern Democrats opposed the measure completely, and many voters apparently agreed. Democrats outpolled Republicans in the congressional election of 1862, held just after Lincoln's announcement. His loudest critics called his action unconstitutional and a high crime; they wanted to impeach him for it. But Lincoln refused to back down. He signed the final proclamation on schedule, assuring witnesses that he had never been more certain that he was doing the right thing. "If my name ever goes into history," he stated, "it will be for this act" (Oates, p. 110).

When slaves heard the news, they began abandoning Southern plantations; they did not wait for the arrival of Union armies. His action also did something for the president himself. In granting freedom to the slaves, the proclamation brought together the private man and the public leader. Now the statesman could stamp out an evil the private citizen had always hated, a blight that had long troubled his conscience.

Perhaps Lincoln's most drastic related act was opening Union armed forces to black volunteers, who numbered more than 100,000. This not only helped solve the army's manpower shortage, it gave black troops the chance to help liberate their own people and to prove they deserved equal rights when the war was over (see **Martin Robinson Delany**). Lincoln was extremely proud of the fighting record of black soldiers.

The president was criticized by some for not writing a defense of liberty into the Emancipation Proclamation. He corrected this oversight in November 1863, when, before a crowd of 15,000 gathered for the dedication of a military cemetery, he delivered his Gettysburg Address at the scene of the great battle. Although he spoke for only two minutes, Lincoln delivered in just ten sentences perhaps the most moving speech in American history. He cast the Declaration of Independence in a new light, speaking of it as the country's founding law. Its basis, he asserted, is the principle of equality, as set forth in the Constitution. His words changed the way the Constitution is interpreted, making equality the country's primary focus.

Lincoln also stressed that the country was one united nation, not just a collection of individual states, thereby changing even the language of politics. Before his address, speakers always referred to the United States as a plural noun: the United States *are*.... After Gettysburg it became a singular noun: the United States *is*.... And when he referred, near the end of his address, to a government "of *the* people, by *the* people, for *the* people," he was doing more than praising popular government. He was stating that the United States *is* one people, and that, "conceived in liberty," they had received a "new birth of freedom," referring obviously to emancipation (Willis, p. 46).

Lincoln as political leader. Emancipation solved some of Lincoln's political problems, but he had to deal with many more. In doing so, he took actions that caused some to call him a dictator. He authorized the military to suspend the right of *habeas corpus,* thereby permitting suspected spies and critics of the Union war effort to be arrested and held without being informed of the charges against them or without a jury trial. Some 14,000 arrests were made without writs of *habeas corpus.*

Lincoln may have allowed his generals too much freedom in arresting suspected enemies, but he was certainly no dictator. He often ordered the speedy release of those who were wrongly detained, and he allowed hostile newspapers to go on attacking him and his policies. Most importantly, he ignored the advice of many of his supporters to cancel the presidential election of 1864, lest it lead to a victory for antiwar forces who might allow the South to stay separated from the Union. He proclaimed the election a necessity, even though he expected to lose. Lincoln said, "We cannot have free government without elections; and if the rebellion could force us to forego, or postpone a national election, it might fairly claim to have already conquered us" (Oates, p. 125). He wanted to prove that popular government could work, even in the midst of civil war. Good news from the battlefront, especially Sherman's capture of Atlanta, helped Lincoln win reelection, an event that doomed the South.

Ford's Theater. Lincoln shared in the joyous celebration that greeted the news of Lee's surrender to Grant. On April 11, 1865, he delivered his last public speech to a crowd celebrating Union victory. He referred to the newly formed government of Louisiana and expressed his hope that this government would correct an oversight and grant the vote to literate blacks as well as black veterans. One listener in the audience was the actor John Wilkes Booth, a Southern sympathizer. Hearing Lincoln's call for at least limited black voting rights, Booth turned to a companion and snarled: "That means nigger citizenship. Now, by God, I'll put him through. That is the last speech he will ever make" (McPherson, *Battle Cry of Freedom,* p. 852).

Booth made good his threat on the evening of April 11, 1865, Good Friday. Lincoln and his wife were attending a performance of the play *Our American Cousin* when the assassin burst into their box and shot the president. Lincoln died the next morning in a room across the street from the theater. Booth's accomplices stabbed Secretary of State Seward, but he survived. Vice President Andrew Johnson was also targeted, but the man sent to kill him lost his nerve. Booth was tracked down and shot in a burning barn. Four others were hanged and several more suspects were sentenced to prison. Lincoln's body was sent by train to New York and then west to Springfield, Illinois. Huge crowds watched in mournful silence as it passed through town after town.

Aftermath

Personal sorrow. Along with the rest of the nation, a shocked Mary Todd Lincoln grieved for her husband of twenty-two years. Though their marriage was sometimes stormy, they had shared a deep bond with each other, and both were devoted to their sons. If some of his wife's habits upset Lincoln (her temper fits and costly shopping sprees), he too had bothersome habits (long silences, brooding moods and a hatred of quarrels). After his death, Mary spent money recklessly and had emotional upsets. Her son, Robert, had her committed to an insane asylum in 1875, where she stayed for four months. A second trial judged her perfectly sane. She lived for seventeen years after Lincoln's death, time failing to soften her grief for him.

Reconstruction. Before his murder, Lincoln had prodded Congress into approving the Thirteenth Amendment, which outlawed slavery throughout the United States. His death probably made the rebuilding more difficult than it would have been with him at the helm. He had produced a plan whereby a Southern state could re-enter the Union once 10 percent of its voting population had agreed, but he was not tied to any one method. Lincoln felt a flexible approach was necessary. He had one plan for Louisiana, another for Virginia, and another for Texas. He also felt no need to punish the South. In a time of bitter hatred, Lincoln never learned to hate and never lost sight of the fact that the Americans were one people. In his second inaugural address, on March 4, 1865, he described the war as God's punishment for slavery, a terrible punishment of a guilty people in the North and South. He called for them to finish the war and to bind up their nation's wounds "with malice toward none; with charity for all" (Ayres, p. 216).

For More Information

Ayres, Alex, ed. *The Wit and Wisdom of Abraham Lincoln.* New York: Penguin, 1992.

Lowenfels, Walter, ed. *Walt Whitman's Civil War.* New York: Alfred A. Knopf, 1960.

McPherson, James M. *Abraham Lincoln and the Second American Revolution.* New York: Oxford University Press, 1991.

McPherson, James M. *Battle Cry of Freedom.* New York: Oxford University Press, 1988.

Oates, Stephen B. *Abraham Lincoln: The Man Behind the Myths.* New York: Harper & Row, 1984.

Willis, Garry. *Lincoln at Gettysburg.* New York: Simon & Schuster, 1992.

Robert E. Lee

1807-1870

Personal Background

Childhood. Robert Edward Lee was born in Stratford, Virginia, January 19, 1807, to General "Lighthorse" Henry Lee and Ann Hill of the prosperous Carter family. Henry had been a brilliant leader in the Revolutionary War, but poor business dealings wiped out the family property. The Lees lived at the Carter estate in Stratford. In the tradition of the day, Anne's mother had willed the property to the oldest male heir, her son, who was not yet old enough to receive the land when his mother died. In 1809, when he became old enough, the family home became his property and Robert's family was forced to move to a small house in Alexandria. Robert was nearly three when they made the move.

Henry Lee and family. Meanwhile, the Lee family had other problems. Henry had spent nearly a year in prison for nonpayment of debts, gaining his release in the spring of 1810. Soon after, Henry was involved in a public disturbance between civilians and soldiers, and he and several others were put into jail. At night, a mob stormed the jail and attacked the men inside. Henry was injured and lay among several dead. Mob members stuck him with knives, tried to cut off his nose, and clipped his ears. He was left for dead, but recovered, scarred and weakened by the affair. In 1813, when Robert was five, Henry left to recover his strength in the West Indies and never returned to the United States.

▲ Robert E. Lee

Event: The Civil War.
Role: Robert E. Lee served as commander of the Army of Northern Virginia and later as military adviser to Confederate president Jefferson Davis before becoming commander in chief of the Confederate army. Although vastly outnumbered in manpower and weaponry, Lee initially won battle after battle until, worn down by inadequate supplies and the size of the enemy, he surrendered at Appomattox Courthouse, Virgina in one of the final events of the Civil War.

The Carter family. Meanwhile, Anne was determined that her children would not fall victim to the weaknesses of their father. She taught them to take responsibility and to help one another. Her tremendous strength of character would influence Robert throughout his life.

Through the generations, the Carters had grown so numerous that the family operated two private schools for its own children. There was one at Eastern View for the boys and one at Shirley for the girls. Robert attended the boys' school near Alexandria. In 1820 he continued his education at Alexandria Academy.

While Robert was still young, his oldest brother went off to Washington to practice law. Another brother joined the navy. His sister had always been sickly and was little help at home. Although strong-willed and dedicated to her children, Anne also grew ill. It fell upon Robert to look after her and his sister, and the responsibility made him a sober young man. Even though he seemed to be popular with people his age, he never participated in any activities that might trouble his mother. At the same time, he did not shy away from friends who might get into mischief. He would watch, refuse to participate, and then refuse to judge his friends.

West Point. Robert grew to be a tall (five-feet-ten-inches), handsome youth with brown eyes and black hair. As he neared his eighteenth birthday, the family lawyer, William Fitzhugh, suggested that a career in the military might suit the strong but quiet and thoughtful young man. Robert agreed, and Fitzhugh gave him a letter of introduction to Secretary of War John C. Calhoun asking for a nomination to the military academy at West Point.

Robert had been taught by his mother that *duty* was the most sublime word in the English language. Now he set about to fulfill his duty as a cadet. He applied himself to his studies, which at the beginning were not very difficult. He had already been taught more mathematics than was covered in the freshman course. He had extra time to read, although cadets were not encouraged to read beyond their coursework. The academy library, in fact, was open for only two hours a day. But Robert checked out books in great numbers and added to his own education by poring over them. He continued his boyhood policy of not becoming involved in the pranks of others. Still, he was popular with his schoolmates while keeping near the top of his class in his studies. After his freshman year, he was named a distinguished cadet. That honor earned him an unheard of appointment as a sophomore: he became staff sergeant and an assistant professor of mathematics. In his senior year, he was appointed adjutant, the highest position for a cadet. Robert graduated in 1829, second in his class of forty-six.

Marriage. His high position in class gave him the right to choose his own branch of the services. The best of the army was thought to be the "Scientific Corps of the Army," which today is the Corps of Engineers. Lee became a second lieutenant in the corps and went home on the leave or furlough usually given to West Point graduates. Just then, his mother died. He stayed home to recover from her death and began to visit the home of George Washington Park Custis, the grandson of Martha Washington. For Lee, the chief attraction at the house was Custis's daughter Mary Anne. Before he could propose marriage, however, he was assigned to Cockspur Island near Savannah, Georgia. This assignment involved four years of building canals, dykes, and forts. Still, Lee managed to court Mary and the two were married June 30, 1831.

Although Mary was quite sickly, the couple had a happy marriage and raised seven children. Throughout his military career, Lee was the chief counsel to his children and through visits and letters actively guided their lives. While he moved about in the armed forces, Mary moved into the Custis home at Arlington, which she would later inherit.

Mexican War. In the army, Lee proved so effective that by 1834 he had been assigned to Washington as assistant to the chief engineer. Promotions arrived on schedule; he was named first lieutenant in 1836 and captain in 1837. As captain, Lee served the corps in many areas: building flood controls at St. Louis, inspecting the forts in North Carolina and recommending improvements on them, and then, in 1841, moving to New York to help rebuild Fort Hamilton. He was still at work building and reinforcing forts when war with Mexico erupted. In January 1847, he joined General Winfield Scott in the capture of Vera Cruz. Part of Lee's work there was to help in the attack on Cerro Gordo, where he took 3,000 prisoners and so impressed Scott that he was mentioned in the reports of the action and was promoted to the rank of major.

The army of about 8,000 men went on to capture Mexico City. Among the officers serving under Scott at Mexico City were Joe Johnston, Pierre Beauregard, and G. J. Pillow, who would later join the Confederate army along with Lee. Also serving under Scott were Franklin Pierce, who would later become president of the United States, and George McClellan, who would be head of the Union army soon after the start of the Civil War.

With the Mexican War ended, Lee returned to Baltimore to supervise the rebuilding of Fort Carroll. Then, in May 1852, he was appointed commander of West Point. During his time there, he tried to strengthen the course of study and make engineering even more important. Like every other job Lee undertook, his work at West Point was highly praised.

Meanwhile, all around him, the debate over slavery and over the rights of states to govern themselves intensified. Lee worried about the nation, which was threatening to break apart. However, he let it be known among his fellow officers that in the event of war, he would have to side with his home state of Virginia.

Harpers Ferry. On October 17, 1859, Lieutenant J.E.B. (Jeb) Stuart delivered to Lee a sealed letter from the secretary of war. Strange happenings were taking place at Harpers Ferry, Virginia.

Harpers Ferry sat on the Potomac River where the Shenandoah River joined it above Washington, D.C. Important as a river crossing, the location was also the site of a government arsenal and a station on the Baltimore and Ohio Railroad. Now, an antislavery raid was in progress at the site. Troops were sent from Washington to put down the disturbance, and Lee, now a colonel, was directed to take charge of leading them. Riding a special locomotive, he caught up with his troops and arrived at Harpers Ferry at eleven o'clock on the night of October 17th.

Lee immediately moved his men into position around the armory, which had been occupied by the renegades, and planned his attack. At two o'clock the next morning he sent a message to the rebel leader, John Brown. Delivered under a flag of truce by Jeb

Stuart, it called for Brown's immediate surrender. When Brown began to argue, Stuart told him there was no room for discussion. Brown persisted, however, and Stuart waved his hat. This was the signal for Lee's men, led by Israel Green, to attack.

Lee had planned so carefully that the whole affair was over in three minutes. Thirteen rebels were captured, four were dead, and Brown lay bleeding from sword wounds.

Texas. Lee was next assigned to command the Department of the Army in Texas. He had now been in the army for thirty-one years. Even so, his pay had risen to just $1,205 a year, which had to support four daughters and his sickly wife. It was a personally depressing time for Lee, who had no choice but to accept an assignment that took him far from home. His personal problems, however, were soon overshadowed by national concerns, as it grew more likely that the South would secede from the Union.

The United States was still a young nation. Most people felt as much or more loyalty for their individual states as for the new nation. Lee valued the Union and did not want to see it divided, but he placed his loyalty for Virginia above the Union.

In 1860, when Abraham Lincoln was elected president of the nation, the states of the South prepared to secede (see **Abraham Lincoln**). War seemed the only course. Winfield Scott, who headed the U.S. army, was about to retire. He hoped that Lee would take his place. Scott told Lincoln that he should persuade Lee to stay in the army at all costs. Keeping him on the Union side, he claimed, would be worth 50,000 men. Lee, however, saw no choice in the matter. On April 20, 1861, after Virginia seceded, he wrote a short note to the secretary of war resigning from the U.S. army.

Participation:
Leading the Southern Army in the Civil War

Confederate army formed. As he had done whenever possible throughout his career, Lee immediately headed for Arlington to talk about this step with his wife, Mary. She agreed that their loyalties must be with Virginia. Officials in Virginia, recognizing Lee's loyalty and his ability, made him commander in chief of the Virginia militia with a rank of major general.

South Carolina led the parade of seceding states. Other Southern states, including Virginia, followed, and another West Point graduate, Jefferson Davis, was chosen leader of the Confederate States of America. Lee and his Virginia army joined the united Confederate army. Other leaders of units in this army were General Joe Johnston, one of Lee's classmates at West Point, and General Pierre Beauregard, another West Point graduate. These three were among the five appointed full generals of the Confederate army. Lee led the Army of Northern Virginia. The first line of defense against invasion from Washington, this army was charged with defending Richmond, Virginia the Confederate capital.

From the beginning, the Confederate cause was a difficult one. The industrial North was able to provide more war materials for its troops. The shipping centers of the north were able to provide ships to blockade Southern ports. One estimate suggests the difference in supplies. At the beginning of his command, Lee had 54,000 rifles for his troops. The opposing army led by General McClellan meanwhile had access to a million rifles. Along with fewer war materials, the South could call on fewer men. Virginia was the most populated state in the South, but was only the fifth most populated state in the United States.

The battles begin. Because of the enormous odds against them, the Confederates' main hope was for the Union to underestimate the South's commitment. This hope was realized in the first battles of the Civil War. The Union army felt that simply setting siege to Richmond would soon break the back of the resistance and the Union would quickly be restored. Northern troops were called up for only three months and went to battle with little training or sense of unity. Each unit of troops even designed its own uniform to mark the region from which it came. Many soldiers took servants to war with them and brought along their own food. Women made picnics to take on the march. Politicians, eager for the publicity that would come from the end of the war, joined the troops on the march. The Southern enemy was taken lightly at first.

Lee's army did not take part in the first defeat of the Union army at Bull Run on July 21, 1861. The battle was led by Beauregard

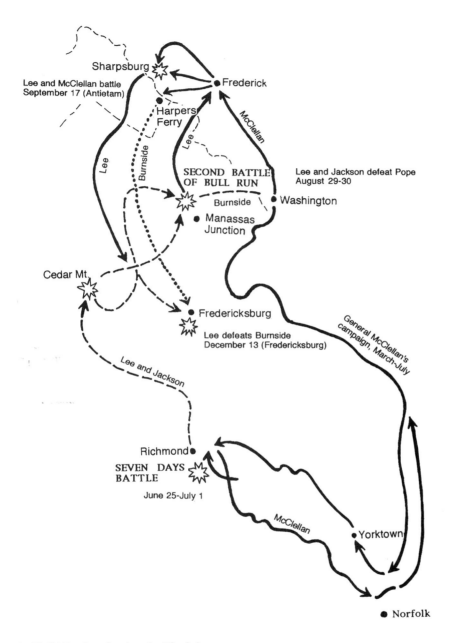

Sharpsburg

Lee and McClellan battle
September 17 (Antietam)

Frederick

Harpers
Ferry

McClellan

Lee

Burnside

Lee

**SECOND BATTLE
OF BULL RUN**

Lee and Jackson defeat Pope
August 29-30

Burnside

Washington

Manassas
Junction

Cedar Mt.

Fredericksburg

Lee defeats Burnside
December 13 (Fredericksburg)

General McClellan's
campaign, March-July

Lee and Jackson

Richmond

**SEVEN DAYS
BATTLE**

June 25-July 1

McClellan

Yorktown

Norfolk

▲ Civil War battle sites in Virginia

and Thomas "Stonewall" Jackson while Lee prepared defenses at
Richmond. On August 28 through 30, Union forces commanded by

General John Pope met the Confederate force at the Battle of Manassas, or Bull Run. So completely were the Union forces routed that one Confederate officer vowed that given 5,000 fresh troops, the South could have continued on to capture Washington, D.C. Had the South been able to garner additional troops, the war might have ended as quickly as the North believed, but without the preservation of the United States.

Lee is promoted. In March 1862, Lee became military adviser to Confederate president Jefferson Davis. McClellan's Union army was then gaining some ground that had been lost in earlier battles with the Confederates. Now Davis wanted to gather the Confederate forces and defend Richmond. Lee preferred an offensive strategy and suggested they attack.

Another Confederate general, Joe Johnston, wanted to attack, too, through the valleys of Virginia. To do this, Johnston felt he needed more men. Lee disagreed with the number he wanted, and Johnston began a gradual retreat pushed by McClellan's forces. By June, Johnston had been wounded in the major but indecisive Battle of Shiloh in April of 1862. Lee took command of the Confederate army.

Under McClellan, the Union forces circled below Richmond and prepared to take the city. Lee sent Jeb Stuart and his cavalry to explore enemy positions. Stuart circled completely around the enemy forces and returned with information that helped Lee drive off the Union army in seven days of battle near Richmond. Then, when McClellan was replaced by Pope, Lee had his opportunity to take the offensive. He engaged the Union forces in a second battle at Bull Run, on August 29, 1862, in which Pope's troops were badly beaten.

Lee then planned to capture Harpers Ferry and march into Pennsylvania. He was defeated in this attempt only when McClellan obtained copies of his plans—showing that Lee had split his army—and fought Lee's army at Sharpsburg with a force nearly twice as large. Known as the Battle of Antietam, this battle was the bloodiest single day's fighting in the Civil War and would eventually prove too costly for the South.

Victorious at Antietam, the Union army now planned again to take Richmond. Lee concentrated his forces at Fredericksburg, Virginia, to stop General Ambrose Burnside and his troops. The confrontation ended in victory for the Confederate forces.

▲ Second Battle of Bull Run

Now General Joseph Hooker took charge of the Union forces. He led his troops across the Rappahannock River, intent on capturing Fredericksburg. Lee's forces turned him back at the Battle of Chancellorsville, thoroughly defeating Hooker's force. In the battle, Lee lost one of his most capable officers, Thomas "Stonewall" Jackson, who was fired upon by his own Confederate troops as he returned from scouting the Union lines.

One skirmish among these major battles revealed Lee's greatest weakness as a military leader. He needed to secure a pass through the mountains where Union troops had established themselves on Cheat Mountain. He placed General W. W. Loring in charge of troops that had an opportunity to surprise and overrun the Union position. However, Loring refused to command his troops into battle, saying they were too weary to make the attack. Lee was too much of a gentleman to override Loring and order the attack.

Meanwhile, he sent a scout, Colonel Albert Rust, to find a way around the mountain so that the Confederates could attack from two positions. Rust found a path up the mountain and asked to be placed in charge of an attack from above the Union soldiers. Lee agreed. However, when Rust reached the peak without harm and captured a few of the enemy, the captives told him that there were 4,000 Union soldiers protecting the mountain. Even though there were actually only 300 of the enemy, Rust believed his prisoners and withdrew. His signal for Lee and Loring to attack from another direction never came, and the cause was lost. In this exercise, Lee had been beaten by his own men and by his gentlemanly attitude toward his officers.

Lee's troops nearly always were outnumbered and just as often were short on supplies. Nevertheless, his troops did major damage to the Union army. The odds were usually against Lee, yet he would only leave a battle when Union reinforcements made his own venture hopeless. He gained the deep respect and admiration of his men because of his ability to organize them and because he often took on the most difficult tasks himself.

Gettysburg. In June 1863, Lee gathered 80,000 men and planned to invade Pennsylvania. General George Meade of the Union army was prepared for the encounter and the two armies met at Gettysburg. Meade's force was too large and Lee's ammunition too little, so after a valiant battle, Lee retreated. The two met again in December in another battle, in which 70,000 Union men fought against 50,000 Confederates. This time it was Lee who forced Meade to withdraw from the battle.

Atlanta. By February 1865, Ulysses S. Grant commanded the whole Union army and took active command of the troops battling Lee's forces. Meanwhile, Union general William Tecumseh Sher-

Robert E. Lee: Greatest General of the Civil War?

Some historians claim that he was. Others say that he was too gentlemanly and too concerned about the feelings of his junior officers to have been a great general. Still, the numbers of soldiers in each battle indicate Lee's greatness.

Estimated Numbers of Opposing Soldiers

	Lee's army	Union army
Battle of Antietam	40,000	50,000
Fredericksburg	78,000	120,000
Chancellorsville	48,000	71,000
Gettysburg	86,000	94,000
Defense of Richmond	62,000	120,000
Dinwiddie Court	57,000	124,000

▲ The Battle of Gettysburg

man was beginning his famous march through Georgia (see **William Tecumseh Sherman**). A smaller Southern force led by Johnston, who by now had recovered from his wounds, stood in the way of Sherman's troops. Lee had planned to help Johnston's force, but was forced to change his strategy when Grant attacked Lee at Dinwiddie Court. Outnumbered by more than two to one, Lee again was undone by others' mismanagement. Supplies he needed badly were misrouted to Richmond. After a bruising battle and difficult withdrawal, Lee had no choice but to negotiate a peace with Grant. The two met at Appomattox Courthouse for the surrender, one of the last acts of the Civil War. At the time of the surrender, Lee had only 27,000 men, only 8,000 of whom had rifles, while Grant had some 113,000 men in his army.

Lee had fought a war he did not welcome, involving an issue, slavery, that he did not favor. (His own home held sixty-three slaves, whom he had begun to think of freeing by the beginning of the war.) In the process, he had acted so bravely and as such a gentlemen that friend and foe alike treated him with great respect. It was said that he was a man who was a foe without hate, friend without treachery, soldier without cruelty, and a victim without murmuring.

Aftermath

Arlington. After the Civil War, Lee needed to find a job and a place to live. His home had been seized early in the war by the

▲ Surrender of Lee

United States government, at which point Lee had freed his slaves. In 1864 the government had sold his home for nonpayment of taxes and bought the land it had taken from him for $26,800. It became Arlington National Cemetery, and later Lee's descendants would collect an additional $150,000 for it.

Lee was invited to participate in the reunited government but felt he could better work to heal the nation by staying out of politics. Holding an office would have been impossible anyhow, for when the war ended, Lee was accused of treason. He felt that the best way to set a pattern for the treatment of Southern soldiers was to ask for a pardon, and he did. Most people of the North and South believed that he had acted honorably throughout the war. However, the pardon for his alleged war crimes was not granted until 1885, fifteen years after his death.

Washington College. When in 1865 Lee was offered the presidency of Washington College, a small college in Lexington, Virginia, that had suffered much from the war, some felt that the position was too humble for such a great general. Lee nevertheless accepted the position at a salary of $15,000 a year. He successfully rebuilt the college into a great school, now known as Washington and Lee University.

The toils of war had taken their toll, however, and in 1870, Lee was too ill to continue at Washington College. He died at Lexington, Virginia, on October 12, 1870.

For More Information

Bradford, Ganaliel. *Lee the American.* Boston: Houghton Mifflin, 1929.

Dowdey, Clifford, and Louis H. Manata, eds. *The Wartime Papers of Robert E. Lee.* New York: Bramhall House, 1967.

Flood, Charles Braelem. *Lee: The Last Years.* Boston: Houghton Mifflin, 1981.

Frassanito, William A. *Grant and Lee.* New York: Charles Scribner's Sons, 1983.

Harwell, Richard. *Lee.* New York: Charles Scribner's Sons, 1961.

Questions and Answers After the War

General Lee, why did you not move on to Washington after the second battle of Bull Run?

"Because my men had nothing to eat. I could not tell my men to take that fort when they had nothing to eat for three days. I went to Maryland to feed my army."

General Lee, who was the best of the Union generals?

"McClellan, by all odds." (Harwell, p. 376)

William Tecumseh Sherman

1820-1891

Personal Background

Early life. Long before 1820, the year that William Tecumseh Sherman was born, Sherman had been a respected family name in America. William's own father, Charles, was a judge of the Ohio Supreme Court and his mother, Mary, had been one of the Hoyts, a highly placed family in New England.

The Sherman family was living comfortably in Lancaster, Ohio, when a baby boy was born on February 8. His father named him William Tecumseh, choosing the name Tecumseh in honor of an Indian chief whom he considered to have been a great warrior. William was the sixth child in the family, which grew to include eleven children before their father died in 1829. His death left Mary Sherman with only a house to live in and an income of $200 per year. This was not nearly enough to care for so many children. Except for the three youngest ones, the children were spread among relatives and friends.

Of them all, perhaps William, or Cump as his brothers and sisters called him, fared best of all. He was taken to live with Thomas and Maria Ewing, next-door neighbors to his own mother. Thomas Ewing was a prosperous lawyer who had turned to politics and had become a United States senator. The Ewings had four children of their own and had already taken in two nieces and one nephew. William was treated as a real member of the family.

▲ **William Tecumseh Sherman**

Event: Sherman's March to the Sea during the Civil War.

Role: After a series of major battles in which he led troops as an aide to General Ulysses S. Grant, William Tecumseh Sherman was assigned to capture the Confederate city of Atlanta, Georgia. He asked permission to extend his march from Atlanta to Savannah and then north along the coast to Durham, North Carolina. His long march of destruction reduced enemy food supplies and hastened the fall of the Confederate States.

West Point. Thomas Ewing wanted the best for each of his children. For William, he thought the right path would be service in the military. As foster father, he began to plan for Cump to attend the military academy at West Point. He asked for a nomination to the academy when the boy was fifteen. A year later, William Tecumseh Sherman was a cadet.

His stay at West Point was filled with friendships that would last a lifetime, with studies, and with his love of pranks. The records show that in his studies he ranked fourth among forty-two in his class. They also show that he received 124 demerits for violating West Point rules (not quite as many as the man he would come to admire). The demerits moved William down to sixth in his class when he graduated in 1840 to become a lieutenant in the U.S. army.

Early army career. As a new second lieutenant, Sherman was assigned to the Third Artillery. He was eager to prove himself in combat, and in 1839, was sent off to Florida to help round up and remove the Seminole Indians. It was, however, the time of the Second Seminole War, and there was not much fighting with the few Seminole that remained in the South. Disappointed with his first assignment, Sherman, nevertheless proved to be a good organizer of men. After two years of very little action, he was made first lieutenant. He was assigned first to Fort Morgan, Alabama, then to Fort Moultrie, near Charleston, South Carolina, and then to New York to recruit soldiers.

In 1846, when the United States went to war with Mexico, Sherman was sent to California, where there was little fighting but heavy quarreling between Admiral Robert Stockton of the navy and General S. W. Kearny of the army. Sherman spent three years in California without seeing battle. Ordered back east, he was promoted to captain and assigned to St. Louis, Missouri, in 1850.

Marriage. From the time he left home, Sherman's best contact with the Ewings and his own mother was through the Ewings' daughter Ellen. She had been eleven when he went off to West Point and was fifteen years old when he was assigned to Florida. The two wrote to each other frequently. On his way to New York, Sherman visited home to find that his foster sister had grown into a mature nineteen-year-old woman. The two talked about marriage before Sherman went to California but had serious disagreements that stood in their way. Ellen wanted Sherman to become Catholic, but he saw little use for any formal religion. She also wanted him to leave the army and take a position in her father's businesses. But Sherman was determined to make a success without the help of Ewing. Finally, when he received assignment to St. Louis in 1850, Ellen agreed to marry him without conditions and the two were wed. Always at odds over religion and army service, they would live sometimes together and sometimes apart until Ellen died in 1888.

Bank manager. So far, Sherman's hope of seeing military action had not been realized. He served as an army officer through a major war but had not fired a shot or seen enemy action. Even though he seemed to be promoted regularly, he was beginning to feel that the army was leaving him behind. By 1853 he was convinced that he had no future in the service and

The Shermans

While Sherman moved from post to post, his wife sometimes moved with him, but most often stayed home to care for their large family. The Sherman family included nine children, five girls and four boys.

resigned his commission to become president of a branch bank in San Francisco, California. He proved to be a very capable manager. Seven of the nineteen banks in the city went bankrupt, yet Sherman kept his bank open even when worried depositors withdrew nearly one-half million dollars in a single day. Despite his efforts, the bank was soon closed by its owners. Sherman then moved to a bank branch in New York. He was there when the depression, or business slowdown, of 1857 caused the owners to close this branch, too.

Odd jobs. Worried about supporting his growing family, Sherman worked first as a surveyor on a new canal and later as a lawyer in Leavenworth, Kansas. Finally, he asked the army for a position, but there was none available. In 1860 he was, however, invited to be superintendent and professor of engineering at the Louisiana Military Seminary in Alexandria, Louisiana. His work there was so successful that the seminary grew, as did his friendships, even though he did not share the views of many Southerners. Although Sherman did not favor an immediate end to slavery, he was totally opposed to the South separating from the Union. He told the directors of the seminary that if the South broke away, he would fight to hold the Union together.

In 1860 Abraham Lincoln was elected president and, almost immediately, South Carolina seceded from the Union. Sherman knew that other states would soon follow. Although he was proud of his work at the seminary, he kept his word to the directors. That same year he resigned from the faculty, and he and the family returned to Ohio, where Sherman worked for Ewing.

He was unhappy in Ohio, however, and was pleased when a year later he was asked to become president of the Main Street Railroad Company of St. Louis. Shortly thereafter, Southern forces fired on Fort Sumter and the war between the states began. Seeing a new opportunity for combat, Sherman wrote to the secretary of war expressing his willingness to fight.

Back in the military. For a short time at the start of the war, Sherman's old friend General Winfield Scott was leader of the army. He brought Sherman to Washington, D.C., and made him a colonel in the Thirteenth United States Infantry. One of Sherman's first assignments was to recruit men for the service.

At first, the leaders of the Union forces, from President Abraham Lincoln down, did not take the secession movement seriously. They thought Union forces would quickly subdue the South. Because of this, the military allowed men to enlist for duty as short as three months. Sherman, however, had spent much time in the South and knew the Southern people. He was sure the war would be a long and bloody one. From the beginning, he refused to recruit men for short periods in which they could not even be properly trained before battle.

Participation: Sherman's March to the Sea

The Battle of Bull Run. Sherman's first Civil War action was as leader of the Third Brigade of the First Division of an army led by General Irwin McDowell. This army of about 30,000 soldiers, many of them three-month enlistees, was met by an equal Southern force led by generals Pierre Beauregard and Thomas "Stonewall" Jackson. Fighting in Virginia about thirty miles from Washington, the Union forces at first seemed to be winning the battle. Jackson, however, stopped the Union advance, and rear forces of the Confederates rushed in to break the Union lines. The Union's new recruits panicked and ran. Sherman and other Union officers tried to rally their men but to no avail. In the effort, Sherman was slightly wounded twice and had his horse shot from under him. The Union forces were severely beaten.

The newspapers of the North made much of this loss, blaming it on poor leadership. Once more Sherman feared his army career was in danger. Instead, the word quickly spread about Sherman's valiant efforts to rally the troops. He returned to Washington expecting to be scorned for the loss but was instead promoted to the rank of brigadier general.

Return to Washington. In Washington, he found the defeated troops ready to give up. Many who had signed up for only three months were planning to quit the army. Sherman succeeded in extending some enlistment periods by counting the three months from when a recruit began training rather than when he enlisted. When one captain still tried to lead some of his men away, Sherman showed his toughness: he threatened to kill the captain if he left camp.

Sherman and President Lincoln. By this time, Sherman's reputation as a tough leader had reached Lincoln. When the president came to visit Sherman's troops in Washington, Lincoln asked the troops not to cheer his presence because General Sherman said it was not military. Then the captain whom Sherman had threatened complained to the president and was told: "Well, if I were you, and he threatened to shoot, I would not trust him, for I believe he would do it" (Marszalek, p. 153).

Kentucky experience. In August 1862, Sherman was assigned as deputy to General James Robert Anderson, who had fought to defend Fort Sumter at the beginning of the war. Anderson commanded the Department of the Cumberland in Kentucky. On October 8, however, he resigned because of ill health, and Sherman took his place.

Sherman assumed that the army with the largest numbers or the best positions would win the war. He had 60,000 men to defend Kentucky but soon said he needed 200,000. Washington politicians, however, still believed the war would be short and did not take him seriously. The secretary of war and others in government thought Sherman was crazy. With rumors spreading that he had gone mad, Sherman was relieved of his command and sent to a training assignment at St. Louis. It soon became clear, however, that defending

Kentucky did indeed require as many troops as Sherman had claimed. He was sent back to that state as commander of the Department of Cairo. Here his greatest job was to secure supplies and send them on to General Ulysses S. Grant, who was having some success in fighting the Confederates. Grant and Sherman established a lasting respect and friendship.

The Union tide turns. Sherman fought in the Battle of Shiloh in Tennessee, participated in the two battles for Vicksburg, Mississippi, and then stood ready to relieve Union troops that took Knoxville, Tennessee. Even though the Union forces almost always had the greater numbers in these battles, they fared badly. The Battle of Shiloh ended with no clear winner (though historians now consider the bloody battle a Union victory because it led to later successes in the West), and in the first Battle of Vicksburg, the Union forces were badly beaten. Again the newspapers questioned the North's quality of leadership. Sherman, however, had captured a nearby fort and saved the Union some embarrassment in the Battle at Vicksburg. Sherman was named major general, becoming the only one of Grant's officers to come out of the campaigns with a promotion (primarily for his actions at Shiloh).

A new view of the war. Meanwhile, Sherman, along with his superior, Grant, had come to a new understanding of war. It was not just between two armies, but between all the people who supported the armies. Using this tactic of total warfare, he began to take supplies for his troops from local citizens, even though they might not be involved with the Confederate military.

Atlanta. By the summer of 1864, Sherman was serving as second in command of the Union army. His orders were to carry the war toward Atlanta in search of a victory over the Confederate army led by Joseph Johnston. Sherman had nearly 100,000 men at his command, but Johnston's force at most numbered 65,000. The Union army had won minor skirmishes against the Confederate general in the past, but his Southern army was still

The Battle of Shiloh

The Civil War was one of the most bitter and bloody wars ever fought. Among the battles in which Sherman was involved was the Battle of Shiloh. It was not a clear victory for either side. The numbers of wounded and dead after this battle are examples of the brutality of the war.

	Dead and wounded
Confederate soldiers	10,700
Union soldiers	13,000
Sherman's troops	2,000

strong. It protected railroads and roads leading from Chattanooga, Tennessee, to Atlanta. Johnston could do this and also protect Atlanta by retreating to ridges and mountain peaks, which gave him defensive advantages over the enemy.

Sherman prepared for the struggle. He would need 130 boxcars of supplies a day for his large army. Because there were not that many boxcars available, he took charge of the routes in nearby Tennessee. Civilians were prohibited from both road and railroad. Supplies were brought up by train or road wherever the army traveled. Sherman had great respect for Johnston. He planned not to attack the Confederate general in his high strongholds directly. Rather, Sherman would weaken the enemy by marching in a series of loops around the Confederate army, forcing them from their strongest positions by threatening attacks from the rear.

Although assigned to defeat Johnston's army, Sherman saw an opportunity to destroy Southern supplies and transportation. His men marched in their series of loops, stopping to fight bloody battles wherever the Confederates took a stand. Meanwhile, practicing the tactic of total warfare, they destroyed whatever was in their path. Railroads used by the Confederates were torn up, the tracks stacked up and burned. Union soldiers took food supplies wherever they found them, even though they were well supplied. After great losses on both sides, Johnston was replaced by General John Hood. Now, nearly within sight of Atlanta, strategies changed. Hood commanded a series of charges on Union forces, but his organization was faulty and he suffered defeat after defeat. Finally he could not hold Atlanta and withdrew from the city.

Sherman took the city that once had numbered 20,000 citizens but now had only 1,000 or 2,000. Even that number was intolerable to the general. He ordered the remaining citizens to leave, because, he said, the Union needed to use Atlanta for the purposes of war. When the city officials protested, he answered that war was cruelty and one could not refine it. As a result, 705 adults, 860 children, and 79 slaves were moved out of the city. Sherman showed another face during the move, treating the evacuating citizens with such kindness that a Confederate officer wrote thanking him for his care.

Still there seemed to be no Union plan for ending the war. Both Grant and Sherman thought there should be one, and Grant sent a

▲ Atlanta destroyed

messenger to Sherman asking for advice. Ahead of Sherman lay the fertile fields that supplied food for the Confederates. Sherman thought it would be wise to march through Georgia to the Atlantic Ocean, laying waste to the fields and carving a path of destruction as he went. Then he would march north to help Grant in the final stages of the war. He sent a message back to Grant: "If you can whip Lee and I can march to the Atlantic, I think Uncle Abe will give us twenty days' leave of absence to see the young folk" (Marszalek, p. 290). He was predicting the end of the war.

March to the Sea. General Hood decided to make the Union army chase him back along the same route that had been taken to reach Atlanta. For a time, it worked. Then Sherman decided that chasing Hood's army was a waste of time and that he should really march to the sea. He asked his commander for permission to

▲ **Georgians fleeing Sherman's March to the Sea**

march, and Grant approved. Sherman knew that the politicians often changed military plans, so before he could receive other orders, he cut the telegraph lines north. There would be no interference with his plan. Hood had retreated to Tennessee, and now Sherman positioned some of his men to hold him there. He divided the rest into two forces to more effectively use the land. They lived mostly off the crops planted by the enemy. They were not to disturb families or destroy any homes. They were, however, to burn any depots, car houses, shops, factories, and foundries. Sherman began his mission in Atlanta.

The Sherman army covered fifteen miles a day, raiding the country with a freer hand than the general's command had authorized. Reported acts of violence were more numerous than acts of kindness, although there were incidents of both kinds.

Sherman thought that war had to be cruel. Still, he wanted to be as kind as possible to the Southern people, but his first loyalty was to his own soldiers. As the large army neared the seaport city of

Savannah, it began to find land mines in its way. When one officer lost a leg to such a mine, Sherman ordered captured Confederate soldiers to sweep the roads ahead of his troops.

From Savannah, the Union army turned north, marching through South and North Carolina to Durham. More than 60,000 men had marched 2,000 miles through enemy territory, destroying the South's ability to manufacture war goods and using enemy food crops in a path that spread across forty miles.

Aftermath

Peace. While Sherman was marching through the South, Grant had been battling the Confederate army under Robert E. Lee in Virginia. When Lee was finally forced to surrender, Sherman prepared to end the war with Johnston in a peace agreement to surrender all remaining Confederate troops to the Union. Sherman had conducted a war that some Southerners felt was one of terror. He had not allowed anyone—soldier or civilian—to interrupt his march to victory. Now he turned from a harsh military leader to a kind victor.

The treaty he worked out with Johnston required the Confederates to deliver their arms to state arsenals but provided no punishment for any soldier participating in the war. It called for the Southern states to again establish state governments and send representatives to Congress. Sherman did not feel that government officials should be limited to people who had not been involved in the war. The South would be restored to its full place in the democracy.

His treaty did not mention the emancipation of slaves, or even refer to the conditions of blacks. After all, Lincoln had already made his Emancipation Proclamation. Why should he, a lesser figure, make his own rules about the matter? Besides, Sherman had always felt that the war was about protection of the Union rather than the freeing of slaves.

An event outside Sherman's control interfered with his treaty making. Just as he and Grant were making agreements with Johnston and Lee, Lincoln was assassinated. The national government was angry. Many thought the South had plotted the assassination. Now, the Washington politicians demanded harsher terms of surrender. Sherman's gentle peace treaty was turned down by the new president, Andrew Johnson. The general himself came under fire from such leaders as Secretary of War Edwin Stanton for his easy terms of surrender. Nevertheless, Johnston surrendered his forces at Raleigh, North Carolina, on April 26, 1860.

Now Sherman prepared his troops for a final march. They moved on to Washington, where masses of people came out to cheer them in one of the greatest parades the city had seen. Sixty thousand men who had marched 2,000 miles, defeating the enemy wherever the armies met, marched in a grand review before the president.

Sherman was very popular with the people, but he was not very popular with government politicians. After being called to explain his proposals for a soft peace, he was assigned to head the army of the West. He spent several years subduing the Indians and protecting the crews building railroads in the West. When the unpopular President Johnson was replaced by Ulysses S. Grant, Sherman became commanding General of the Army.

Sherman moved his family to St. Louis to get away from the politics of Washington. His popularity was so great that collections were started to buy the Shermans a fine home. (Citizens raised more than $100,000 for the Shermans, making the family wealthy for their time.) Meanwhile, Sherman continued to receive a salary of $15,000 a year. He remained so well liked that some years later he was proposed as Grant's replacement as president. He still did not like politics or politicians, however, so he refused, content to remain General of the Army. In 1884 Sherman retired from the army, still so popular that Congress voted to retire him at full pay.

The Sherman family lived comfortably in St. Louis until 1890, when Ellen Sherman died. Sherman then moved to New York, where he died on February 14, 1891.

For More Information

Marszalek, John F. *Sherman: A Soldier's Passion for Order.* New York: Free Press, 1993.

Merrill, James M. *William Tecumseh Sherman.* Chicago: Rand-McNally, 1971.

Sherman, William T. *Memoirs of General W. T. Sherman.* New York: Literary Classics of the United States, 1990.

Martin Robinson Delany

1812-1885

Personal Background

Early life. Martin Delany was born on May 6, 1812, the fifth child of a free black mother, Pati, and a slave father, Samuel. Slave rules in Charleston, Virginia, where Martin was born, did not allow the father to live with his family. The leadership role normally held by a father was partly filled by Martin's grandmother Graci Peace, who thrilled her grandson with stories of his proud African grandfather, Shango. She told how Shango had been captured into slavery in Yorubaland in West Africa, where he had been a prince among his people. As was proper for a prince, he struggled with his captors before being forced to stand in the slave trading market.

Martin's father probably acted in the same proud way, for he was in prison before Martin was ten years old. Samuel Delany had been convicted of fighting a white man who had tried to beat him. Martin was eleven before his father managed to buy his freedom and join the family.

Move to Pennsylvania. A Virginia law passed in 1819 had made legal a long-standing policy preventing black children from attending school and making it a crime for anyone to teach a black child to read and write. Nevertheless, a kind white peddler left a primer (a beginning reading book), and a spelling book with the family, and with these the Delany children taught themselves to

▲ **Martin Robinson Delany**

Event: Involvement of black troops in the Civil War.

Role: For years before the Civil War, Martin Delany had championed black independence and black pride. His own experiences had, by the beginning of the war, led him to believe that African Americans would improve their status more rapidly by leaving the country. He changed his mind after Abraham Lincoln issued the Emancipation Proclamation, however, and sought to improve the positions of black people by establishing a black army. When this effort failed, he became a major in the Union army to help the newly freed blacks of the South.

read. In 1822 some white people of Charleston found out the children could read, and Pati Delany was brought into court and accused of aiding the children in this "crime." Although she was not guilty, Pati had no way to defend herself, for black people could not testify in the white court. Therefore, before she could be tried and jailed, Pati took her five children and left the state. They settled in a growing black community in Chambersburg, Pennsylvania. It was a year later when Martin's father, now a free man, joined the family.

Education. Martin was able to attend a school for free black children in Chambersburg, but his best education came at age nineteen after he left his family to seek his fortune in Pittsburgh. The African Methodist Episcopal (AME) Church there provided schooling under the direction of Reverend Louis Woodson. For five years, the young Delany worked at various laboring jobs during the day and attended Woodson's school at night. When he was twenty-four, Delany felt he was ready to study for a career in medicine. There were few schools of medicine at that time, and even fewer that admitted black students intending to practice in America. Delany studied medicine by becoming an assistant to Dr. Andrew McDowell. Medicine, however, was not his only, or even his first, interest.

In fact, Delany was most interested in helping black people gain equality in America. As a young man in Pittsburgh, he had begun to participate in clubs and associations formed for that purpose. He became a respected speaker among these groups.

Commitment to emancipation. Delany had arrived in Pittsburgh in 1831, the year that Nat Turner tried to organize a rebellion. This event was a turning point in his life. He became fully dedicated to fighting for equality for black people and to speaking out for black pride. He had already seen the violence that some Northern white people used to suppress free blacks whom they saw as threats to their own jobs. In 1839 he visited the South, where he saw firsthand the problems of slavery. After this visit, Delany wrote his first book, a novel about slavery called *Blake; or, the Huts of America.*

Joining other black abolitionists such as Frederick Douglass, Delany began to travel around the North speaking out for black pride and for emancipation. His ideas, however, differed from those of the already famous Douglass, who along with many other black leaders felt that success was impossible without the support of white abolitionists. Delany, on the other hand, believed that as long as black people looked to white people for help they would remain a lower-class people in society. His speeches urged black people to organize their own society and to create their own factories, farms, and stores. He told them to pay attention to their churches but not to depend on prayer alone. Delany viewed organized religions as a sort of pacifier of blacks, teaching them to accept their positions meekly. Black people, he thought, were capable of and should become independent of white people.

Delany was as often mistreated and shunned by both white listeners and black people as he was praised. Nevertheless, in 1843 he began to publish a four-page newspaper, *The Mystery,* dedicated to publicizing black causes. The paper also discussed the causes of other groups who did not have full rights as citizens, such as women, who were not allowed to vote. In *The Mystery* as well as his speeches, Delany took issue with mistreatment of black people everywhere regardless of the intent or even the color of the offender. Once he wrote a blistering article about a black man suspected of helping white bounty hunters capture fugitive slaves. For this he was sued for libel, found guilty, and fined $150, the largest amount ever awarded in a libel suit in Pittsburgh.

Marriage and family. The year he started to publish *The Mystery,* Delany married. His bride was a mulatto woman named Catherine Richards, the daughter of an Irish mother and an African father. Over the years, Catherine and Martin had thirteen children and raised nine of them to adulthood. In keeping with his great pride in black people, Delany gave each child the name of a famous black person in history. In spite of his speaking campaigns, which often kept him away from home, Martin found time to be a good father and always to provide for his family. His marriage to Catherine had expanded the scope of his crusade; now Delany also spoke for combining the causes of full-blooded blacks with those of mixed bloods.

With Frederick Douglass. Through his travels and speaking engagements, Delany became a friend of Douglass. In 1848 he gave up his own newspaper to join Douglass in publishing the *North Star.* Although this newspaper was published in Rochester, New York, Delany stayed in the West and wrote his reports and columns from there. Soon, however, the two partners saw that their views were radically different, and Douglass worried that Delany would drive away white people who wanted to help in their cause. Delany thought this was a necessary risk for the advancement of blacks. Within less than a year, the two agreed that they had best sign their articles so that readers would not confuse their ideas. Finally, the partners in the *North Star* agreed to break up.

Delany decided to renew his studies of medicine by working with two Pittsburgh doctors. Meanwhile, he applied for admission to medical schools. Two years later, in 1850, he was admitted to Harvard Medical School. His stay there was short, however, since white students were not happy studying with a black man who was planning to practice medicine in the United States. The few other black students who had studied at Harvard planned to practice in a foreign country. After one term, the faculty committee, headed by Oliver Wendell Holmes, told Delany that he could not return to Harvard.

Published Works of Martin Delany

Martin Delany wrote several books advancing the cause of black equality:

The Condition, Elevation, Emigration, and Destiny of the Colored People of the United States, 1852.

The Origin and Objectives of Ancient Freemasonry; Its Introduction into the United States, and Legitimacy Among Colored Men, 1853.

The Principia of Ethnology: The Origin of Races and Color..., 1879.

Pan-Africa. By this time, Delany had started to feel that the situation for blacks in the United States was hopeless. His second book, *The Condition, Elevation, Emigration, and Destiny of the Colored People of the United States,* published in 1852, recommended that blacks move from the United States. He organized some conferences, one of which was the Cleveland National Emigration Convention, and attended others to propose that black people leave the United States to find freedom, equality, and independence in another part of the world. The passage of the Fugitive Slave Act in 1850 had threatened to put all Northern free black people in jeopardy. For a few years afterward, Delany protested by moving his family and his cause to Canada. Life there was very different from life in Ohio. They rented a home in Chatham, and Delany became involved in politics. In 1856 he helped a white liberal, Archibald McKellar, win election to parliament and became a member of his executive committee.

THE

CONDITION,

ELEVATION, EMIGRATION, AND DESTINY

OF THE

COLORED PEOPLE

OF THE

UNITED STATES.

POLITICALLY CONSIDERED,

BY MARTIN ROBISON DELANY.

PHILADELPHIA
PUBLISHED BY THE AUTHOR.
1852.

▲ Title page of Delany's 1852 political tract

While the Delanys were in Canada, the Dred Scott case came to trial in the United States. Dred Scott was a black slave who had lived in the northern United States for five years with his master. Abolitionists had convinced him to sue for his freedom because his master had taken him to live in a free state. Chief Justice Roger Taney, however, ruled that blacks were not citizens and so had no right to sue in a federal court even if they were free. Certainly slaves were not and could never become citizens of the United States, according to Taney. Taney's decision increased Delany's belief that black people needed their own homeland.

While still in Chatham, Delany met with another famous crusader for freedom, an already aging white man named John Brown. Brown, too, had a plan. He wanted to pick a few strong men and establish armed camps in the Appalachian Mountains. From these camps, they would make raids on Southern plantations, freeing slaves and encouraging them to join in a revolution. Abolitionist Harriet Tubman had already met Brown and found him "the most of a man I ever met with" (Sterling, p. 168). She decided to support the plan however possible. Delany wanted to help, but he was already forming his own plans. He did, however, offer to organize a meeting for Brown and his followers.

Delany realized, however, that he could accomplish little from Canada. He did not plan to establish a separate black American colony in another land, as was being suggested by some of the white abolitionists. He hoped rather to take black Americans to another country, join with the people there, and build an entirely new black society. Some who agreed with him would have chosen to move to Haiti. Others chose Central America. Delany had a greater dream, however. He wanted to move the black people of America back to Africa and unite all of Africa to build a great economically rich black continent.

In 1859 he and a friend traveled to what is now Nigeria and Benin, visiting nearly every town and talking with many of the chiefs of Yorubaland. Their idea of building a great African economy was well received by many, but by this time it was too late for action. Europeans were conquering and dividing Africa and the sounds of civil war were ringing in the United States.

▲ 107th U.S. Colored Infantry Guard

Participation: Recruiter in the Civil War

Black soldiers in the war. At the beginning of the war between the states, black men were discouraged from joining the Union army. Because the North was heavily populated, Northern leaders thought there would be plenty of white volunteers to fight a short battle to subdue the South. The South, most Northerners thought, would be quickly defeated.

The war proved more difficult and bloody than anticipated, however. As time passed, Northern recruits grew more difficult to find. Union soldiers, moreover, signed up for only three months at the beginning of the war, after which many wanted to return home. After the Emancipation Proclamation the Union army began to recruit black men, separating them into totally black regiments led by white officers. Officials soon realized that getting black men to serve in these fighting units would be more effective if there were black leaders recruiting them. The army turned to well-known black leaders. Douglass was hired to enlist soldiers for the Union army.

The Northern states were still enlisting men and organizing them under their state flags to form units of the Union army. There were, for example, Massachusetts divisions and Connecticut divisions. Douglass recruited men for the New York and Massachusetts militia. Each man who enlisted received a bonus of about $100, a uniform, and about $15 per month. The recruiter received a payment, something on the order of $20, for each man he enlisted. In contrast, the bonus for a white volunteer sometimes grew to $1,000. Nevertheless, by 1863, black participation in the war had grown to twenty regiments. There was a Bureau for Colored Troops in the war department, and the regiments had an official name, the United States Colored Troops. By war's end there were 185,000 black soldiers in the Union army.

Delany lived in the United States during the Civil War. Working from an office in Chicago, Illinois, he at first worked for other recruiters who had contracted with the government to supply troops. He was so successful that he was soon able to get his own contract with the state of Connecticut. For Delany, however, recruiting men for an army that would keep them segregated was not enough. Always looking for ways to advance the cause of black equality, Delany developed a new idea when it appeared that the Union army would eventually win the war.

Black army. On September 22, 1862, President Abraham Lincoln proclaimed that all persons held as slaves in the South would be free on January 1, 1863 (see **Abraham Lincoln**). This Emancipation Proclamation had a great effect on Delany. He planned to create a whole black army with black officers to serve the Union. This army would march through the South making sure the freed slaves were fairly treated. He saw his plan as a great statement of black independence and equality that would build the morale of Southern black people who found themselves free but still treated unfairly. To achieve his goal, Delany needed an official rank, money, and government approval. He hurried to Washington to propose his plan to

Lincoln. The president listened to the suggestion and seemed interested. He asked Delany to explain the plan to the secretary of war.

Meanwhile, government plans were already being formed for a Freedman's Bureau as part of the Union army. This bureau would care for the freed people of the South, particularly those with no land, for a period of a year after the war ended. The bureau would provide food, clothing, and bedding for needy ex-slaves and even give them farmland for as long as three years. The land would be taken from areas that had been abandoned by white owners during the war. Delany's plan would have been a much larger step. He proposed that his all-black army would take charge of breaking up the large Southern plantations into twenty– or forty–acre farms to be given to the freed slaves who had worked there.

Whether Lincoln and Secretary of War Stanton really liked the idea or thought it was too far-fetched is not known. However, Delany was made a major in the army and assigned to the Freedman's Bureau. Under the leadership of General O. O. Howard, the bureau was to become the guardian of freed slaves, and it would direct the reorganization of Southern society. The task proved more difficult than at first imagined, however, and government support of the Freedman's Bureau had to be extended for several years after the war.

Delany was assigned to duties in South Carolina. Another dream of his had at least been partly achieved. There was no all-black army, but he must have been delighted when he arrived in Charleston. Two days earlier, the city had seen the arrival of the Union troops that would keep order in the state, the Massachusetts Fifty-fifth regiment. It had been the second all-black regiment recruited in that state. The dismay of white South Carolinians was countered by the joy of freed blacks when this unit came into town to the tune of a song praising John Brown. A reporter asked one elderly black woman if she was glad the Yankees had come. "O child," she said, "I can't bless the Lord enough, but I don't call you 'Yankees.' I call you Jesus' aids, and I call your head man the Messiah" (Quarles, p. 328).

On April 5, 1865, a great event was scheduled to occur outside Charleston. General Robert Anderson, who had been forced to surrender Fort Sumter in Charleston Harbor at the beginning of the war, was to raise the same old Union flag over the recaptured fort. Among the many black people who rode to this event aboard the ship *Planter* were Delany and his son Toussaint L'Overture Delany, a member of the famous Massachusetts Fifty-fourth regiment, the first black regiment to be recruited from that state. The next day, 3,000 black citizens gathered to celebrate in the only Negro Presbyterian Church in the South, Zion Church. The featured speaker at this affair was William Lloyd Garrison, perhaps the leading white abolitionist. Garrison was taking great joy in touring the South and making speeches from platforms that had once been used to exhibit blackss for sale as slaves. A joyous Delany joined the great white leader as a speaker.

His duties over. Delany had accepted his commission as the best compromise to his own plan. He served in the army in South Carolina for three years, helping freed black families adjust to the new society. In the course of this service, he had enlisted enough ex-slaves in the Union army to form two regiments. Even three years after the war, however, having a black major in the army still rankled some people. Also, by that time, white people in the North had begun to worry about black dominance in the South. Already white workers were being shipped into South Carolina to do the work slaves had previously done. Delany thought that within five years, the black majority in the state would be overcome by the immigration of white workers. He called for the new black citizens to immediately establish their position in the economy and politics of the state. Perhaps concerned over this turn of events, Delany's superiors in the Union Army decided that they no longer needed his services and let him go.

Aftermath

Politics. Delany remained in South Carolina as a private citizen. For a short time, he served as a judge, but then his old dreams began to resurface. Having always held a warm feeling for Africa, he now petitioned to become ambassador to the colony of Liberia. He by this time had come to support the movement of black Americans to Liberia, but the ambassadorship was not given to him. Next, he ran for the position of lieutenant governor of South Carolina two times and lost each time. Black people who admired him were free, but few of them could vote, and most white people did not trust Delany.

Medicine. Delany was nearly fifty-five years old and the fires of rebellion were fading. For the remaining two decades of his life, he returned to the practice of medicine. In 1880 he moved to Ohio, where he continued to serve black people by providing them with the best medical service available. He joined his family, which had been living on the campus of Wilberforce University in Xenia, Ohio. Delany died January 24, 1885, at Wilberforce, leaving behind his wife and six children.

> ### Martin Delany, Candidate for Lieutenant Governor of South Carolina
>
> "I do not intend to lower my standard of manhood in regard to the claims of my race one single step. I do not intend to recede from the rights that have been given us by a just Congress one single hairsbreadth; but I do intend to demand the same equal rights and justice to every citizen, black and white, of the state of South Carolina." (Sterling, p. 297)

For More Information

Griffith, Cyril E. *The African Dream.* University Park: Pennsylvania State University Press, 1975.

Mays, Joe H. *Black Americans and Their Contributions Toward Union Victory in the American Civil War, 1861-1865.* New York: University Press of America, 1984.

Quarles, Benjamin. *The Negro in the Civil War.* Boston: Little, Brown, and Company, 1953.

Sterling, Dorothy. *The Making of an Afro-American.* Garden City, New York: Doubleday, 1971.

Anna Ella Carroll

1815-1893

Personal Background

Influential ancestry. On August 29, 1815, Anna Ella Carroll was born in a lavish, twenty-two-room manor called Kingston Hall, which rested on a large Maryland plantation stocked with cotton, wheat, and tobacco. Anna was a bright, blue-eyed baby with dark red curls and a fair complexion. She had in girlhood a fierce temper and an independent spirit, balanced with an equally strong tendency to shower her family with love. Her sense of independence would remain with her, carrying her through the adventures that lay ahead.

For generations, the Carrolls had been an influential family in America. Thomas King Carroll and Juliana Stevenson Carroll, Anna's parents, were extremely wealthy and well-respected people of the South. As a teenager, Juliana had been an accomplished organist for the Episcopal church. Thomas Carroll was a powerful lawyer whose partners included Francis Scott Key, the composer of America's national anthem. Anna Carroll's paternal grandfather, Charles Carroll, signed the Declaration of Independence. Her maternal grandfather, Doctor Henry Stevenson, served as an officer and a surgeon in the British navy during the Revolutionary War. He operated on Tory soldiers and American prisoners of war alike, earning the respect of men on both sides.

▲ Anna Ella Carroll

Event: Military campaigns of the Civil War.

Role: As an aide to President Abraham Lincoln, Anna Ella Carroll was one of the first women to work for the U.S. government. During the Civil War, she devised a key battle plan that benefited the Union army at a critical point in the war.

Life at Kingston Hall. Anna Carroll was the first of eight children, only two of whom were boys. She soon became Anne to her family and friends, rarely using her real birthname, even in adulthood. Anne led a privileged life as a child, with a slave caretaker, Milly, to care for her every need from the time she was born. She also had a personal servant, a beautiful slave girl her own age named Leah, who tended her for many years. Anne and Leah became friends, yet they always observed the boundaries of their positions as mistress and servant.

From a very early age, Anne was the favorite of her well-educated father. In his eldest daughter, Thomas Carroll recognized the thirst for learning he had had as a boy. Proving that he did not subscribe to the popular notion that girls should not be educated, Thomas spent many hours reading Shakespeare's plays to his daughter. His readings continued as she grew older so that by the age of eleven she was reading with her father essays by the Scottish historian Alison. By the age of twelve, Anne had learned to assist her father in his work by finding legal passages from his law books for use in his debates with Southern legislators.

In the spring of 1829, when Anne was thirteen, democrat Andrew Jackson was elected president, and Thomas ran for and was elected governor of Maryland by a Jackson-supporting legislature. His new position took him to Annapolis, Maryland, away from his family. Back at Kingston Hall, Anne took on new responsibilities as her father's secretary, screening visitors and answering letters on his behalf. She even started a book of newspaper clippings for him, selecting articles dealing with the ever-increasing tension between the Southern planters and the peo-

A Teenager Discusses Politics

The following is from one of Carroll's letters to her father when he was away in Annapolis serving as governor of Maryland. In it, she criticizes the fact that some of her father's appointed advisers were considered too radical, or favorable toward change, and therefore were not readily accepted by others in his political party. The man she refers to in the letter, Lycurgus, was a Greek lawmaker in the ninth century B.C. "The hall" is Kingston Hall. She wrote the letter at the age of fourteen.

"It is my principle as well as that of Lycurgus, to avoid mediums—that is to say people who are not decidedly one thing or another. In politics, they are the inveterate enemy of the state."

"I hear there has been a committee appointed to visit you on your return to the hall and present a petition for the removal of some whom you have recently appointed. They call themselves reformers ... to be forever reforming reform is absurd." (Greenbie and Greenbie, p. 36)

ple in the North, whose views and life styles were very different. In the spring of 1831, Anne and her family traveled to Annapolis to visit Thomas. She was excited by this opportunity to observe firsthand the workings of the government.

Several years later, in 1837, after Thomas had returned home from his governorship, the nation fell into a terrible depression, and the Carrolls lost much of their fortune. The plantation and Kingston Hall were becoming too much to afford financially. Though they had at least 200 slaves to account for, they were not willing to sell them to slave traders who would separate the families that had been kept together. Luckily, a distant relative returning to the States from South America had enough money to buy the house and well over half the slaves. The remaining slaves went with the family to a smaller plantation, up the Choptank River, called Warwick Fort Manor.

Off to Baltimore. After her family was settled in their new environment, Carroll decided it was time to leave home and try to make her own way in the world. Now twenty-two, she announced to her parents that she and Leah would head for Baltimore, Maryland, the second-largest city in the United States at the time. She hoped they could not only support themselves but have enough money left over to send back home.

Leah, a skilled seamstress, found employment almost immediately working for wealthy families in Baltimore. As she worked in their homes, she would listen carefully to their gossip about new businesses and bring the word directly to Anne. Anne learned to act quickly on Leah's leads, tracking down new business owners and using her writing ability to compose letters for mailing lists, generate publicity, and create advertising. Her public relations work soon earned her enough to send home a few extra dollars to her brothers and sisters. She worked steadily for seven years in Baltimore, making a name for herself as a skilled publicity writer.

From railroads to politics. At the age of twenty-nine, Carroll began writing press releases for railroad companies in Baltimore. Her work for the railroads, as well as her family's strong political background, allowed her to easily slip into the world of politics that was so familiar to her. She became affiliated with the Whig party, meeting such people as the army chief of staff Winfield Scott. With Carroll, Scott discussed his war strategies in the invasion of Mexico, which resulted in the acquisition of California, New Mexico, and parts of Utah, Arizona, and Colorado.

Because of her acquaintance with Scott, Carroll began sitting in regularly at the visitors' gallery in the Senate, where she met many powerful men and future presidents, such as James Buchanan, whom she briefly dated. She also became close friends with Millard Fillmore in the early 1850s, shortly after he was sworn in as president following Zachary Taylor's death.

In the midst of her budding political career, Carroll had many discussions with Northern abolitionists about slavery. To satisfy her personal belief that slavery was wrong, Carroll freed all twenty of her slaves, whom she had inherited from her father. This was a dangerous move in 1853, a year in which any freed slaves were considered fair game for recapture. So Carroll used her political influence to persuade abolitionists to accompany her former slaves to safety in Canada.

In 1854 Fillmore began seeking Carroll out as a confidante and, because his first wife had died, as a possible second wife. But Carroll had a personal agenda to fulfill. She wanted to make an impact in the political world but not as the president's wife. Although she refused Fillmore's proposal, she continued to help him in his campaign for the presidency in 1856, which he lost to James Buchanan.

Also in 1856, Carroll met railroad mogul Cornelius Garrison. Her knowledge of railroads, which she had gained from writing press releases for various railroad companies, impressed Garrison so much that he hired her as an assistant planner for new railroad lines. Railroads, in fact, prompted Carroll to write her first major political essay, "The Star of the West," in which she discussed the importance of building railroad lines in order to keep the Union together and improve the economy.

"The Star of the West" was quite successful among Union supporters when it was published in 1856. Carroll's writing caught the interest of Republicans, many of them former Whigs, who shared her earnest desire for the Union to stay together. She met with

Republican senators, wrote other pro-Union essays, and, in 1860, optimistically watched Abraham Lincoln sworn in as president of a nation divided by the argument over secession and slavery (see **Abraham Lincoln**).

Participation: The Civil War

When she was forty-five, Carroll became romantically involved with Lemuel Evans, a member of the secret service assigned to protect President Lincoln. Evans offered Carroll her second marriage proposal, which she refused. She was concentrating on her political writing at the time. Carroll began working on a new document, *Reply to Breckenridge*, in which she spoke out against the anti-Lincoln Southerners, headed by such people as Senator Samuel Breckenridge, who wanted the nation divided. She even touched on strategies for keeping the nation united. In one part of the *Reply*, Carroll stated, "There can be no equivocal position in this crisis; and he who is not with the Government is against it, and an enemy to his country" (Wise, p. 110). Her powerful writing caught Lincoln's eye and, in the summer of 1861, he not only demanded government funding to publish 50,000 copies of the manuscript and distribute them throughout the states, but he also sent Carroll a telegram inviting her to the White House for a confidential interview.

A woman advises the president. Upon meeting Lincoln, Carroll was impressed by his loyalty to the Union, a sentiment which she fully shared. Although they had met in social situations before, this was the first time they were able to talk in depth about the state of the nation. Lincoln spoke frankly with Carroll about his need for her expert strategical mind and extensive political background. He had a war on his hands and he needed all the help Carroll could offer. Lincoln asked her to become an unofficial member of the Cabinet, acting as a top adviser to him, with access to the White House at any time of the day or night. She enthusiastically accepted the offer.

Carroll was immediately assigned to work directly with the Assistant Secretary of War Thomas Scott. Her first assignment was to travel by train to St. Louis, Missouri, to observe and report the general sentiment of the soldiers stationed along the Mississippi River. As a woman, she probably would not be suspected of being an informer to the president, for women in government were unheard of at the time. The trip proved to be a strenuous one for Carroll, with hours of traveling in hot, overcrowded railroad cars. The farther along the river she traveled, the more she discovered that hopes in the Union army were not high. Many of the soldiers confessed to her that the current plan of attack, to move down the Mississippi and take the Southern army head-on was simply too obvious. The Confederate army was ready and waiting at the mouth of the river. In the event that a Northern gunboat became disabled, it would float, with the southerly flowing current, right into the hands of the enemy. The soldiers feared that too many lives would be lost with this unimaginative battle plan.

By the time she arrived at her hotel in St. Louis, Carroll felt an impending sense of doom for the Union army. She knew that too much blood had been shed already and sought to hasten the end of the war. Under the light of an oil lamp, she studied the crude maps of the land for a better route, one that would take the South by surprise. After many hours, a brilliant alternative dawned on Carroll: the Tennessee River!

The Tennessee River Plan. Carroll worked all night on her discovery, devising a plan that would cut the Southern forces in half by intercepting the very railroad lines she had helped design years earlier. The South was now using these lines to transport supplies to their troops. If troops could not get food and ammunition from the Charleston and Memphis railroads, they would be forced to surrender immediately. The Union army could use the Tennessee River to surprise the Confederate army from an angle they were not expecting. Moreover, the Tennessee River flowed north, so any troubled gunboats would float with the current back to the safety of the Northern army bases.

Carroll had masterminded an amazing plan, but she still had some crucial questions to answer: Was the Tennessee deep enough to hold gunboats? What were the water current speeds? Where were the points of landing? She wasted no time in seeking out a river pilot loyal to the North. Charles Scott knew the Tennessee River well and he gave Carroll the information she needed to

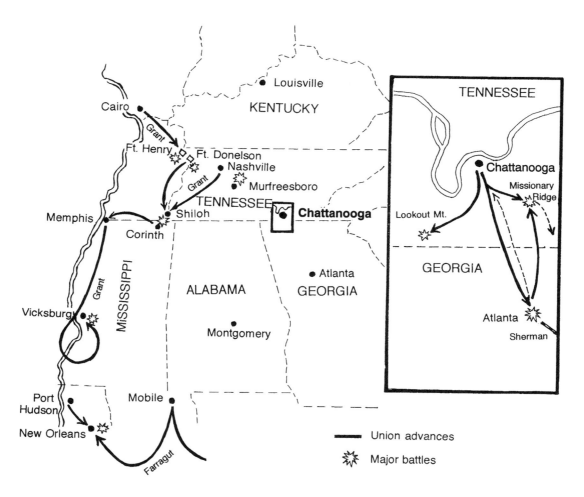

Union advances

🔆 Major battles

▲ **Civil War battle sites in the Mississippi River Valley**

ensure that her plan would succeed. He even pointed out that the Tombigbee River, which flowed directly to Mobile, Alabama, was a short distance from the middle of the Tennessee. With this information, Carroll added to her outline the taking of Mobile via the Tombigbee. Wasting no more time, she drew up a comprehensive version of the Tennessee River Plan, and sent one copy to the secretary of war and one to the president in mid-November 1861.

According to Secretary of War Scott, when Lincoln received Carroll's proposed battle plan, he expressed "overwhelming relief, joy and hope" (Greenbie and Greenbie, p. 295). The president ordered the plan to go into effect as a military strategy in February 1862, keeping very silent about whose idea it was. Many gunboats under the command of Ulysses S. Grant were ordered up the Tennessee River and, within two weeks, two Confederate forts, 13,000 prisoners, and sixty-five guns were captured. The enormous success of the mission made people across the nation want to know who could have come up with such a successful scheme. There were rumors of a woman working in Washington, but Carroll's name was not leaked to the public. Meanwhile, Kentucky had been defeated, Tennessee was struggling, and, in accordance with Carroll's plans, Northern troops were heading for Vicksburg, Mississippi.

The war was far from over, however. As it raged on, Carroll continued to work side by side with Lincoln and Grant until the war's end in 1865. During the final months of war, Lincoln began planning the reconstruction of the country, with Carroll at his side offering advice.

On March 1, 1865, while Carroll and the president looked for ways to pick up the pieces of the shattered country, she received an anonymous letter from Fort Delaware. It read:

> Madame: It is rumored in the Southern army that you furnished the plan or information that caused the United States Government to abandon the expedition designed to descend the Mississippi River, and transferred the armies up the Tennessee River in 1862. We wish to know if this is true. If it is, you are the veriest of traitors to your section, and we warn you that you stand upon a volcano. Confederates. (Greenbie and Greenbie, p. 415)

Civil War Heroines

Mary Livermore worked for the Sanitary Commission, which distributed medical goods to hospitalized soldiers. Livermore risked her life, sailing down the Mississippi River in a rickety wooden boat, to bring comfort to Union soldiers in their hospital beds. With the clothes on her back and a pair of knee-high boots for wading through the river, Livermore visited at least 10,000 soldiers individually. She dressed wounds, gave sips of brandy, told stories, and sang songs to the thousands of soldiers, many of whom did not make it through the war.

Kady Brownell was born in a British military camp during the Revolutionary War. She married a Union soldier, and instead of watching her husband march off to the Civil War, she marched with him, proudly carrying a flag bearing the Union colors. In the Battle of Bull Run, she marched on the deadly front lines, her flag held high for the Union men to see. At one point, she became separated from her husband. Riding on an abandoned horse, she searched for days through enemy lines and raging battles until she found him. Miraculously, neither she nor her husband were harmed in the war.

The warning worried Carroll, but everyone, it seemed, was receiving threats from bitter Confederates. She was never harmed in any way, unlike Lincoln. His plans for reconstruction were cut short with his assassination in April 1865. Exhausted from work and grief, Carroll was now fifty. Yet she by no means intended to quit the business of government simply because of the war's ending.

Aftermath

Carroll advises Grant. Grant, with whom Carroll had communicated by telegraph from Washington many times when he was in the battlefield, was being backed by an overwhelming number of people for the office of the presidency. Grant asked Carroll to do what she did best—advise him from his post as general of the Union army to his job as president of the United States.

The quest for recognition. Carroll needed Grant as much as he needed her. Feeling that the time had come for her to be officially recognized for her invaluable duties to the United States government, Carroll sought Grant's support. Also, she still had unpaid bills to printing companies, who printed copies of her speeches and pamphlets, equaling over $6,000. The Carroll family fortune had been used up, and Carroll had lived very modestly throughout her period of service to several presidents.

Carroll prepared a statement for Congress, "A Memorial," and published it on June 8, 1872. In it were quotes from some of the most influential men in government, who argued that she be given the recognition and monetary compensation she was rightly due. She quoted such statements as this one from Benjamin Wade, president of the Senate in 1869:

Civil War Heroines

Mary A. Bickerdyke, known to soldiers as Mother Bickerdyke, used to sneak onto Union hospital ships to nurse and comfort the wounded soldiers. She often had to be escorted off because her loud orders for food and supplies became too much for the ship captains to bear. While visiting the ships, she worked for days at a time, never giving in to fatigue. She became the subject of this poem, written by Eliza Pitzinger:

"Behold the light! It moves around
Through all the dreary night!
Whence comes that slow and muffled sound?
Who bears the charmed light?

'Twas neither angel, sprite nor elf,
Nor spectre; it was like
The dear, good, kind and loving self
Of faithful Mother Bickerdyke!"
(Young, p. 150)

I know that some of the most successful expeditions of the war were suggested by you, among which I might instance the expedition up the Tennessee River.... I also know in what high estimation your services were held by President Lincoln ... I [hope] that the Government may yet confer on you some token of acknowledgement for all these services and sacrifices. (Greenbie and Greenbie, pp. 436-37)

Carroll also had the backing of Thomas Scott and Lemuel Evans, who was now chief justice of the supreme court of Texas. To their testimonies, she added her own: "I cannot ... detract from our brave and heroic commanders to whom the country owes so much; and ... I believe that ... they would be gratified to see me or anyone properly rewarded" (Wise, pp. 189-90). This may have been true, but unfortunately there were too many men in the government who wanted this secret of a woman military adviser to remain just that. They would not recognize her role in any official sense.

Although Grant knew the truth about Carroll's responsibility in the war, other top advisers chose to bury the truth and promote Grant as the real war hero. Grant did not argue with this decision, causing Carroll to lose her faith in her former friend. Her "Memorial" and other claims for recognition disappeared from government files several times over, drawing the process out for years. In fact, Carroll did not receive any promise of payment from the government until James A. Garfield was elected in 1880 and Congress considered a bill demanding that Carroll receive back-pay as a major general in quarterly installments from November 1861 to the end of her life. However, this bill disappeared at the same time that Garfield was shot, and it was replaced with another in 1881, offering fifty dollars a month from the passage of this new bill until the end of Carroll's lifetime. This offer was financially incomparable to the salary of a major general, and an insult to such an important political figure. Nevertheless, Carroll had no choice but to accept it, for during her nine-year fight for recognition, she had grown ill and needed the money to take care of herself.

Carroll and her younger sister, Mary, lived together in Washington, D.C., on Carroll's meager government pension. Under Mary's devoted care, Carroll continued her writing well after she was bedridden. In a room piled high with books and letters, next to a vase of fresh flowers Mary brought almost daily, Carroll enjoyed the last years of her life by a window that gave her a view of the West. She accepted visitors until her last days, including her long-time love, Lemuel Evans.

On the morning of February 19, 1893, Anna Ella Carroll died, surrounded by family and friends. In accordance with her wishes, she was buried in the churchyard of the Old Trinity Church in Cambridge, Massachusetts, next to her father, mother, and other members of the Carroll family. She remains revered by those who recognize her selfless devotion and vital contributions to her country.

For More Information

Greenbie, Sydney, and Marjorie Barstow Greenbie. *Anna Ella Carroll and Abraham Lincoln*. Tampa: University of Tampa Press, 1952.

Wise, Winifred E. *Lincoln's Secret Weapon*. New York: Chilton Company, 1961.

Young, Agatha. *The Women and the Crisis: Women of the North in the Civil War*. New York: McDowell, Obolensky, 1959.

Mathew B. Brady

c. 1823-1896

Personal Background

Farm boy. Little is known of Mathew Brady's early life. Even the exact date of his birth is not known, though he thought he was born about 1823 or 1824 in Warren County, New York. His parents, Andrew and Julia, were farmers whose families traced their heritage to County Cook in Ireland, although both parents seem to have been born in America. Apparently, Mathew had a typical upstate New York boyhood, his days a mixture of farm work and play. He probably attended just enough school to learn to read and write. At the age of sixteen, he left home to seek his fortune in the large town of Saratoga. It was there that he met the man who would lead him to his life's work—William Page, a young and well-known artist.

Artist. Page took an interest in young Brady and encouraged him to try painting. The two traveled together to Albany, where Page painted portraits and Brady practiced his art skills.

Earlier, Page had studied art in New York under Samuel F. B. Morse. President of the National Academy of Design, Morse supported himself by painting portraits while he perfected the invention that would later make him famous—the telegraph. Page saw talent in the seventeen-year-old Brady and decided to take him to New York City to meet Morse and see if he would take the young

▲ Mathew B. Brady

Event: Photographing the Civil War.
Role: At the onset of Civil War, Mathew B. Brady, a successful photographer with studios in New York and Washington, used his savings of $100,000 to build special wagons and train crews to photograph the war. Brady and his crews toured battle grounds and sent their photographs to journals and newspapers across the United States.

man on as a student. Page and Brady met with the old teacher at a time of great excitement.

The birth of photography. From 1829 to 1833, two French experimenters, Joseph-Nicéphore Niepce and Louis-Jacques-Mondé Daguerre, had been trying to perfect a way to take photographs. Before they succeeded, Niepce died. Daguerre spent several more years, from 1833 to 1839, perfecting the photographic method by himself. The French government recognized the great value of the final method. For an annual pension, the government persuaded Daguerre and Niepce's son to give the right to their method to the world.

Samuel F. B. Morse was in France when the method for creating photographs, called daguerreotypes, was released to the public. Morse was trying to get a French patent for his telegraph invention. He immediately saw that taking photographs in a few minutes would save his customers hours of posing while he painted their portraits. He could paint from the daguerreotype.

America and daguerreotypes. Morse bought a daguerreotype camera in France and headed home to experiment. He also wrote an account of the new method for the *New York Observer.* Morse's first photograph, and perhaps the first one in America, was of the Unitarian Church in New York. Within a year, news of the discovery had attracted the attention of many people in America. Morse saw another opportunity and opened a school of photography in 1840. Brady, who had intended to study art with Morse, enrolled in the new school at the cost of fifty dollars.

The Brady studio. In 1844 Brady opened a studio in New York to use the new photographic method. One of his first customers was Daniel Webster, an important American politician. Webster's portrait was one of the first in what became a very profitable business for Brady—taking portrait photographs of famous people.

Method for Making Daguerreotype Photographs

1. Clean and polish a copper plate.
2. Coat the plate with a thin coat of silver.
3. Subject the silver plate to vapors of iodine.
4. When ready, use a camera obscura (basically a black box with a pinhole opening in one end).
5. Expose the iodine-treated silver to light for five or ten minutes, then put the plate in a container of mercury vapor.
6. Finally, "fix" the picture using sodium hyposulfate (hypo).

In this first year, Brady entered his daguerreotypes in a contest held by the American Institute and won a bronze medal. The following year he was awarded the top prize in the contest, an honor he won for five straight years.

Photographer of leaders. Brady wanted to publish a book containing photographs of every great man and woman of the time. To accomplish this goal, he moved to the Astor House, a high-priced New York hotel where most of the famous and wealthy New York visitors stayed. Brady worked quickly to execute this plan, photographing important New Yorkers as well as all the presidents from John Quincy Adams to William McKinley except for William Henry Harrison, who died after only one month in office. In 1850 *The Gallery of Illustrious Americans* was published, filled with photographs and short stories of famous people.

By 1850 Brady's studio and work had gained a reputation in America and abroad. For an exhibit of his work at the Crystal Palace in London, England, Brady selected forty-eight of his best photographs and tinted them to add color. The show was such a success that he was awarded a medal for his photographs. Now his fame spread even further, and he opened a second studio and gallery in Washington, D.C., still hoping to photograph everyone of importance.

Marriage. Sometime during this period, Brady got married, though no record of the event exists. Brady met Juliet Elizabeth Handy, the daughter of a Maryland lawyer, at a party on a plantation. Some accounts say the couple married in the late 1840s, while others place the date as late as 1860. At any rate, Julia, as she preferred to be called, was a nearly perfect mate for Brady. First, she loved to entertain, which helped her husband meet the people he hoped to photograph. Second, Julia preferred to live in hotels. The two made their permanent home in the National Hotel in Washington and stayed at the Astor House when in New York.

Although the couple had no children, they often cared for Julia's young nephew, Levin Handy. The boy spent much of his time with the Bradys and became involved in the photography business as a teenager. When he was about thirteen, Levin participated in a prank at school and was suspended. Levin went to Brady's Washington studio to report his predicament, and Brady began to teach the boy photography. By the age of fifteen, Levin was a photographer in his uncle's business. He took over the business when Brady gave it up long after the Civil War.

Wet plates. During this period, photography changed a great deal. Making daguerreotypes was really only useful for landscapes and portraits. A person sitting for a portrait was placed in a well-lighted area, and a head clamp prevented movement for the three to five minutes required to make the picture. Even then, the picture could not be easily reproduced. Brady had published his book by having an artist copy the daguerreotypes into etchings. Now, new discoveries expanded the use of photography. Alexander Wolcott invented a way to use a curved reflector to concentrate more light and reduce the time needed for taking the picture. John Draper found a way to tint the photographs to give them near-living colors. Then, in 1851, Frederick Archer developed a method that used a glass plate and collodion to hold the silver and iodine picture materials. This method, known as the wet plate method, quickly replaced the older and more difficult daguerreotypes. Brady was slow to change to the new method because his daguerreotype business was successful. By 1853, however, he began using wet plates; later, he used this process in his greatest venture—making a pictorial history of the Civil War.

Participation: Photographing the Civil War

Beginning of the war. By the time the Civil War erupted, Brady had managed to save the large sum of $100,000 from the profits of his business. He decided to invest money in a project to photograph the war's battles. As he was to say in a later interview, he felt he had to go.

The Civil War began with some false expectations on the side of the North. The first soldiers came to Washington prepared to put a quick and easy end to the fight. Fort Sumter had been taken by the South and some small battles fought when, on July 20, 1861, the Union army set out to meet the main forces of the South. It was more like a glorious parade. Bands played. Banners flew. Columns

▲ Brady photograph of a meeting of Union officers

of troops formed, each wearing their own uniforms: kilts for the New York 79th Regiment, French uniforms for the New York 11th, and lumberjack uniforms for soldiers from Minnesota. Others wore sports clothes and straw hats. Among them all were a few army regulars in standard blue uniforms. The more prosperous recruits came with trunks of clothes, a store of food, and other fineries, causing the line to straggle out endlessly. Wives and sweethearts came along with picnic baskets to watch the fray.

Brady had asked Lincoln for permission to take photographs of the event (see **Abraham Lincoln**). The photographer had prepared two special wagons covered with gray canvas and equipped with cupboards for chemicals, storage for the large cameras, and a dark room for developing. Soldiers saw these contraptions and, slurring their words together, asked, "Whatsit?" Brady wagons carried the name Whatsit throughout the war.

Some senators went along, hoping to make political gain by being associated with the easy victory. The Union generals waited impatiently while senators Wade, Chandler, Trumball, Wilson, and Grimes made their speeches. Then the large and colorful procession headed up the road to Bull Run, where Confederate generals Pierre Beauregard and Thomas "Stonewall" Jackson were ready for the First battle of Manassas (Bull Run). The North was seriously miscalculating the South's willingness to defend its right to secede.

The battle at Bull Run quickly became a disaster for the North. The Union lines were soon broken, and the untrained and unprepared Union recruits threw away their gear, abandoned their guns, and fled back to Washington. Brady was forced to turn his Whatsit around and head back, too, but not without taking pictures of the abandoned weapons and the clothing and food left by the Union army.

The Battle of Bull Run was a great embarrassment to the Union. Everyone looked for someone to blame for the loss. Even Brady was accused of helping to create the panic, as were the women and the senators who had come along. One reporter, George William Curtis, however, summed up the problem: "As for blame and causes, they are in our condition and character. We have undertaken to make war without in the least knowing how" (Meredith, p. 14).

Regrouping. Lincoln began to believe his generals, Winfield Scott and William Tecumseh Sherman, who felt that the war would be a long one (see **William Tecumseh Sherman**). He called for an additional 400,000 men. Brady, too, saw the horrors and problems that would come from such a war and felt that the new method of photography could be used to make a record of the war. It would, however, be a larger venture than anyone had at first believed.

▲ **Brady photograph of a dead soldier**

Brady invested his life savings in the project. He recruited photographers and trained them. Soon he had twenty-two Whatsits and twenty crews of photographers that he had trained and that he directed to the scenes of war activity. Beginning in 1851 his own eyesight had begun to fade so that he seldom was the man behind the camera, but he was always the director. He or his men traveled by road, rail, and ship to make a pictorial record of the Civil War. Many of the Brady men hired to actually take the pictures became great photographers in their own right, including T. H. O'Sullivan,

William R. Pywell, J. B. Gibson, George Cook, David Knox, D. B. Woodbury, J. Recker, and Stanley Marrow. O'Sullivan is often given credit for the most vivid of the Civil War photographs.

Documenting the fighting. Brady, even with his failing eyesight, was present at the end of some major battles of the war. He directed the photographing of dying and dead Confederate soldiers after the Battle of Antietam, which had driven the Southern forces into retreat. When the armies of Robert E. Lee and General Ambrose Burnside met at the Battle of Fredericksburg, Brady and his crew photographed the battlefield after the fight. Again at Chancellorsville, Brady directed the photographing of the frozen bodies of the dead. These vivid photographs of bloody battlegrounds littered with dead soldiers showed the world the true horror of war.

One famous Brady photograph shows a Southern soldier lying dead in a stone trench at Gettysburg. Others show the fields strewn with bodies of soldiers on the morning of the last day of fighting there. On July 21, 1864, Brady arrived at Petersburg in time to come under cannon fire from Confederate troops led by Beauregard. But the threat of death did not keep Brady's crew from photographing Union troops and gun placements in the siege of the city.

Documenting the hidden tragedies. Wherever the Union army went, Brady or one of his crews followed. They took pictures of troop movements, of buildings destroyed in the war, of the destruction of railroads and bridges, and of landmark places, such as Confederate winter quarters at Centreville, the field at Massaponax where General Ulysses S. Grant met with his generals to plan strategy, field hospitals, and prisons for captured troops. Some of Brady's most dramatic photographs showed the horrors of the prison camp. Although both Union and Confederate governments were guilty of mistreating prisoners, if only by failing to provide food, clothing, and shelter for them, the Confederate prison at Andersonville was Brady's chief target. Here 33,000 Union soldiers were held in a large tent city that did not provide shelter for all of them. With little or no clothing, few blankets, small and rotten rations of food, and no medical care, more than one-fourth of the prisoners died in captivity. Conditions at Andersonville, as photographed by Brady and others, showed the evils of war at its worst.

▲ **Brady photograph of soldiers dead in the trenches**

Photographs of the conditions raised a furor in the North, resulting in the arrest of Henry Wirz, the prison superintendent. Accused of brutality, he was convicted and hanged, even though records showed that he had earlier written to his superiors protesting the lack of provisions and even though mistreatment of prisoners was common on both sides of the war.

CIVIL WAR

Photographer of generals. Throughout the war, Brady remembered his first goal—to photograph every prominent American. He photographed General Grant and, later, General Lee, along with most of their highest ranking officers. As the war neared its end, he asked General Sherman to sit for a photograph and to bring along his staff. In an unusual Civil War photograph, Sherman and his generals posed for Brady in Washington in 1865.

Aftermath

Brady's downfall. By war's end, Brady had taken photographs of every phase of the conflict with his twenty-two crews. He had invested his own savings in a project that he felt compelled to carry out, hoping to regain the cost from the sales of his photographs. But the costs had proven too high. Brady returned to his two studios in New York and Washington and began to try to regain his fortune. He disbanded the twenty-two crews, but even a slimmed-down staff could not be supported. Then, too, the war years had established even more competition in the photography business. With few customers, failing eyesight, and increasing rheumatism, Brady could not reestablish his business. In 1866 he offered to sell his photographs of the war to the United States government, but there was no interest.

Friends tried to secure government support for his war expenses. Brady began to sell bits of his land in order to pay creditors. Finally, in 1873, he could hold on to his business no longer. The New York studio declared bankruptcy and was sold at auction to pay back taxes. The next year, Brady offered many of his photographs for sale at a public auction. The government was now interested and bought most of his photographic plates for $2,840. Later, his friends General Benjamin Butler

> ### Oliver Wendell Holmes on the Brady Civil War Photographs
>
> "These terrible mementoes of one of the most sanguinary [bloody] conflicts of the war, we owe to the enterprise of Mr. Brady of New York. We ourselves were upon the battlefield upon the Saturday morning following the Wednesday when the battle [at Antietam] took place. The photographs bear witness to the accuracy of some of our sketches ... the 'ditch' encumbered with the dead as we saw it ... the Colonel's gray horse ... just as we saw him lying ... let him who wished to know what war is, look at these series of illustrations." (Holmes, pp. 11-12)

250

and James Garfield persuaded Congress to provide another $25,000 as reward for Brady's service to the Union. However, the money arrived too late to help.

Brady handed over his Washington studio to his beloved nephew, Levin Handy. The remaining photographic records of the Brady studios sat in Handy's office in dusty boxes for decades. In the end, the greatest photographer of one of the United States' darkest periods died a pauper on January 15, 1896, in the alms ward of the Presbyterian Hospital in New York City.

For More Information

Holmes, Oliver Wendell. "Doings of the Sunbeam". *Atlantic Monthly,* vol. XII (July 1863).

Horan, James D. *Mathew Brady, Historian with a Camera.* New York: Crown Publishers, 1955.

Meredith, Roy. *Mr. Lincoln's Camera Man.* New York: Charles Scribner's Sons, 1946.

Walt Whitman

1819–1892

Personal Background

Early life. Great American poet Walt Whitman was born into a large and poor family. His father, Walter Whitman, Sr., a laborer, married Louisa Van Velsor, and the couple had nine children. Walter, Jr., called Walt, was the second child, born May 31, 1819, on a farm in Long Island, New York. Much of what is known about his early life has been gleaned from memories he later set down in poems—details of farm life (lilacs, grass, a sow's faint-pink litter, apple trees) as well as city scenes (heavily loaded ferries, schooners, bustling men and women).

The memories are probably accurate since Walt's father tried many occupations to keep the family fed. He farmed, worked at odd jobs, and when Walt was four, moved the family to Brooklyn to try house building. Walt attended Brooklyn schools until age eleven. He then dropped out to work as an office boy and educated himself by reading the classics and books on history and Eastern and Western philosophy.

Because his father was a laborer, Walt had spent his childhood with working-class people. In 1830 he became part of this labor force. His job as an office boy led to another as a printer's devil (apprentice) and finally to a job as a printer. In 1836, at age seventeen, he took a job in rural Long Island as a schoolteacher; it lasted

▲ **Walt Whitman**

Event: The Civil War.
Role: Forty-two years old when the Civil war started, Walt Whitman spent three years tending the wounded in makeshift hospitals on the battlefields and in Washington, D.C. The poems, speeches, letters, and newspaper articles he wrote at this time recount the horrors of war and the struggles of a nation divided. Some of the writing found its way into Whitman's ground-breaking volume of poetry *Leaves of Grass*.

for three years. In those days, a teacher was partly paid by "board-ing around," staying for a day or a week at the homes of people in the community who could afford to feed and house the teacher. Boarding around gave Walt the opportunity to meet some of the more prosperous and better-educated citizens of Long Island.

Meanwhile, he was beginning to write. Young and full of life (and some would say of his own importance), his first poems dealt with himself. He would continue to write about his own experiences all his life, in the process developing a deep appreciation for the American people and celebrating their experiences and character.

First writing. By 1842 Whitman had published his first book, a story about the evils of drinking alcohol. Called *Franklin Evans; or, the Inebriate: A Tale of the Times,* the venture was not very suc-cessful. Four years later, however, his writing and printing experi-ence won Whitman a job as editor of a Brooklyn newspaper, the *Daily Eagle.* He by now strongly believed that the Americans would rise to greatness only by becoming a more moral people. Whitman was strongly in favor of democracy precisely because he had faith in the common people, whose lives he had come to know so well. An out-spoken opponent of slavery, he considered its existence a disgrace in a country that boasted of its humanity. His sympathy for slaves would later surface in his poetry.

> ### From "Song of Myself"
>
> The runway slave came to my house and stopt outside,
>
> I heard his motions crackling the twigs of the woodpile....
>
> I am the hounded slave, I wince at the bite of the dogs,
>
> Hell and despair are upon me, crack and again crack the marksmen.... (Lowenfels, pp. 228–29)

Through his writing as editor of the *Eagle,* Whitman's hatred of slavery became public knowledge. He also strongly opposed admitting into the Union any new state that allowed slavery. These views and others cost him his position at the paper, and he began job hopping, much as his father had once done. Whitman traveled, became editor of a New Orleans, Louisiana, paper for a time, then returned to Brooklyn to edit the *Daily Times,* a paper that competed with his old employer, the *Eagle.*

Leaves of Grass. Meanwhile, Whitman kept a journal and experimented with his own style of verse. Finally, in 1855, he published the first edition of *Leaves of Grass*. A ninety-four-page poem, the whole small volume was written in a new style of unrhymed poetry called free verse. Not only was the format new, so was the autobiographical subject matter. The book concerned Whitman's feelings about his own and working people's experiences. It began with a section on his personal life, later called "Song of Myself." Unafraid to praise the beauty in people and nature or to show sorrow and pain, Whitman openly expressed his feelings, raising the eyebrows of people who thought only women should discuss such emotions. At first people did not know what to make of the book, and it attracted hardly any readers. Soon, however, a leading thinker and writer of the day, Ralph Waldo Emerson, sent a letter to Whitman in praise of the work. Here was the true American poet, felt Emerson, whom the nation sorely needed. People respected Emerson and began to buy *Leaves of Grass*.

The work became even more popular when in 1856 Whitman published a second edition, including the letter by Emerson and his own response. Emerson liked the poetry but felt that some passages were not decent. He advised Whitman to take out passages about the body and sexuality, but Whitman refused. Just as such talk would boost sales in the present day, this suggestion that the book was daringly different made it popular in Whitman's time.

Whitman's Job Experience	
1848–49	With brother Jeff, edited the *New Orleans Crescent*.
1850	Edited Brooklyn's *The Freeman*.
1850–54	Managed a stationery store.
1854	Began housebuilding and carpentry jobs.
1857	Edited Brooklyn *Daily Times*.
1857–58	Traveled and wrote in the West and Canada.

From 1855 on, Whitman continued to add more verses to *Leaves of Grass*. Generally, some event would inspire him to write a long poem, which he then would publish in a small book. Finally it would become part of the larger volume, as in the case of a series of poems called *Drum-Taps,* inspired by Whitman's experiences in the Civil War. Nearly ninety pages long, *Drum Taps* was first published in 1865.

Few writers caused such a stir as Whitman, who slyly promoted himself. Writing three unsigned reviews of *Leaves of Grass* in 1855, he showered his own work with praise: "An American bard at last," his review declared, and "politeness this has none" (Kaplan, p. 208). In

▲ Portrait of Whitman used as the frontispiece in the first edition of *Leaves of Grass*

addition, two authors of the time, wrote books—*The Good Grey Poet* by John Burroughs and *Notes on Walt Whitman as Poet and Person* by W. D. O'Connor—defending Whitman's work. Whether celebrated or ridiculed, the poet doggedly continued to publish new versions of *Leaves of Grass*. After 1859 he found outside publishers who were willing to invest in the book. Before Whitman died, it would be published nine times: in 1855, 1856, 1860, 1867, 1868, 1871, 1876, 1881, and 1889. In the 1881 edition, the parts of the book were set in final order according to the chronology of the poet's life. The volume had 156 smaller poems before the Civil War, which Whitman credits with having the greatest impact of all on the book.

Participation: Wound Dresser in the Civil War

Not a soldier. Whitman did not enlist for active duty at the start of the war. His age was one reason. Already forty-two, he was too old to serve in the ranks and untrained as an officer. (Most soldiers were twenty- to thirty-years-old). He had trouble anyway with the thought of firing a gun or drawing a sword on another man. Furthermore, the war at the outset was expected to be a quick affair. President Abraham Lincoln called for only 20,000 volunteers to bolster the Union's small regular army, and they were expected to take the South's chief city, Richmond, Virginia, in short order (see **Abraham Lincoln**). Finally, there was the matter of Whitman's mother. He felt very close to her ("How much I owe her! It could not be put in a scale" [Lowenfels, p.133]), and after Whitman's father died in 1855, Whitman felt obligated to care for her. So he stayed out of the fighting, but his younger brother George was drafted. Whitman would later describe the call to arms:

> Beat! beat! drums!—blow! bugles! blow!
>
> Through the windows—through the doors burst like a ruthless force,
>
> Into the solemn church, and scatter the congregation. (Allen, p. 200)

George must have fought well, for within a year he was leading troops into action as a first lieutenant in the Battle of Fredericksburg.

Early battles. The early fighting of the war did not go well for the North. The Southern secessionists, or Secesh as Whitman was fond of calling them, seemed to pick more capable military leaders than the North. Confederate generals P.G.T. Beauregard and Thomas "Stonewall" Jackson beat the Union army in the first great battle at Bull Run. General Robert E. Lee had some early success around Richmond, Virginia, the Confederate capital (see **Robert E. Lee**). Much of this fighting took place on battlegrounds between the two capitals, not far from Washington, D.C.

The early 1800s had seen the development of rifles, guns that gave the bullet a spin out of the barrel (making them more accurate), and explosives that sent that bullet off when the charge was struck. These new weapons, which could be fired again and again quickly and at long range, produced heavy casualties. Four of every ten soldiers in the Civil War were wounded in battle. At first, most of the casualties were on the Union side. However, the wounded from both sides were sometimes sent to Washington hospitals. Whitman himself encountered enemy brothers in a hospital there:

> One was a strong Unionist, the other Secesh; both fought on their respective sides, both badly wounded, and both brought together here after a separation of four years. Each died for his cause. (Lowenfels, p. 125)

The city became a massive hospital site. Even the railroad station was devoted to medical care. Endless rows of cots became beds for suffering soldiers, who lay dying or hurt. New medical sites were hurriedly set up by erecting tents in open spaces throughout the city.

The Battle of Fredericksburg. Several major battles had been fought before the Battle of Fredericksburg, December 11, 1862. By then, the Confederate army in Virginia had grown to 78,000 soldiers while the Union force swelled to 120,000. Some 18,000 were killed or wounded in the four days of fighting at Fredericksburg. Northern newspapers wrote daily accounts of war events, publishing casualty lists of the Union soldiers who were wounded in battle. Listed among the wounded was a Lieutenant George Whitman.

Volunteer wound dresser. Whitman caught a train for Washington, D.C., and from there planned to travel to Fredericksburg to find his brother. In Washington, the center of Union activity, Whitman could hardly avoid seeing the hospitals with wounded soldiers in desperate need of care. Everywhere, he saw crippled, hungry, and thirsty young men.

Whitman hurried on to Fredericksburg, where he found that his brother had only been slightly wounded and was already back in action. He spent a week in his brother's tent and wrote to his mother:

> When I found dear brother George and found that he was alive and well, O you may imagine how trifling all my little cares and difficulties seemed … George is about building a place, a half hut and half tent for himself…. Every captain has a tent in which he lives, transacts company business, etc., has a cook (or a man of all work); and in the same tent mess and sleep his lieutenants and perhaps the first sergeant. (Lowenfels, pp. 31–32)

Whitman described the battle, explaining that everyone from the colonel on down was forced to lie full length on his back or belly in the mud, protected, until they lifted their heads, using the slightly raised ground as shelter from Southern sharpshooters. And after the battle, he described the destruction:

> Death is nothing here. As you step out in the morning from your tent to wash your face, you see before you on a stretcher a shapeless, extended object, and over it is thrown a dark gray blanket. It is the corpse of some wounded or sick soldier of the regiment who died in the hospital tent during the night; perhaps there is a row of three or four of these corpses lying covered over. No one makes an ado. (Lowenfels, p. 36)

Such scenes weighed heavily on the poet. For the next three years, he took it upon himself to give physical and spiritual comfort to the wounded. He meanwhile wrote down some of his impressions in letters, poems, and newspaper articles.

In one case Whitman's writing testifies to the brutal handling of some Union soldiers after they surrendered. Two Union lieutenants, already wounded, were dragged on the ground and surrounded by some Confederate guerrillas.

A Glimpse of War's Hell-Scenes

[Each guerrilla fighter] was stabbing them [the lieutenants] in different parts of their bodies. One of the officers had his feet pinned firmly to the ground by bayonets stuck through them.... These two officers, as afterwards found on examination, had received about twenty such thrusts, some of them through the mouth, face, etc. (Lowenfels, p. 41)

The Union army, in response, captured and shot some Confederate officers. Whitman described the whole incident, and then asked the reader to multiply the scene a few hundred times to get some inkling of the horrors of this war.

After touring the camps for a while, Whitman felt a need to return to Washington to nurse all the injured there. He took various part-time jobs, every day or evening working somewhere among the wounded. He wrote his mother, describing how the wounded and sick got more plentiful all the time. He debated how to make money in the meanwhile for his hospital and soldiers visits. From 1862 to 1865, Whitman wrote a selection of pieces published in New York papers describing the hospitals and wounded. His articles were based on a mass of personal experiences. Whitman befriended more than 1,000 young men in this time, making more than 600 visits to hospitals and military fields:

> I adapt myself to each case and to temperaments—some need to be humored; some are rather out of their head; some merely want me to sit with them and hold them by the hand. One will want a letter written to mother or father...; some like to have me feed them...; some want a cooling drink...; others want writing paper, envelopes, a stamp, etc. (Lowenfels, p. 113)

In the poem "Wound Dresser," Whitman explains how their pain became his own: the fractured thigh, the knee, the wound in the abdomen, the countless amputations. He felt their suffering, and they responded: "Many a soldier's loving arms about this neck have cross'd and rested/Many a soldier's kiss dwell'd on these bearded lips" (Whitman, p. 319).

Whitman's clear and detailed descriptions of events provide a vivid picture of a nation at war. He pointed out, for example, that there were more Southerners, especially from the border states, in the Union army than most people suspected. He described huge droves of cattle passing through the streets of Washington during the war. He explained how soldiers warmed their battlefield tents by digging a long trough in the ground under them, covering it over with old railroad iron and earth, then building a fire at one of the open ends to let it draw through to the other. He said of prison camps, "Starvation is the rule. Rags, filth, despair" (Lowenfels, p. 211). He visited black troops and questioned how well the Republican party would look out for them, repeating a comment he had heard: "The Negro will get his due from the Negro—from no one else. I say so, too; that is the whole story, from beginning, middle, and end" (Lowenfels, p. 227).

The war had turned Whitman from a poet preoccupied with his own actions to one who wrote with deep feeling about the surrounding conditions and people and their effect on him.

Lincoln's death. Whitman was still caring for the injured when news arrived that President Lincoln had been assassinated. This too the poet documented in a final speech about Lincoln. He had seen the president almost every day, happening to live where Lincoln passed to and from some lodgings just outside the city. Whitman considered Lincoln America's most moral personality, allowing for his faults but celebrating his honesty, shrewdness, conscience, goodness, and sense of Unionism. In a lecture describing Lincoln's murder, Whitman recounted that Lincoln heartily enjoyed watching plays. A scene had just been performed in which two ladies were told by a Yankee that he was not a wealthy man, and therefore poor marriage material. The actresses then exited, leaving only the actor on the stage for a moment, at which point the fatal gun was shot.

> The actual murder, transpired with the quiet and simplicity of any commonest occurrence…. Through the general hum following the stage pause … came the muffled sound of a pistol shot, which not one hundredth part of the audience heard at the time … and then through the President's box, a sudden figure, a man raises himself with hands and feet, stands a moment on the railing [of the second tier] leaps below to the stage (a distance of perhaps fourteen or fifteen feet) …. Booth, the murderer, dressed in plain black broadcloth, bareheaded, with full, glossy, raven hair … holds aloft in one hand a large knife …. (Lowenfels, p. 275)

Whitman also wrote two poems about the event: "When Lilies Last in the Dooryard Bloom'd" and "O Captain! My Captain!," which cap-

261

tures the mood of the country after the murder: gloom dampening the sweet joy that had come with the ghastly war's end.

In the end, it was Whitman's ability to communicate with the soldiers that so greatly affected his post-war versions of *Leaves of Grass.* He did not ask a wounded person how he felt. Instead, as the poet explains, someone else's agony was one of his changes of garments. He became the wounded person, and the patient felt it.

Aftermath

Government clerk. At the end of the war, people began to recognize the valuable work Whitman had done as an army volunteer. Some persuaded the government to find employment for him, and he became a clerk in the Treasury Department. James Harlan, the secretary of the treasury, read parts of *Leaves of Grass,* however, and decided that Whitman wrote too freely about sex in the book. He fired the new clerk, but friends in Washington came to Whitman's rescue. Soon he was hired as a clerk in the office of the attorney general.

Leaves of Grass. Whitman continued to add to and to print new versions of *Leaves of Grass.* The war had sobered and shocked him; now he focused more on the wonders of nature and the glory of living in America. He encouraged others to work toward the betterment of the country. For thirty-seven years Whitman continued to travel and write about new events, adding his experiences to this one book. He also wrote other smaller pieces, many of which found their way into revised editions of *Leaves of Grass.* He made it clear that he was describing his personal feelings and observations. In some farewell lines to the volume, he wrote "Camerado, this is no book. Who touches this touches a man" (Miller, p. 349).

Wartime writings. Most of Whitman's wartime writings were published after the fighting stopped. One of the newspapers that had published his wartime articles was the *New York Times.* In 1867 that paper collected his letters and published *Memoranda During the War.* His wartime letters to his mother were also collected and published in 1868 in a volume called *The Wound Dresser.* Some of these letters too became part of *Leaves of Grass.*

Final years. Double misfortune struck Whitman in 1873. All his life, he had remained close to his mother. In 1873, she died, and in the same year he suffered a stroke. He afterward began to grow more feeble and paralyzed. Whitman spent his remaining days in Camden, New Jersey, living with his brother George's family until his death on March 27, 1892.

For More Information

Allen, Gay Wilson and Charles T. Davis. *Walt Whitman Poems.* New York: New York University Press, 1955.

Kaplan, Justin. *Walt Whitman: A Life.* New York: Simon and Schuster, 1980.

Lowenfels, Walter, editor. *Walt Whitman's Civil War.* New York: Alfred A. Knopf, 1960.

Miller, James E., Jr. *Walt Whitman.* New York: Twayne, 1962.

Bibliography

Blair, Walter, ed. *The Literature of the United States.* Glenview, Illinois: Scott, Foresman & Co., 1971.

Bode, Carl. *The Portable Thoreau.* New York: Viking Press, 1964.

Bradford, Ganaliel. *Lee the American.* Boston: Houghton Mifflin, 1929.

Brewerton, George Douglas. *Overland with Kit Carson.* New York: Coward-McCann, Inc., 1930.

Bruns, Roger. *Abraham Lincoln.* New York: Chelsea House, 1986.

Capers, Gerald Mortimer. *Stephen A. Douglas: Defender of the Union.* Boston: Little, Brown, 1959.

Chalfant, W. A. *Outposts of Civilization.* Boston: Christopher Publishing House, 1928.

Commager, Henry Steele, and Milton Cantor. *Documents of American History.* Vol. 1. Englewood Cliffs, New Jersey: Prentice-Hall, 1988.

Creel, George. *The People Next Door: An Interpretive History of Mexico and the Mexicans.* New York: The John Day Company, 1926.

Dowdey, Clifford. *Death of a Nation.* New York: Alfred A. Knopf, 1962.

Dunbar, Edward E. *The Romance of the Age.* New York: D. Appleton & Co., 1867.

Freedman, Russell. *Lincoln: A Photo Biography.* New York: Clarion Books, 1987.

Freeman, Douglas Southall. *Robert E. Lee.* 4 vols. New York: Scribner's, 1935.

Frémont, Jessie. *Mother Lode Narratives.* Ashland, Oregon: Shirley Sargeant, 1970.

Gigelshiffer, Saul. *The American Conscience: The Drama of the Lincoln-Douglas Debates.* New York: Horizon Press, 1973.

Goodwin, Cardinal. *John Charles Frémont: An Explanation of His Career.* Palo Alto, California: Stanford University Press, 1930.

Greenbie, Marjorie Barstow. *My Dear Lady.* New York: McGraw-Hill, 1940.

Griffith, Cyril E. *The African Dream.* University Park: Pennsylvania State University Press, 1975.

Hawthorne, Nathaniel. *The Complete Short Stories of Nathaniel Hawthorne.* Garden City, New York: Doubleday & Co., 1959.

James, Laurie. *Men, Women, and Margaret Fuller.* New York: Golden Heritage Press, 1990.

James, Marquis. *The Raven.* New York: Blue Ribbon Books, 1929.

Lavender, David. *Climax at Buena Vista.* Philadelphia: J. B. Lippencott, 1966.

McKinley, Silas Bent. *Old Rough and Ready: The Life and Times of Zachary Taylor.* New York: Vanguard Press, 1946.

Miers, Earl Schenck. *The General Who Marched to Hell.* New York: Alfred A. Knopf, 1951.

BIBLIOGRAPHY

Milton, George Fort. *The Eve of Conflict: Stephen A. Douglas and the Needless War.* New York: Houghton Mifflin, 1934.

Oates, Stephen B. *With Malice Toward None.* New York: Dorset Press, 1952.

Pearce, Roy Harvey, ed. *Whitman.* Englewood Cliffs, New Jersey: Prentice-Hall, 1962.

Peters, Dewitt C. *Kit Carson's Life and Adventures.* Hartford, Connecticut: Dustin, Gilman & Co., 1875.

Schyberg, Frederik. *Walt Whitman.* New York: Columbia University Press, 1951.

Wagenknecht, Edward. *Nathaniel Hawthorne: Man and Writer.* New York: Oxford University Press, 1961.

Walters, Jolen B. *Merchant of Terror.* New York: Bobbs-Merrill, 1973.

Whitman, Walt. *Leaves of Grass.* New York: Aventine, 1931.

Whitman, Walt. *Walt Whitman: Complete Poetry and Selected Prose.* Edited by James E. Miller, Jr. Boston: Riverside Press, 1959.

Williams, T. Harry. *Lincoln and His Generals.* New York: New American Library, 1977.

Index

Boldface indicates profiles.